POLAND

WESTVIEW PROFILES • NATIONS OF CONTEMPORARY EASTERN EUROPE

Poland: Socialist State, Rebellious Nation, Ray Taras

† *Czechoslovakia: Profile of a Socialist Republic at the Crossroads of Europe,* David W. Paul

Hungary: A Nation of Contradictions, Ivan Volgyes

Romania: A Developing Socialist State, Lawrence C. Graham

Yugoslavia: Tradition and Change in a Multiethnic State, Lenard Cohen

The German Democratic Republic: The Search for Identity, Henry Krisch

Bulgaria, William Welsh

† Available in hardcover and paperback.

ABOUT THE BOOK AND AUTHOR

Over the centuries Poland has been characterized by a combination of romanticism and realpolitik, of religious fervor and rebellion. In this comprehensive introduction to one of Europe's largest and most troubled nations, Dr. Taras examines the country's checkered history from its conversion to Christendom in the tenth century to its great-power status in the sixteenth century and from the loss of independence and statehood three centuries later to the resurrection of the Polish state following World War I.

The turbulent politics of Communist-ruled Poland, beginning with the little-known civil war of 1944 to 1948 and ending with Solidarity, martial law, and beyond, are carefully analyzed. Next the author examines Poland's international relations, which are determined largely by its geopolitical position between East and West, the dependence of Regime and Party on Soviet power, and the traditional allegiance to the West of the intellectual elite and the middle class. He also focuses on Poland's economic system—unusual because it combines Soviet-type nationalization and central planning with widespread private agriculture and a thriving private economy—and on its changing social structure, including a discussion of social problems and minority groups. Dr. Taras then presents a survey of the nation's rich cultural heritage and contemporary achievements in the arts, music, and letters. He concludes with an assessment of the country's political and economic prospects.

Ray Taras is assistant professor of political science at Tulane University. He is the author of *Ideology in a Socialist State: Poland, 1956–83.*

POLAND

Socialist State, Rebellious Nation

Ray Taras

Westview Press / Boulder and London

943.8
T177p

87-3863

Westview Profiles/Nations of Contemporary Eastern Europe

Published in 1986 in the United States of America by Westview Press, Inc.; Frederick A. Praeger, Publisher; 5500 Central Avenue, Boulder, Colorado 80301

Library of Congress Cataloging in Publication Data
Taras, Ray, 1946–
    Poland, socialist state, rebellious nation.
    (Westview profiles. Nations of contemporary Eastern Europe)
    Bibliography: p.
    Includes index.
    1. Poland. I. Title. II. Series: Nations of contemporary Eastern Europe.
DK4040.T37 1986   943.8   86-9060
ISBN 0-8133-0181-5

Printed and bound in the United States of America

The paper used in this publication meets the requirements of the American National Standard for Permanence of Paper for Printed Library Materials Z39.48-1984.

10   9   8   7   6   5   4   3   2   1

Contents

Tables and Figures

xi

Illustrations

Preface

The purpose of this study is to introduce the reader to diverse aspects of contemporary Poland. This country, located in the heartland of Europe, possesses a stormy history, and developments in the 1980s have proved no less tumultuous. Socialist by geopolitical fate rather than choice, intensely nationalistic, devout, independent, and insurgent, Poland has repeatedly followed the clarion cry—"Oh, seize the sword of history and strike! and strike!"—words of the poet Krzysztof Baczyński (1921–1944) who perished in the uprising in Warsaw in 1944.

In completing this book the author is indebted to a number of individuals for their direct and indirect assistance. Professor Jerzy Wiatr of the University of Warsaw read the entire manuscript, uncovered factual errors, and challenged unconvincing interpretations, in these ways greatly enhancing the quality of the final product. Colleagues at Tulane University—Radomir Luza, Sam Ramer, and Robert Robins—offered helpful criticism of individual chapters, as did Anna Kolyszko, an editor of the Polish literary journal *Literatura na Swiecie*. The University of Michigan's Slavic Librarian, Joseph Placek, supplied indispensable research materials that are not readily found in New Orleans. Pat Smith made available her revealing and professional photographs, reproduced here with her permission. Two kind editors at Westview, Barbara Ellington and Miriam Gilbert, encouraged and advised me at various stages of publication, and a third, Libby Barstow, added the professional finishing touch. All the shortcomings that remain can be safely heaped upon the author.

As this is a general work on Poland, I would also like to acknowledge the influence of several personal sources. Inspiration for becoming and remaining a student of Poland derives from my late father, Mieczyslaw Taras ("Sarat"), who served Poland in a dual capacity as an R.A.F. squadron leader and wartime bomber pilot and as propagator of the nation's most honorable values. To an equal degree my mother, Stanislawa, contributed to the upholding of Polish traditions in the family. During the years the author spent in Poland, Waclaw Taras, an officer in the Home Army's Róg unit during the 1944 Warsaw uprising and a fervent Polish patriot until the time of his death in 1985, was always an invaluable source of information and inspiration.

When the inevitable doubts about Poland's fundamental wisdom and virtue have surfaced, my wife, Malgorzata, and older son, Michal, have imbued me with renewed fascination and affection for things Polish. It seems appropriate to dedicate this book to my younger son Krzysztof, however, because he was conceived at the same time it was. Moreover, in faithfully waking the author up every morning at six for the better part of a year, he ensured that I had an early start to each day's work. Krzysztof's contribution to this study is immeasurable.

Ray Taras

Guide to Pronunciation

Polish is widely held to be a difficult language for foreigners to learn and to pronounce. As in Latin (and Russian), nouns are declined and verbs conjugated. Special declension forms of nouns often take the place of prepositions to denote syntactical relations. In turn, adjectives have to agree with the noun's case (nominative, genitive, dative, etc.). Conjugational forms of verbs are also abundant, and the reflexive form is widely used. This great number of inflexional forms makes Polish a challenging language to master.

To make matters somewhat easier, however, Polish spelling is basically phonetic, and one letter of the Latin alphabet corresponds to one particular sound. Moreover, as a rule, stress falls on the penultimate syllable, for example, So-li-DAR-noshch.

The Polish alphabet consists of thirty-two letters, of which nine are vowels. In addition to vowels found in English (including "y"), Polish has three instances of vowel sounds that are denoted by letters of the Latin alphabet with added diacritical marks. These include two nasal vowels:

- ą, approximating the sound "awn," as in Śląsk (SHLAWNSK)
- ę, approximating the sound "en," as in Wałęsa (Va-WEN-sa)

An additional vowel, ó, is equivalent to the English sound "oo," as in Kraków (KRA-koof).

The twenty-three consonants are divided into soft and hardened categories, and each has special stem endings and other spelling rules. Although they do not constitute separate letters of the alphabet, a number of digraphs can be added to the list of consonants, for example, "cz," "sz," "ch," and combinations with "i," such as "ci," "si," and even "ni." A guide to the pronunciation of the consonants and digraphs peculiar to Polish follows:

xvii

- c = "ts," as in Cyrankiewicz (Tsi-ran-KEI-vich)

- $ć$, ci, cz = "ch," as in Czechoslowacja (Che-ho-swo-VA-tsya)

- ch = "h," as in Lech (LEH)

- dz = "g" (like "Germany" in English), as in Dzerżyński (Ger-ZHIN-skee)

- j = "y," as in Jaruzelski (Ya-ru-ZEL-skee)

- $ł$ = "w," as in Woytyla (Voy-TY-wa) (this letter will not show up, however, in the typography used in this book)

- $ń$ = Spanish $ñ$ (niño), as in Poznań (POZ-nany)

- r = trilled "r," as in Rosja (RRRO-sya)

- rz = "zh," as in Krzysztof (KZHY-shtof)

- $ś$, si, sz = "sh," as in Szymanowski (Shy-ma-NOF-ski)

- $szcz$ = "shch," as in Szczecin (SHCHE-chin)

- w = "v" or "f," as in Walewska (Va-LEF-ska)

- $ż$, $ź$, zi = French "j" (*jour*) or English "zh" (measure), as in Boże (BO-zhe)

One final remark on Polish usage in this book: The Polish nouns cited here are presented in the nominative singular case.

R.T.

Contemporary Poland. Source: *Poland Watch*, no. 1 (Fall 1982). Used by permission of the Poland Watch Center, Washington, D.C.

Introduction

Poland is a socialist state located in the Soviet-controlled part of the European continent. Although in a geographical sense the country can be considered part of Central Europe, the convention generally employed since World War II is to classify individual European states in terms of the political division agreed upon by the "Big Three" powers—the United States, the Soviet Union, and Great Britain—at the 1945 Yalta conference. Accordingly, by virtue of its political and military membership in the Soviet bloc, Poland is currently treated as a constituent part of Eastern Europe.

Political geographers might add that such a superimposed political boundary also represents a culture-molding boundary: That is, Poland's original cultural landscape was Central European if not, as certain Polish intellectuals have argued, fully Western European. The Yalta order caused this landscape to become increasingly Eastern European and more similar to Russian culture. The true basis of Poland's cultural heritage and its cultural values remains a fiercely debated subject among the Polish intelligentsia.

The Polish People's Republic, as the country is officially called today, is the largest state in Eastern Europe both in population and surface area. In 1981 its population numbered 36 million, more than 98 percent of whom were ethnic Poles. The proportion of Roman Catholics is slightly less—90 percent—with most of the remainder adhering to Orthodox and Protestant faiths. The Polish language belongs to the West Slavonic group and employs the Latin alphabet. No serious linguistic barriers exist in the country despite the use of several regional dialects. Poland's capital, and its most populous city, is Warsaw, which has 1,700,000 inhabitants. Other cities with populations of more than five hundred thousand include Lódz, Kraków, Wroclaw, Poznań, and the tricity port region of Gdańsk, Gdynia, and Sopot. One significant demographic feature of postwar Poland has

1

been the massive urbanization of the population: The last prewar census, taken in 1931, revealed that 73 percent of the population was rural. By the mid-1980s this figure had been halved, and the proportion engaged directly in agriculture had fallen to 20 percent. Despite these tendencies, Polish culture continues to bear the mark of its peasant heritage.

Poland's local administration is divided into forty-nine provinces, each with its own capital. Contrasts abound, from the highly industrialized Katowice province to the extremely rural Siedlce province. Postwar economic development has not been uniform throughout the country, and regional differences extend to the quality of education, health care, and social services. The country's basic unit of currency is the zloty, which is nonconvertible. At the beginning of 1986, a base rate of about 180 zlotys to U.S. $1 was set; unofficial (black market) rates of exchange are generally four to five times higher.

Poland's surface area measures 121,946 square miles. Poland is the size of New Mexico and is roughly hexagonal in shape. The climate is continental, with substantial snowfall in winter and warm, dry summers. Lowlands are the principal topographical feature, but in the south the Carpathian and Sudety Mountains, together with their foothills, offer a contrasting landscape. Several peaks in the Tatra range of the Carpathians rise to more than eight thousand feet and display Alpine characteristics (though they do not have glaciers). Two major river systems, the Vistula and the Odra, drain the country's basins northwestward into the Baltic Sea.

Because much of Poland lies in the great central lowlands, the country does not enjoy any natural borders either in the east or the west. The Polish plain itself is internally differentiated, ranging from the Mazury lake region in the north, through the fertile alluvial floodplains farther south, to the vast uninhabitable Pripet marshlands in the east. The richest agricultural lands are located in the south-central region, which extends to the foothills of the Carpathian Mountains dividing Poland and Czechoslovakia. The earliest Polish cities—among them Kraków, Lublin, and Wroclaw—were established in this area and became centers of commerce in medieval times. The grain trade along the Vistula was booming, and in this period Poland served as Europe's breadbasket. To this day the country ranks among the world's top producers of some agricultural commodities such as potatoes (1983 production was 33 million tons—nearly thrice the U.S. figure) and sugar beets (16 million tons).

Poland's chief mineral resource is coal. In 1980 it was estimated that minable and prospective reserves of hard, or bituminous, coal amounted to almost 200 billion tons. Actual production in 1983 was

The Polish countryside—an enduring stillness on the Northern European Plain

187 million tons. The Upper Silesian coal basin contains the second-largest total reserves in Europe (after the Ruhr), has perhaps the heaviest concentration in the world (most seams lying within 1,000 yards of the surface), and is continental Europe's largest continuous coalfield (mined since the mid-eighteenth century). The high quality of Silesian hard coal has allowed Poland to earn much-needed hard currency. Moreover, until the late 1970s coal mining ensured the country's energy sufficiency.

In addition to hard coal, substantial brown coal, or lignite, reserves are found in Upper Silesia. This variety can be gasified and used both as fuel and for chemical synthesis. In 1983 some 42 million tons were produced in Poland. Also located in the northern part of the basin are significant deposits of lead ore and zinc: According to the *Europa Year Book 1985*, the country's production of these minerals in 1981 was 44,000 tons and 202,000 tons respectively. Poland ranks fifth in the world in the mining of these two ores.

The coalfield in Lower Silesia, which is separated from Czechoslovakia by the Sudety Mountains, contains less abundant reserves than its northern counterpart, but the coking coal remains of equally high quality. One of Europe's largest copper deposits (yielding 350,000 tons of ore production in 1982) was discovered in the vicinity in

1957. Other parts of southern Poland contain further natural riches—
iron ore (50,000 tons) near Częstochowa, rock salt (1 million tons)
near Kraków, and sulphur (5 million tons) near Tarnobrzeg.

Despite occasionally promising exploratory drillings, known petroleum reserves are small, and natural gas is found in modest
quantities. Both are located principally in the Carpathian foothills.
In the nineteenth century Poland stood as one of the pioneering
countries in Europe in exploiting crude oil. Reserves were quickly
depleted, however, and production fell by 50 percent in the interwar
period. The loss of the main oil basin to the USSR in the postwar
territorial adjustment brought output to nil by 1950, but it has since
risen (210,000 tons of crude in 1983), and total known extractable
deposits are thought to be about 100 million tons. Exploratory drilling
continues in the Baltic Sea, and an important deposit (estimated at
20 million tons) has been uncovered 50 miles north of the port of
Leba. But Poles are cautious about all potential findings because an
initially promising discovery near Karlino in the 1970s proved a dud.
Likewise, before World War II Poland was a large supplier of natural
gas to Western Europe, but loss of the fields to the Soviet Union has
only recently been offset by discoveries of new fields, producing more
than 200 billion cubic feet annually in the 1980s.

Wood is no longer used as a significant energy source, and the
timber industry of the mountain region peaked some time ago.
Nonetheless, the country has been able to export limited quantities
of wood pulp, and efforts have been made to expand fast-growing,
cellulose-yielding tree plantations. Another potential source of energy—atomic power stations—has, until now, not been developed.
But the Jaruzelski administration has committed itself to the completion
of Poland's first atomic reactor, first announced in 1971, at Zarnowiec
(near Gdańsk) by 1993. Preliminary research has also been commissioned on the feasibility of constructing a second nuclear reactor
near Pila.

1

One Thousand Years of History

Many nations are profoundly driven by their history, but perhaps those with a tragic one are more affected than others. The case of Poland appears to substantiate this proposition. An acute consciousness in individual Poles of the nation's turbulent past helps fashion the contemporary collective mentality of Poland while it also inspires Poles' recourse to action. In the first part of the nineteenth century, the great Russian poet Pushkin remarked that the history of Poland was and ought to be a disaster. Events in this country in the one hundred and fifty years since his time have largely confirmed this view. Strangely, perhaps, Poles themselves appear to share this understanding of their homeland's peculiar relationship with history. Oftentimes they seem fatalistic about where history is taking their nation. On other occasions, they seem to invite disaster through an irrational and romanticized form of bravado. The seemingly contradictory roles performed by history—both an immutable *factum* and an exhortatory call to action—must, therefore, be at the center of an examination of this Eastern European nation.

Because history represents both an objective and subjective constituent of the Polish nation, it is a natural starting point for the study of this country. Let me begin this profile of Poland with a look at the historical personages and events that appear to have left the greatest imprint on Poland's present collective memory.

EMERGENCE OF THE POLISH NATION

The Poles are a Slavic nation, and some historians hold that they have a strong claim to be considered the "kernel" of all Europe's Slavic peoples (now so far-flung they reach from Russians who have settled on the frontiers of China and Mongolia to Slovenes living on the Italian border). Much historical evidence suggests that the original home of all the Slavs was in the lands bounded by the Pripet River (a tributary of the Dnieper) in the north, the Carpathian Mountains in the south, the Vistula River in the west, and the Dnieper River in the east. Virtually all this territory was under the rule of Polish kings between the fourteenth and eighteenth centuries. At the time of the Great Migration of peoples in the third and fourth centuries, groups of Slavs moved westward toward the Oder River, which presently constitutes Poland's western border; later large groups pushed southward and westward, too. The evolution of different dialectics, the Magyar invasions of the tenth century, and religious disputes following the schism in the Catholic church served to separate these groups. The result was the emergence of three distinct Slavic language groups: the western, which includes the Poles, Czechs, and Slovaks; the southern, composed of Serbo-Croatians, Slovenes, and Bulgarians; and the eastern, made up of Russians, Belorussians, and Ukrainians.

The term *Slav* originally derived from the word for *glory* or perhaps *speech*. Later Greek usage transformed the meaning of the term into *captives of Slavonic nationality*, and this distorted sense of *slave peoples* was invoked by the racist Hitlerite leadership to help justify conquest of the Third Reich's eastern neighbors. The conflict between Slavs and *Niemcy* (the Polish word for Germans, which may originally have meant "nonspeaking" or unintelligible peoples) is basic to an understanding of the history of Eastern Europe.

The ancestors of the Poles were themselves drawn from various ethnographic groups, such as the Polanie (literally, "dwellers of the plain"), Mazovians, Silesians, and Pomeranians ("coast dwellers"). In order to resist German invasions the other tribal groups acquiesced to the leadership of the Polanie, and this latter term came to designate all these groups. It was some time, however, before anything resembling an organized state was established. Historians disagree about which was the first Slavic state to emerge: Some hold it was the Slovene duchy of Carenthia (a region located in modern-day Austria) at the turn of the eighth century, others contend it was independent Greater Moravia founded about 830, and still others claim it was either Kievan Rus or the Bulgar state in the late ninth century. Any of these antedate the first German kingdom, which came into being in 911. But most historians concur that as a result of the geographical dispersion of the Polish tribes, the founding of a Polish state was delayed until the second half of the tenth century.

The first written evidence pointing to the existence of a Polish state dates from 963, and it suggests that at least two generations of princes had been ruling over these lands. But Polish history is generally considered to begin in 966, the year that Mieszko I of Poland's Piast dynasty converted to Christianity following his marriage to the daughter of a Bohemian duke and became the nation's first king. External relations during Mieszko's twenty-six-year reign prefigured much of future Polish history. His marriage and conversion were designed to strengthen the alliance of Poland and Bohemia in the face of a threat posed by a powerful neighbor, Germany, under whose overlordship Mieszko eventually fell. In 981 Poland was invaded by Russians and stripped of lands. Quarrels also broke out with other neighbors, such as the Czechs and Danes. In 985, therefore, the exasperated Mieszko undertook an act of donation of all Poland to Pope John XV, seeking in this way the protection of the Apostolic See and also its recognition of Poland as an independent church province and separate kingdom.

The country indeed became Christianized very quickly after 996, when Saint Adalbert (Wojciech), bishop of Prague, undertook the mission of bringing Christianity to the Polish peoples. Henceforth, Rome took greater interest in "the fate of that distant and almost unknown country," a description invoked a millenium later in the first public speech of the first Polish pope, John Paul II. Poland, in return, began to pay a tribute to Rome that became known as Peter's Pence.[1] It is a sublime irony of history that one thousand years later—after entering into a series of different international alliance systems and security pacts—Poland still looks to the Vatican for moral and spiritual protection.

POLAND OF THE DYNASTIES

In addition to bequeathing its name to the Slavic peoples of the Northern European Plain, the Polanie also provided the first dynasty of rulers—the Piast, named after a semilegendary ninth-century prince. Mieszko may have been the fourth or fifth in this line, but it was his son Boleslaw the Brave (Chrobry) who did most to consolidate Piast rule over the Polish tribes. In the year 1000 Rome finally permitted the foundation of an archbishopric in Poland, which made the church dependent on Rome alone and suggested that the country would soon obtain a royal crown and kingdom. As a result of a series of intrigues, it was Stephen of Hungary who on Christmas Day 1000 obtained the crown intended for Boleslaw. When a metropolitan, or ecclesiastical province, was created in Gniezno, Boleslaw entertained Emperor Otto III and convinced him to extend German recognition of the sovereignty of the Polish state. It was only after successful military campaigns against the Germans, which were crowned with the favorable peace treaty of Budziszyn in 1018, and the conquest of Russian territories, culminating in the capture of Kiev, that the Polish state became consolidated.

Boleslaw's greatest success may have been, however, Pope John XIX's consent to his coronation, which took place Easter Day 1025. The coronation symbolized the full sovereignty of Boleslaw's state, its internal unity and indivisibility, and, not least, its Christian character. Poland's first chronicler, Gallus Anonymus, described Boleslaw, accordingly, as "the father of these lands, defender, lord."[2]

The next Piast rulers had to contend with pagan revolts, centrifugal tendencies, and Bohemian invasions that tore at the young state. In 1058 Boleslaw II became ruler. Like his earlier namesake, he reasserted Poland's independence from the German Empire, undertook an expedition to recapture Kiev (which had in the interval between the two Boleslaws—and not for the last time in history— slipped away from Polish dominion), and was also crowned king of Poland. In internal politics he wished to replace the seniorate system— by which an elder prince would be given suzerain power, but younger members of the dynasty could inherit independent provinces within the state—with primogeniture as the principle of dynastic succession. The magnates of Poland, descendants of the early tribal dynasties, who had lost their independent standing under the Piasts, opposed any increase in the autocratic powers of the king and organized a conspiracy against Boleslaw.

One of the conspirators was alleged to be Stanislaw, bishop of Kraków. He was accused of treason against the crown, found guilty by the royal court (which included the head of the Polish church, the metropolitan bishop), and dismembered in 1079. Stanislaw was soon proclaimed a martyr; he was canonized in 1253 and became the patron saint of the country. In political terms this Polish antecedent of "murder in the cathedral" led to the victory of the magnates over absolutism. Boleslaw was forced into exile, the primogeniture system was not introduced, and for the next two hundred years no Polish ruler was to assume the title of king.

The rulers that followed presided over the disintegration of Polish unity and the emergence of a number of major principalities (though ecclesiastical unity was preserved under the archbishop of Gniezno). Extensive German colonization of Polish territories followed. The strategy of Kazimierz the Just in the twelfth century was to seek compensation for losses in the west with extensions of the eastern frontier at the expense of Russian principalities. Poland remained receptive above all, however, to Western ideas and machinery of government: This occurred through the forced, and occasionally welcomed, contact with German knights and artisans and through close cultural links with France and Italy. Therefore, the twelfth century might have shown "a decline from unity to disintegration. Closer investigation reveals the genuine moral and material progress that is beginning beneath the crumbling political structure."[3]

The political structure indeed continued to crumble in spite of the revival of the Polish kingdom in 1295. Ironically, it was the last ruler of the Piast dynasty, fittingly called Kazimierz the Great, who reversed the fortunes of the country and helped usher in its Golden Age. Crowned in 1333, Kazimierz had to contend with Bohemian pretensions to all of Poland and territorial losses of Pomerania and Silesia. In the north Kazimierz sought to Christianize still-pagan Lithuania and obtain its cooperation against a common enemy, Prussia. Expansion of Polish influence in the east led to the acquisition of the city of Lwów. Skillful diplomacy produced the cementing of an alliance with Hungary, whose ruling dynasty was promised the Polish crown upon Kazimierz's death. A rapprochement was also reached with Bohemia, based on the recognition of the latter's interests in Silesia.

Most importantly, Kazimierz had to confront the Order of the Teutonic Knights at the height of its power. This crusading military-religious order, composed largely (though not exclusively) of German knights, was first invited to Polish lands by a Mazovian duke in 1226. Soon its military conquests resulted in the establishment of a Teutonic state that effectively cut Poland off from the Baltic Sea. For nearly two centuries, up to the time of its final defeat in 1410, the order menaced Poland's territorial integrity. Under Kazimierz a peace treaty was concluded with the order that restored Pomerania to Poland.

Intense diplomatic activity was maintained at this time with the Holy See in Avignon. As a result, papal nuncios and collectors based in Poland, together with the local Polish ecclesiastical hierarchy and most of the clergy, threw their support behind Kazimierz's efforts to improve the country's international position as well as to consolidate unity within the kingdom. Not least of Kazimierz's achievements were the establishment of Central Europe's second university, in Kraków in 1364 (a university in Prague was established in 1348), the first codification of Polish law, the promotion of commerce between the far-flung Polish cities, the colonization of previously uninhabited regions, greater protection for oppressed peoples (such as Jews fleeing persecution in Western Europe and the masses of peasants constantly threatened with famine), the construction of fortified castles along the Polish borders, and the creation of a permanent force of mercenaries to defend these borders. The Polish saying that Kazimierz inherited a Poland built of wood and bequeathed to posterity a Poland made of stone is more than just figuratively true.

The Jagiellon Dynasty

After Kazimierz's death in 1370 the Polish nobility was obliged to offer the crown of the Piasts to the Hungarian dynasty, as Kazimierz's accord had specified. This did not signify that Polish representatives were bereft of influence in choosing the successor: Quite the contrary, the nobility determined that the twelve-year-old Hungarian princess Jadwiga should marry its nominee, Jagiello, grand duke of Lithuania. In one stroke this marriage was destined to alter the internal and external profile of the Polish state.

The union with Lithuania brought to Poland peoples possessing different racial origins and religious backgrounds, including Belorussians and Ukrainians. The Kingdom of Poland and Lithuania was to be heterogeneous in a way Piast Poland had never been. The new state extended from the Baltic Sea and approached the Black Sea in the south. Needless to say, it was much better prepared to deal with the threats of the Muscovy state in the east as well as the still troublesome Teutonic Order in the west. The structure of power within the new Kingdom was also dramatically changed: Just as Jagiello had been chosen by the nobility, so in the future the Polish throne was to be subject to elective confirmation by this group. In 1386 Jagiello was formally elected king, baptized into Catholicism, married to the initially disconsolate Jadwiga, and formally crowned—all within a month. In short, the dynastic transfer consummated in that year represented drastic territorial, ethnic, and structural adjustments in the Polish state.

It also made possible one of the most glorious and significant military victories in Polish history—the defeat of the Teutonic Order in the battle of Grunwald (in German known as Tannenberg) in 1410. Germanic supremacy along the Baltic was given a mortal blow. Following further defeats inflicted by Jagiello's son Kazimierz, the order formally lost its independence. By the Peace of Toruń concluded in 1466, Prussian lands were either fully incorporated into the Polish state (for example, Danzig) or were turned into a fief of the Polish crown (such as East Prussia). The Kingdom now stretched from sea to sea—the Baltic to the Black.

Although it is possible to find earlier references to the concept of Poland as an eastern *antemurale christianitatis*—Christianity's outpost and bulwark—it was not until the mid-fifteenth century that the country's rulers appeared to become fully conscious of this role. Hitherto Poland displayed little enthusiasm for the Crusades, but in

1443 an ill-fated expedition was launched against the Ottomans that resulted in the death at Varna of King Wladyslaw III. His head was stuck in a honeypot, and the expedition proved not an auspicious start to Poland's defense of Christianity. Skirmishes with the marauding Tartars at this time came to be viewed, too, as a tribulation and test of Poland's faith, and the struggles with Muscovy in the Livonian wars a century later (and all subsequent conflicts with Russia) were generally viewed as efforts to defend the faith in the face of the menace posed by the Byzantine church. The greatest symbol of Poland as a bulwark of Christianity came two centuries later when King Jan Sobieski defeated the Turks by laying siege to Vienna in 1683. Consciousness of Poland's Christianizing mission has remained very strong to this day.

The Reformation in Poland during the sixteenth century was largely inspired by German settlers scattered throughout the country. In East Prussia it even took a legalized form. Some members of the royal court as well as large sections of the gentry, the so-called *szlachta*, became imbued with Reformation ideas. Measures taken by the church against the heretical movement were largely ineffective, and Calvinism in particular gained new adherents. By 1555 Protestantism was given legal recognition, and Protestant churches were allowed to keep property they had already acquired. The religious question exacerbated the power struggle between the nobility and the Catholic clergy, especially about the legitimacy of tithes, and the conflict ultimately led to the victory of the first group: In 1573 the Confederation of Warsaw officially established religious toleration and religious equality, making Poland one of Europe's most liberal societies. But once proponents and sympathizers of the Reformation had scored their political victory over the Catholic church, Reformation ideas quickly dissipated in the country due primarily to the lack of a popular base in the peasantry and the existence of deep internal divisions between Lutherans, Calvinists, and Unitarians.

The sixteenth century also marked the Golden Age of Polish civilization and was contemporaneous with the Polish Renaissance. The international standing and power that had been achieved under Kazimierz Jagiellon following the Peace of Toruń in 1466 provided the basis for a flowering of the arts, culture, literatures, and intellectual thought as well as for unprecedented economic prosperity, which was linked closely to the Vistula grain trade. This period was notable for the enlightened rule of the last two kings of the Jagiellon dynasty, the humanists Zygmunt I the Elder (1506–1548) and Zygmunt II August (1548–1572). The contribution of the Italian princess Bona Sforza, who married Zygmunt I, was also remarkable. Her encouragement of many of her gifted compatriots (especially Florentines) to visit and work in Poland linked the Polish Renaissance directly to the Italian. Artists and architects such as Quadro, Canavesi, Padovano, Berrecci, and Italus made enduring contributions to Polish culture. Poland's capital at this time, Kraków, and its royal court set in the Castle of Wawel became a cosmopolitan center for the arts, this at a time when Ivan the Terrible was ruler of Russia. This was the age of the astronomer Copernicus, native of Toruń, who demonstrated that the earth circled the sun; of the lyric poet Kochanowski, father of Polish drama; of the writer Rey, who was the first to write in Polish rather than Latin; of Modrzewski and Zamoyski, whose political works were at once socially progressive and linked to antiquity (notably Roman republican ideas) and were to exert an important influence on politics of the post-Jagiellon period. The Golden Age marked the ascendancy of Poland in many different spheres.

THE REPUBLICAN COMMONWEALTH AND ITS DEMISE

Polish entry into the Livonian wars in 1561 signaled the beginning of a confrontation with Muscovy, which deeply coveted an outlet to the Baltic. The Polish-Lithuanian Kingdom had hitherto been based on a union personified by the king, but the Kingdom required more durable foundations to challenge Muscovite ambitions successfully. In 1569 the Treaty of Lublin was concluded by which the separate parliaments, or Seyms, of Poland and Lithuania were obliged to meet jointly and enact legislation. The site of the meetings was to be Warsaw, a town roughly equidistant from the capitals of Poland and Lithuania, Kraków and Wilno respectively. A few decades later, in 1596, Warsaw officially was proclaimed the country's new capital.

This union proved to be particularly important when, three years later, Zygmunt II died without leaving an heir, thereby ending the Jagiellon dynasty. It was at this point that Zamoyski, grand hetman of Poland and fascinated with political theory, convinced the assembled nobility to adopt the principle of "one nobleman, one vote" as the method for choosing the Polish monarch. This concept became the basis of the Republican Commonwealth (more accurately, Democratic Kingdom) until the time of the partitions. Power was effectively transferred from the aristocracy to the *szlachta*. Accordingly, in 1573 some fifty thousand members of the nobility, representing all its ranks, convened in Warsaw and elected a Frenchman, Henri de Valois, to be king.

This first democratic election produced not a wise choice, as events were to prove. Within a year Henri had had enough of an extraordinarily democratic system that seemed to produce only strife and chaos, and he fled to his native France where a throne awaited him. In 1575 another convocation was held, and divisions over potential candidates—such as the Habsburg emperor Maximilian II and certain Polish nobles—became so acrimonious that civil war loomed. The *szlachta* again looked to Hungary and again was not disappointed. The Transylvanian prince Stefan Batory ruled Poland for only ten years, but he became a legendary figure for his exploits in the wars with Russia, which produced a consolidation of the Commonwealth's eastern territories.

Until now, successive Polish rulers had perceived their role in the east as providing a rampart against Muscovy, the Ottoman Empire, and the Tartars. At the turn of the seventeenth century, however, the Commonwealth adopted a more aggressive design. A series of plots to extend Polish influence into the tsarist court was undertaken. The plots originated in royal support for the False Dimitri, a rather obscure person who had arrived in Poland with claims to the throne of Muscovy. This brief, complex, significant episode has been recounted in the Russian composer Mussorgsky's magnificent nineteenth-century opera *Boris Godunov*. False Dimitri served as a convenient pretext for the ambitious Polish king Zygmunt III Vasa to mount a campaign against Russia in order to unite it with the Commonwealth and convert the heathen people to Christianity. Zygmunt's successes were as impressive as they were temporary: Smolensk was captured and Moscow briefly held, and his son Wladyslaw was elected tsar of Russia. In 1613 False Dimitri became tsar and his Polish wife, the ambitious Marina Mniszech (who had no qualms about marrying a second False Dimitri when the first was overthrown), tsarina. They occupied the Kremlin for all of ten days. Shortly afterward the Polish garrison was driven out of Moscow, and the Russian boyars chose what they expected to be another interim tsar, Michael Romanov. The dynasty he founded ruled for the next three hundred years and allowed Russia to emerge from its time of troubles and invasions. The Romanov dynasty was finally overthrown in 1917 and subsequently replaced by Bolshevik rule. Poland was to get no closer to turning Russia into a satellite state than during Zygmunt's reign. Unsuccessful Polish imperialism was, during the next centuries, to give way to successful Russian imperialism.

Poland was not directly engaged in the Thirty Years War (1618–1648) but did enter into conflicts with Muscovy, Sweden, and Turkey. By the middle of the seventeenth century the Republic was, paradoxically, more expansive than ever, yet more vulnerable to the enemies surrounding it. Poland had overextended itself and did not possess the military capability to police all its lands. Moreover, it became the isolated party in a tripolar power struggle that also involved Sweden and Russia: The latter two states were weaker and naturally gravitated toward each other in order to undermine the power of the stronger country, Poland. The Commonwealth steadily began to lose military and political encounters as a result of the intrigues hatched by its neighbors.

Szlachta *Democracy*

Although the balance of military power was a crucial factor determining Poland's ultimate fate, the country possessed one advantage that delayed the Commonwealth's collapse. That was its constitutional laws, which incorporated the ideas of liberty, equality, and government based on the consent of a significant part of the nation. Such progressive ideas were readily embraced by peoples who otherwise might have had little love for Polish rule. The Polish state might more quickly have collapsed and been partitioned, it could be argued, had it possessed the type of autocratic political system most of its neighbors had.

However, what may have been a positive factor in allowing the Polish state to manage peoples of different ethnic and religious backgrounds proved also to be a factor in the erosion of the Polish government's structure. From the outset the Commonwealth could be characterized as the "democracy of the gentry." Already in the second half of the fifteenth century, land diets, or regional assemblies (*Seymiki*), began to assert their influence in central affairs. With it, gentry encroachment on the power of the magnates steadily increased. Although the entire *szlachta* had generally accepted the legal equality of everyone belonging to it, regardless of individual wealth or power, this did not preclude a struggle for power between strata in this order. Thus, by 1493 the Seym (or national Diet) had been divided into an upper chamber, or Senate, consisting of bishops and high-ranking magnates, and a lower Chamber of Deputies representing the lesser gentry (who made up close to 10 percent of the population—the largest franchised class in Europe) and a symbolic representation of burghers (drawn exclusively from Kraków). Conflict between the two chambers, and the strata they represented, became more frequent—for instance, when it was necessary to find a successor to Henri de Valois.

It is important to stress that at this time the Polish nobility was an extremely heterogeneous class. As one Polish historian observed, "In it were the great lords, holders of the highest positions in the state, owners of substantial landed estates, possessors of considerable wealth. . . . At the other end of the spectrum were the poor gentry descendants of medieval knights, warriors or courtiers, entitled to noble rank and privileges but frequently possessing little or no land."[4]

The first group, the magnates, disposed of exceptional power as a result of wealth and office. Accordingly, they "acted as the focus of political activity, as the center around which factions formed; they were the bridges between the central government and the provincial nobility. . . . In many spheres of activity they simply replaced the functions of the royal court and the central government."[5] Not surprisingly, the monarchy often sought the lower nobility as allies to check the power of the magnates, but the royal pursuit of *absolutum dominium* was incompatible with the narrower self-interests of the *szlachta*.

In addition to such a precarious balance of political power, certain institutions determining the operation of government contributed to the breakdown of all authority and the propagation of the idea that *Polska nierządem stoi* ("Poland is governed by unrule"). One such institution was, obviously, the procedure for electing kings, whether to confirm them in office as under the Jagiellon dynasty, or to choose them from a slate of candidates as after 1572. The intrigues and infighting this system engendered among the electors proved extremely divisive, and the system compelled the monarch to earn power and prestige rather than to assume them *ex officio*.

Another mechanism was the Pacta Conventa: It identified the personal obligations of the king to Poland in the crucial areas of foreign policy and finance and formally guaranteed before his coronation that he would abide by the terms set by the lower chamber. The related Henrician Articles accepted by Henri de Valois in 1573 also obliged the monarch to convene the Seym regularly and to obtain the advice of its permanent council at all times. Failure to abide by the articles freed the gentry from the oath of allegiance and officially sanctioned opposition to the king (*de non praestanda obedientia*). As if these were not enough controls on monarchical power, the principle of *neminem captivabimus* was respected by Polish rulers as early as the mid-fifteenth century: That is, that all noblemen had immunity from confiscation of land or arrest until a court had passed sentence. In this way monarchs faced considerable legal obstacles in trying to deal with political opposition.

There were other institutional arrangements that promoted "szlachta democracy." At the beginning of the sixteenth century the Seym passed the act of *incompatibilitas* that prohibited any individual from holding more than one high state office. Furthermore, lands belonging to the crown were to be disposed of by the Seym, not according to the will of the king. In 1505 the famous principle of *nihil novi* found expression in Polish jurisprudence: It meant that "nothing new" in the way of legislation could be enacted by the king unless it received the consent of both chambers. Finally, the execution of law movement in the sixteenth century sought to hold high state officials accountable to the gentry or its representatives. All this made the Polish state far more democratic (some would say anarchic) than probably any other state in existence then.

Over time such procedures inevitably began to engender chaos and disorder and were increasingly interpreted by some strata of the nobility as signifying *liberum conspiro* ("the right to conspire against authority"). The institution of *confederatio* had first been employed early in the fourteenth century (its actual origins in Poland were even more remote) to mobilize any group of citizens (primarily the nobles and burghers) to seek redress of its grievances. A group could also declare itself a confederation in order to advance specialized interests. All that was required was a majority vote among those attending an assembly convened for that purpose. In short, "confederation was a legal procedure. It was undertaken in the name of the common good, by citizens acting in defense of the law, and conscious of its protection."[6]

By 1606 confederation had given way to the notion of *rokosz*, "a legalized insurrection whereby the nation in arms could even impeach the king."[7] In that year Zygmunt III Vasa, another imported monarch (this time from Sweden) accustomed to much broader royal authority than the Polish nobility allowed, was threatened with deportation for failing to pay adequate attention to the caprices of the gentry. Although this episode was subsequently glossed over as a regrettable misunderstanding that had produced unnecessary bloodshed between royal forces and rebels, fear bordering on paranoia of absolute government remained acute among the nobility and led to the enshrinement of the most famous principle of the Polish Commonwealth, *liberum veto*.

The crucial feature of this mechanism was the ability of one member of the Seym to veto any act under consideration by the Parliament. For some time, resort to the *liberum veto* was unnecessary because agreements were carefully worked out prior to Seym sessions in order to secure unanimity. In 1580, however, the ability of the Seym to impose taxation was quashed when a disgruntled representative invoked this principle. In 1652 all legislation approved during a session of the Seym was nullified when one nobleman cast a veto. Six years later *liberum veto* was employed before the session had even begun, thereby paralyzing the central government, and under

August III (1733–1763) just one session of the Seym was able to pass any legislation at all. This so-called golden freedom of the Polish nobility, the Russian tsars soon realized, could guarantee that the Republic would remain weak, disorganized, and divided. Accordingly, it became a device cleverly exploited to serve the cause of the Russian autocracy. Members of the Polish nobility were played off against each other, a number of prominent nobles came to serve the interests of the Romanovs, and inherent centrifugal forces in the system of government were exacerbated. Although the Polish state devised for itself an ingenious system of checks and balances meant to preserve the democracy of the nobility, one can only wonder at the folly of a system founded upon a premise that engendered self-destructive tendencies.

The Fall of the Republic

If the Polish Republic's internal political mechanisms appeared fundamentally irrational, it was the series of armed insurrections and invasions that directly produced the decline and final disintegration of the state. The revolt of the Ukrainian Cossacks in 1648 triggered the Great Deluge: In quick succession the Tartars, Turks, Russians, and Swedes went to war against Poland. The Swedish army, in particular, was able to overrun the country very rapidly, in 1655, and only the miraculous last-ditch defense at the monastery of Częstochowa—attributed by many Poles to the intercession of the Blessed Virgin whose representation in the icon of the Black Madonna was kept there—turned the tide of war. This troubled period of invasions was aggravated by the treasonous conduct of a number of magnates that produced a short, bitter civil war in 1665–1666. The last of the Vasa kings, Jan Kazimierz, sought to introduce sweeping political reforms such as centralization of the state and emancipation of the serfs, but the nobility blocked these projects. In this period the Sarmatian myth was rekindled: The *szlachta* more consciously identified itself with the descendants of the ancient Sarmatians, inhabitants of the proto-Slavonic lands who had conquered local tribes and became the ruling class. It was now considered to be the duty of the gentry—who were increasingly equated with the Polish nation, thereby precluding other social classes—to defend the state and its religion. Kazimierz's designs were frustrated, and the embattled king abdicated and left for France.

Jan Sobieski, the vanquisher of the Turks at Vienna in 1683, temporarily halted the erosion of the Republic but also failed to modify the constitutional arrangements where it mattered most—the need for a stronger dynastic form of monarchy. He was bogged down

Devotion to Poland's Black Madonna on the edge of a forest

in wars for seventeen years, and his successes ultimately promoted the resurgence of the Habsburg Empire more than they did that of his native country. Moreover, his lack of concern for the eastern border was to cost Poland dearly. As the historian Davies wrote, "In 1686, at the whim of one wayward ambassador, the entire Ukraine, provisionally assigned to Muscovy since the truce of 1667, was needlessly abandoned. This one step . . . marked the transformation of little Muscovy into 'great Russia' and tipped the scales of power in Eastern Europe in Moscow's favor."[8] Along with the Ottoman Empire, Poland became the recognizable invalid of Europe.

The reign of Saxon kings from 1697 to 1763, who were generally absent from and uninterested in the country, only accelerated the process of degeneration. Although receiving the backing of only a minority of the Polish nobility, the two Augusts enjoyed the support of the great powers including Prussia, Austria, and, above all, Peter the Great's Russia. The Poles did present their only candidate, Stanislaw Leszczyński, whose claim to the throne was supported initially by Sweden and later by France and Spain. But the War of the Polish Succession (1733–1735)—whose principal protagonists included France, Spain, and Austria, though not the Poles—confirmed the Saxon in power. The Saxon period was marked by double elections, rival candidates, and eventual dethronements, and it weakened further the prestige of the Polish monarchy in Europe. Although unprecedented peace from foreign wars reigned in the country, Poland became vulnerable to the designs of the northern system—the emerging coalition of Catherine the Great of Russia and Frederick II of Prussia. This sixty-six-year Saxon reign also had an impact on social mores. Foreign fashions were adopted by many noble families, traditional Polish and Catholic customs lost their attraction, and fashionable marriages in which both sides agreed to full sexual freedom were in vogue.[9]

In plotting the decline of Poland we should not overlook the significance of factors embedded in the very nature of Polish society. There were separate social estates, such as the burghers (making up approximately 7 percent of the Polish population in 1791) and the clergy (about 0.5 percent), who enjoyed considerable autonomy from the nobility, possessed legal positions protected by royal charters, but played virtually no part in central government (with the inevitable exception of the church bishops). Moreover, though a few wealthy burghers could buy their way into *szlachta* ranks, social mobility between the estates—from peasant to burgher to nobleman—was negligible in the two hundred years preceding the partitions. Triggered by this immobility and by the unreformed system of serfdom, some peasant rebellions took place in the early seventeenth century, particularly among the Cossacks in the Ukraine. But *szlachta* democracy stubbornly refused to yield to reform of this rigid social stratification system and continued its refusal right up to the death throes of the Republic.

The ethnic makeup of Poland also contributed to the erosion of any sense of national unity. Although the gentry was almost completely polonized by the late eighteenth century, about half of the peasantry was non-Polish and was composed of Ukrainians, Belorussians, and Lithuanians. In turn, the supremacy of the gentry and the primacy of a farm economy based on serf labor adversely affected the growth of Polish towns. Although largely Polish until the early sixteenth century, these towns became multicultural centers following the influx of German burghers, Dutch Mennonites, Silesian Protestants, and Jewish and Armenian merchants during the next century. The concentration of Jews in urban areas was particularly marked in this period: In escaping persecution from Western Europe, Jews increased their share of the Polish town population from approximately 10 percent in the early sixteenth century to as much as 70–80 percent in towns in eastern Poland by the eighteenth century. Given such a social and ethnic structure, therefore, it is not surprising that the survival of the Polish nation (as opposed to Polish state) is most closely identified with the *szlachta* order residing in the countryside, and the contribution of other social and ethnic groups is minimized.

Poland's last king was Stanislaw August Poniatowski (1764–1795), whose reign corresponded to the Russian protectorate of Poland and who also had to preside over the series of partitions that eliminated the Polish state from the map of Europe. Historians disagree whether he was merely a "creature" (as well as lover) of Catherine the Great or whether he set out on an independent course that was terminated by the first partition. From the outset, he had to contend not only with the powerful empress and with Frederick, but with the incorrigible *szlachta*. The Seym of 1767–1768 declared, for example, that the Polish state was based on five "eternal and invariable" principles applicable to the gentry: 1) the free election of kings; 2) the *liberum veto*; 3) the right to renounce allegiance to the king; 4) the exclusive right to hold office; and 5) the domination over the peasantry.[10]

These principles were put into practice when the Confederation of Bar rose against the king and had to be crushed by Russian troops in 1771. Although quickly defeated, the confederation had extraordinary political significance: It represented a final assertion of the *szlachta*'s political independence before the partitions, and it constituted the beginning of modern Polish nationalism. The confederation revealed the military genius of Kazimierz Pulaski, who became an important figure in the American struggle for independence. It served as the pretext for the first partition undertaken by Russia, Prussia, and Austria of what had become known as the Republic of Anarchy. Finally, the confederation evoked the support of the French political philosopher Jean-Jacques Rousseau who, in his *The Government of Poland*, reached this understated conclusion: "It is hard to understand how a state so oddly constituted can have survived for so long." Sensing imminent disaster for the Republic, Rousseau urged: "Establish the republic in the Poles' own hearts, so that it will live on in them despite anything your oppressors may do."[11] This was precisely what Poles were required to do for the next century and a half.

PARTITIONS AND THE STRUGGLE FOR INDEPENDENCE

Specific plans for annexation of various parts of Poland were initiated by Frederick II as early as 1768, but it was only in 1772 that a formal treaty specifying the partitioned lands was signed and one year later that Stanislaw August and the Polish Parliament officially rendered their consent to the partition act. The ostensible reason for the first partition was given in the preamble to the treaty: "In the Name of the Most Holy Trinity! The spirit of faction, the troubles and intestine war which had shaken the Kingdom of Poland for so many years, and the Anarchy which acquires new strength every day . . . give just apprehension for expecting the total decomposition of the state. . . . At the same time, the Powers neighboring on the Republic are burdened with rights and claims which are as ancient as they are legitimate."[12]

The more that the government of what remained of Poland tried to reform the country in the next two decades and the clearer it was that a veritable age of enlightenment in the arts and culture was taking place in the country, the greater was the interest of the partitioning powers to have done with Poland as quickly and completely as possible. The same Seym that had been compelled to sanction the partition went on to create the world's first Ministry of Education—the Commission of National Education—in 1773 and to initiate a veritable educational revolution in the secondary school system. The four-year Seym that sat from 1788 to 1792 passed a series of important reforms: Unprecedented taxes on incomes from land and on ecclesiastical property were introduced, local administration modernized, and a standing army approved. The famous constitution of 3 May 1791, was inspired by the emancipatory ideas flowing from the French Revolution; it granted rights to the third estate, allowing burghers to have access to public office and to the Seym.

Although serfdom was not abolished, peasants were now extended "the protection of the law and the government." Extensive central governmental machinery was created, including a Council of Ministers and a national bank. Such radical measures were only enacted because the Seym adopted the procedural device of constituting itself a confederation, thereby circumventing the use of *liberum veto*. Under these circumstances it became possible, too, for the Seym to abolish formally the principles of *liberum veto* and elective monarchy. The only problem with this audacious reform package was that it came much too late.

A Poland reformed in this way would have resurrected the threat to the partitioning powers. The anarchy and decomposition of the state that had been cited in 1772 as justification for partition would have been rectified by this remarkable constitutional document. Accordingly, the new standing army, under such able leaders as its commander in chief Józef Poniatowski, the king's nephew, and a divisional commander Tadeusz Kościuszko, who was destined to fight in the American War of Independence, was confronted by Russian military forces within a year. More insidious was the signing of an act of confederation by several Polish magnates at Targowica in 1792. The confederation condemned the 3 May constitution and the Polish "revolution" it had spawned and requested the help of Russian troops to put down what was viewed as a rebellion. Soon the unfortunate king cast his lot with the confederation. It is hardly surprising that much later Targowica became a term used by many Poles to describe any form of sellout solution.

The second partition concluded between Russia and Prussia in 1793 further reduced Poland to the status of an unviable rump-state. Kościuszko's national insurrection of 1794 foundered and led to bloody reprisals and massacres by Russian troops. It also produced the third partition, which was signed by Russia, Prussia, and Austria in October 1795. All remaining Polish lands were divided up, the king was forced to abdicate a month later, and, by agreement of the three powers, the name of Poland was to disappear forever from international law.

. From our historical outline we have seen how the system of oligarchical anarchy that had become institutionalized in Poland for at least three centuries was primarily responsible for the final disappearance of the Polish Republic. Let me stress, too, that many Polish magnates frequently pursued their own narrow interests even though this meant forging alliances with powers inimical to Poland's national interest. The Confederation of Targowica was merely the most visible symbol of this ongoing process. Presented with the alternatives of reforming the constitutional arrangements or passively acquiescing to foreign partition, however, the Polish nobility opted for a remarkably radical variant of the first. In the last years of the Republic, therefore, an unprecedented feature of Polish political life was "the desire to resurrect the Polish State by internal reform, in alliance with the European revolutionary movement, in defiance of the defenders of the old order, the very powers which had partitioned Poland."[13]

For the next one hundred twenty-five years, the Polish nation was able to survive where the Polish state had not. This occurred in spite of a methodical process of Germanization of the lands occupied by Prussia and, to a lesser extent, Austria, and in spite of the violent repression sporadically applied by Russian rulers. It is true that institutional vestiges of the dismembered Polish state continued to appear in the nineteenth century. So long as Napoleon posed a threat to the partitioning powers, for example, Poles held hopes of national resurrection. The Duchy of Warsaw, which Napoleon carved out from Prussian-occupied lands, seemed both a partial realization of these hopes and yet another partition of the country by a foreign power. The French emperor's attitude to his Polish supporters was cynical at best: He used them to buttress his forces in Lombardy, Spain, and even distant Haiti; he engaged them in fighting Austria and marshalled Polish troops in his famous campaign against Russia in 1812; Napoleon even took a Polish mistress, Maria Walewska, who sought favors from him for her compatriots. Yet he doggedly resisted making a firm commitment to help the Poles in their struggle for independence. Napoleon's defeats in Russia and then at Waterloo simultaneously put an end to the duchy's existence. At the Congress of Vienna in 1815 Polish territories were redistributed for a fifth time, among Austria, Prussia, and Russia, with the insignificant concession that a small Congress Kingdom of Poland was established with Tsar Alexander I as its king.

Congress Poland represented at once an expansion of Russian influence westward as well as an implicit acknowledgment by the tsar of the Poles' rights to certain autonomy in local matters. A fascinating aspect of this period was the way in which Poland became the scene of a struggle for power between the tsar and his brother Grand Duke Constantine, who harbored imperial ambitions as well. Constantine was given to irrational and troubling caprices, such as hiring only giants and dwarfs to act as his servants and chaining university students to wheelbarrows and forcing them to clean the streets of Warsaw. This did his cause little good. Likewise, he divorced his Russian wife for a Polish woman, which required him to renounce his royal rights in Russia. His seeming intention was to become a "good Pole," and, accordingly, upon the death in 1825 of Tsar Alexander and the Decembrist revolt that ensued, it was his more ruthless brother Nicolas who came to power. Constantine subsequently attached himself even more closely to Congress Poland.

His dilemma was, however, that by acting as a "good Pole" he fed demands for greater independence. In late November 1830 a group of infantry cadets stormed the duke's Warsaw residence and demanded full independence for Poland. Constantine's fortuitous escape and lapse into greater insanity has been dramatized by the playwright Wyspiański in his haunting *November Night*. The cadet revolt produced a political crisis that was resolved, in the end, through an armed struggle between Polish and Russian military units. The much weaker Poles were beaten in September 1831 with the capitulation of Warsaw.

The November insurrection put an end to the shaky *modus vivendi* between Poles and Russians in the Congress Kingdom and gave way to a period of bitter repression and forced Russification. The constitution was abolished by Nicolas, state lands were confiscated and handed to Russian generals and government officials, and the cultural vanguard of Polish society was driven into exile. The failed insurrection fired the creativity of Polish poets and artists of the romantic period, most notably Mickiewicz and Chopin. The Polish revolutionary tradition was now immortalized even as national independence was turned into an improbable dream.

This is not to suggest that the nationalist movement had been fully destroyed by emigration and repression. In quick succession other uprisings were organized. In 1846 Austrian-occupied Galicia rose, expecting other regions to follow suit. But the cagey Austrian leadership played on the ingrained conservatism of the peasantry and persuaded it to massacre much of the Kraków nobility who had issued the call to arms. Two years later, during the "springtime of nations," revolts were staged in various parts of Poland, extending from Poznań to Lwów. No less a figure than Prince Metternich, the Austrian chancellor, advanced a characteristically sophistic distinction between what were regarded as understandable rebellions by other European nations and those instigated by the Poles:

> Polonism is only a formula, the sound of a word underneath which hides a revolution in its most glaring form; it is not a small part of a revolution, but revolution itself. Polonism does not declare war on the monarchies which possess Polish territory, it declares war on all existing

institutions and proclaims the destruction of all the common foundations which form the basis of society.

Poles were viewed as conspirators, revolutionaries, anarchists, and even barbarians, inhabiting "swamps, woods and marshes on which wolves and bears swarm in packs and endanger the roads."[14]

From the viewpoint of the supposedly civilized, partitioning nations, the worst was yet to come from the Poles. In January 1863 Polish insurgents attacked Russian garrisons, bringing to a head several years of nationalist agitation in the occupied territories. By May a national government had been proclaimed, and it quickly received the moral support of Western European states such as France, England, the Vatican, and even Austria. Unfortunately, the Polish leadership was fragmented into opposing factions. The "reds," or radicals, stressed the indispensability of an insurrection to attain independence and the centrality of an agrarian revolt in order for such an insurrection to succeed. Among the leaders was Korzeniowski, father of the novelist Joseph Conrad. In contrast, the "whites," led by members of the nobility, sought, initially at least, to reach accommodation with Russia. Eventually they, too, demanded a national government to govern the Congress Kingdom as well as Poland's borderlands—Lithuania and Ruthenia.

Without outside help the uprising had little chance of success. By October 1863 it had been brutally suppressed and its leaders, including the eloquent nobleman Traugutt, hanged. In 1864 Congress Poland was officially abolished and its territories incorporated as a province of Russia. The reign of terror instigated by Russian officials was designed to eradicate Polish nationalism once and for all, but the atrocities were so massive and the Russification drive so brutal that world opinion was horrified. Sensing advantages for Germany in this repression, Bismarck instituted his own *Kulturkampf* in Prussian-occupied lands: It too sought to eliminate all manifestations of Polish language and culture. By contrast, Austria, following the 1867 *Ausgleich* with Hungary, granted virtual autonomy to Galicia, which dovetailed well with the intentions of Kraków conservatives who were willing to cooperate with Vienna anyway. The differential treatment meted out by the partitioning powers shaped the attitudes of Poles to these countries to this day.

These series of insurrections left the Poles exhausted and forlorn. Following an analogy drawn by their national poet Mickiewicz, many now believed that Poland, like Christ, was destined to suffer in order to redeem the sins of other nations so that they, too, could become worthy of liberty. Poles in the second half of the nineteenth century came to believe this cross should be borne heroically and stoically.

In this period various parts of Poland underwent rapid industrialization. In the Russian-occupied lands the size of the emergent working class doubled, and the value of industrial production increased sevenfold between 1864 and 1892. Leading the way in industrial growth were textiles (whose output in these years increased fivefold), coal mining (increased tenfold), metallurgy (increased thirty times), and sugar refining (increased ninefold). The so-called Vistulaland province soon became the most advanced region of the whole Russian Empire. By 1890 those employed in the industrial sector here represented 0.7 percent of Congress Poland's total population; in Prussian-occupied Poznania and Austrian-occupied Galicia the proportions were only 0.1 percent and 0.3 percent. A further indicator of the increasing significance of the former Congress Kingdom was its demographic growth: While the population of Poznania grew by 36 percent and that of Galicia by 59 percent in the second half of the nineteenth century, that of the Kingdom rose by 108 percent.

The industrialization process was reflected in the values of the intellectual movement that emerged in this period. Its main current was positivism—the belief that reason and intelligence determine the pace and direction of expansion. The doctrine was readily embraced by students, who saw a sorry tale in the insurrectionary tradition. It also engendered a new realism that stressed triloyalism: reconciliation of Polish provinces with their foreign governments, apoliticism, and, above all, "organic work"—a spirit of industriousness that would raise the social, economic, and cultural level of the nation and, in this way, make Poland strong again.

In practice, organic work was designed to strengthen the position of the embryonic capitalist class, along with that of the petite bourgeoisie, the intelligentsia, and the wealthier peasants. The birthplace of organic work—and perhaps its cradle to this day—was Poznań. The concept of organic work was first elaborated in 1840, and certain of its characteristics colored the program of the "whites" in 1863. In the aftermath of the January uprising, members of the Kraków Learned Society and Warsaw's Main School became adherents. Perhaps nowhere more than in literature were positivist values dominant, as in the writings of Prus, Konopnicka, and Orzeszkowa (the latter concerned above all with a central aspect of positivism—the emancipation of women). The dichotomy between the romantic revolutionary tradition and the pragmatic realistic approach was now fully developed, and much of subsequent twentieth-century Polish history can be viewed through this prism.

POLONIA RECONSTITUTA

At the turn of the twentieth century, economic development led in Poland, as in many other European nations, to the rise of mass political movements, in particular those of the left. In 1893 a Polish Socialist Party (PPS) was secretly formed that emphasized the primacy of national independence over proletarian internationalism. It argued that socialization of the means of production could only be achieved if national oppression was removed and capitalism allowed to flourish. This would lead, in turn, to the eventual overthrow of the capitalist order by ineluctable socialist forces. PPS leaders such as Pilsudski were reluctant to subordinate the Polish socialist movement to a Russian one, thereby replicating Poland's inferior status in socialist institutions. In contrast, the Social Democratic Party of the Kingdom of Poland and Lithuania (SDKPiL), founded in 1894, was more internationalist and its leaders, such as Luxemburg (who became a central figure in the German Spartacus League) and Dzerżyński (who became Soviet Russia's first security chief) held that the struggle for national independence was anachronistic. In the case of Poland, a poor capitalist state far removed from a socialist revolution would result.

On the right, the movement known as National Democracy (ND) was formed in 1887 and was always closely identified with its leader, Dmowski. It was extremely nationalist, not in the sense of advocating Polish independence by any means possible but in stressing the need to maintain a national, homogeneous, all-Polish character. For Dmowski, Poland's past failures were related to its religious toleration, ethnic equality, and humanitarianism. In particular, the sizable Jewish and Ukrainian minorities had weakened the social fabric of Poland and made it an "effeminate nation." Minorities had to be fully assimilated if a strong all-Polish nation was to come into being. Dmowski remained equivocal about national independence but underscored the importance of collaboration with the Russian autocracy, which he justified in terms of Neoslavism. After Russia had become a constitutional monarchy, Dmowski's party took part in the 1906 elections to the Duma (in contrast to the socialists). However, the ND was not involved in the general strike and revolutionary upheavals that hit Poland in 1905 and 1906; these were principally the work of the socialist parties.

In short, on the eve of World War I Polish political leaders envisaged very different alliances that could lead to the reemergence of a strong state. Dmowski's scenario foresaw a pro-Russian policy as alone being capable of offering an opportunity for statehood, but Pilsudski's conception was predicated on the total collapse of the ian Empire. The fortunes of war were to prove the latter's views correct. But Pilsudski's approach was also very praxeological: Five days after the war began he led a company of riflemen—a precursor of his famous Legions—against Russian troops. This display of decisiveness, together with his popular anti-Russian sentiments, contributed considerably to the emergence of Pilsudski as the first leader of independent Poland.

During the next four years offers made by the warring parties to enlist Poland on their side became ever more enticing. As Davies has put it, "In 1914–16, the Tsar, the Kaiser, and the Emperor-King proposed mounting degrees of autonomy. By 1917, the President of the United States, the Provisional government in Petrograd, and even the leader of the Bolsheviks declared themselves in favor of Polish independence. In 1918, they were copied by France, Italy, Japan, and, last of all, Great Britain."[15]

Notwithstanding such promises, the reemergence of a Polish state was ultimately contingent on the outcome of the war and more specifically, on a weakening of the partitioning powers. The Bolshevik Revolution of October 1917 represented a step in this direction; Russia withdrew from the war, signed an unfavorable peace treaty with Germany and, more importantly, annulled all the tsarist partition treaties. The approaching collapse of the central powers, in turn, presaged a much weakened Germany and a collapse of the Habsburg Empire. On 8 January 1918, President Woodrow Wilson put forward his plan for a general peace in his Fourteen Points. The thirteenth point foresaw a "united, independent and autonomous Poland with free unrestricted access to the sea" and situated on "territories inhabited by an indubitably Polish population." On 7 November of that year, just prior to the armistice, a provisional government was set up. Four days later Pilsudski officially became head of state as well as supreme commander of the army. The Polish state had finally been reconstituted.

The interwar Polish Republic emerged, therefore, as a result not of a national insurrection or of military victories scored by Polish troops, but of an extremely fortuitous combination of external events. This is not to suggest Poland played a negligible part in the war effort: 90 percent of the country had been directly affected by the military hostilities, and much industry and agriculture had been requisitioned by occupying forces. But the establishment of statehood certainly did not proceed along the lines envisaged by either the nineteenth-century romantic or positivist theorists. Neither was it simply the brainchild of Woodrow Wilson, nor the creation of the 1919 Versailles treaty (which merely confirmed the *fait accompli* in Central Europe), nor the consequence of the Bolshevik policy of national self-determination, as Soviet propaganda is wont to present the event.

The formative years of the interwar republic also did not generate the universal support or enthusiasm among Poles one might have expected, given the one hundred fifty year interval since the first partition of the Republic. The constitutional system was modeled on the French Third Republic and reproduced all its shortcomings: a weak president, a powerful legislature, a profusion of political parties (in 1925 there were ninety-two registered parties and thirty-two actually represented in the Seym), and a rapid turnover of governments. To indicate the precarious nature of the new political order, the premier of the first national government was Ignacy Paderewski, more famous as a concert pianist than as a founding father of the so-called Second Republic. The first president, Gabriel Narutowicz, was assassinated in 1922, two days after he was sworn in! No Polish king had ever suffered such an indignity. The first elections held in January 1919 demonstrated deep political divisions between Poles who had lived under differing partitioning powers. In the former Kingdom of Poland the right-wing National Democrats scored a clear victory, while in Galicia the centrist Polish Peasant Party (Piast), led by the indomitable, self-educated peasant Wincenty Witos (who thrice became premier in the interwar years), was the winner.

What was more, Poland quickly became involved in no less than six conflicts between 1918 and 1921, all occasioned by its uncertain frontiers. Thus, the Poles took on the Ukrainians regarding eastern Galicia, the Germans twice concerning Poznania and Silesia (where three national uprisings broke out between 1919 and 1921), the Lithuanians about the city of Wilno, the Czechs about the Cieszyn region and, most importantly, the Russians regarding much of the Ukraine and, ultimately, the very fate of the Polish Republic.

In the so-called "forgotten war" between Poland and Russia, Pilsudski's troops, which were not associated with the White Armies fighting the Bolsheviks, initially captured Kiev in May 1920. Then a Russian counteroffensive drove them back to Warsaw itself by August. Lenin even established a Polish Provisional Revolutionary Committee at Bialystok headed by the Polish Communist Marchlewski. Throughout this war Lenin seemed more interested in creating a red Poland than in annexing lands for Soviet Russia. In the end his hopes were frustrated by Pilsudski's military genius and, in the eyes of some Poles, divine intervention: By adopting some intricate troop deployments, Pilsudski was able to snatch victory when defeat seemed imminent and drive the Bolsheviks back into Russia. Following this "miracle on the Vistula," Pilsudski allegedly contemplated striking

at Moscow itself but in the end agreed to a peace treaty that was
concluded in Riga in 1921, which still gave Poland more territories
than the British intermediary Lord Curzon had suggested. Success
in this war was to have its price later, however: So confident was
the Polish officer corps of its genius that little effort was made in
the interwar years to modernize the army or update military doctrine.
The ill-fated 1939 campaign against the German invasion underscored
these weaknesses. At the same time, the Soviet leaders bided their
time and awaited propitious conditions to regain the lands they had
lost. The Ribbentrop-Molotov pact, concluded on the eve of World
War II, more than offset Russia's 1920–1921 losses. The pact's secret
protocol gave the Soviet Union all of eastern Poland, with Germany
obtaining the remainder of the country. Soviet foreign minister Molotov
asserted this was the logical fate reserved for the "bastard of the
Versailles treaty."

Interwar Poland turned out to be ethnically more heterogeneous
than Wilson had anticipated. In 1921 about 70 percent of the population
was Polish and the rest minority groups. The latter included approximately 5–6 million Ukrainians, 3 million Jews, 1.5 million Belorussians, and more than 1 million Germans. Deprived of statehood
for so long the Poles became more concerned with an assertion of
national goals than with the status of minorities. The gradual lurch
to the right in interwar politics had serious consequences for the
Jewish population in particular: Although Poland had displayed more
tolerance toward this group during the centuries than most other
European countries, many chauvinists in Poland (as in other parts
of Europe in the 1930s) increasingly saw the Jews as scapegoats for
growing economic ills. Anti-Semitism never became official government policy, but neither was it combated with much energy by
Pilsudski's governments.

The parliamentary system was afflicted by a number of incon-
clusive elections and a plethora of weak governments between 1922
and 1926 so that, in the end, Pilsudski lost patience and undertook
a coup. It took place in May 1926 and involved several days of
fighting in Warsaw, which cost some five hundred lives. The new
regime strengthened the power of the executive—Pilsudski was even
prevailed upon to become premier for several years—but for the most
part his dictatorship was well concealed in parliamentary guise. His
political program was also well disguised. At one time he claimed
that he had taken a streetcar named socialism and got off at a stop
named Poland. He also spoke vaguely of the goal of "the diminution
of robbery and the pursuit of honesty." But increasingly, more rigged
elections, harassment, and even internment of oppositional officials

and more widespread censorship brought even these aspects of his misnamed *sanacja* ("purification") regime into question. Parliamentary support was drummed up by forming in 1928 a "non-party bloc for cooperation with the government," in which the conventional procedure of a cabinet emerging from an elected legislature was reversed.

Following the stock market crash of 1929, national income in Poland fell; by 1933 income had declined by 25 percent. Economic conditions led to worker unrest and even peasant radicalism (as in the agricultural strike of 1937). In turn, the government became simultaneously more authoritarian, run by Pilsudski and his inner circle of legionnaires, and ineffective, unable to translate brute power into a much-needed reform program. Little changed when Marshal Pilsudski died in 1935. A colonel's regime surfaced, buttressed by a realigned parliamentary group calling itself the Camp of National Unity. Economic recovery did not take place: In 1936 the country's industrial output had not even attained the 1914 level, unemployment remained high (40 percent of the labor force in 1935), more than two-thirds of the population continued to work in agriculture, and an indigenous capitalist class was virtually nonexistent (52 percent of joint stock companies were owned by foreigners and another 42 percent by the Polish state). In addition, relations with minority groups continued to deteriorate.

But it was in the foreign policy area that the *sanacja* regime showed itself most incompetent. Pilsudski had resisted overtures to align himself with one of Poland's great neigbors, Russia or Germany, though nonaggression pacts were concluded with each (1932 and 1934 respectively). In particular, Pilsudski seemed unconcerned by the rise of the Nazis in Germany and described them as "nothing but windbags." Poland's foreign minister from 1932 to 1939, Colonel Beck, exuded greater confidence and sought great power status for his country through the creation of a Third Europe, to consist of the small Central European states under the leadership of Poland, of course. Even after the 1938 Munich conference, which ceded the Sudetenland to Germany, and after signals from Moscow that a Soviet-German rapprochement was being contemplated, the Polish government appeared oblivious to the threat and did nothing to prepare itself for the increasingly inevitable war.

Poland's fate was effectively sealed by the Ribbentrop-Molotov pact concluded by the Third Reich and the Soviet Union on 23 August 1939. A provisional partition line was agreed upon, and nine days later the Germans invaded Poland, leading to declarations of war against Germany by Britain and France. On 17 September the Russians marched into Poland from the east, claiming their spoils. Polish resistance on both fronts was quickly crushed. Although partition was nothing new to Poland, World War II was to pose a threat to the existence of the Polish nation itself.

The war proved a holocaust for Polish Jews, 3 million (or 90 percent) of whom were killed. Some 3 million ethnic Poles also lost their lives, only a small proportion (10 percent) of whom were military casualties. Total battle deaths were about six hundred sixty thousand, approximating the number suffered by British and U.S. forces combined in the war. Civilian populations were transported to extermination camps in Auschwitz-Birkenau (where 4 million human beings of various nationalities, mostly Jews from various countries of Eastern Europe, were slaughtered), Treblinka, and Majdanek. Summary mass killing took place on city streets and in small villages throughout the country, and many others died of starvation and in labor camps in Poland and the Reich. The Nazis found very few willing collaborators in the country (nor did they particularly search for them) and met valiant resistance. It took one month of bitter fighting for the German forces to liquidate the Jewish ghetto of Warsaw in April–May 1943: Close to sixty thousand Polish Jews were killed in the uneven struggle. In the sixty-three days of fighting between August and October 1944 that marked the Warsaw uprising, nearly two hundred thousand Poles lost their lives. The remaining eight hundred thousand survivors were forcibly removed from the capital, and the city was methodically razed to the ground.

In sum, one-fifth of Poland's prewar population, or more than 6 million people, was killed between 1939 and 1945, the highest attrition rate of any nation in the war. Only fifty thousand Polish Jews lived through the Holocaust. Hitler's policy was aimed at genocide, but the Russians also contributed to the nation's suffering. The Soviets sent more than 1 million Poles into forcible exile in distant Siberia and Asiatic Russia. Moreover, some ten thousand Polish officers were executed by Stalin's security forces in 1940, in part because of their "bourgeois" origins, in part to weaken Polish fighting forces. Several thousand of their graves were uncovered by the German army in the forest of Katyn in 1943. Economically, Poland's wartime losses were estimated at 38 percent of national wealth and 70 percent of grain production.

After the German-Soviet invasion the country was divided into three parts. The northern and western regions were annexed to the Reich, and the central lands were put under the administration of a murderous German governate-general. Territory east of a line running close to Curzon's earlier proposal was incorporated into the USSR in November 1939. Most of the population here was not ethnically

Polish: There were more than 4 million Ukrainians, 1 million Belorussians, and 1 million Jews. The obstinate demand by the wartime Polish government in exile, based in London, that all these territories be returned caused continuous friction between Western leaders and Stalin during the course of the war. Relations were further strained when Poland's premier Sikorski demanded an investigation of the Katyn atrocity.

It has been argued that "Poles were perhaps more united under foreign occupation than they were under governments of their own election."[16] Although in large measure true, this view may exaggerate the degree of political unity among Poles at that time. By 1942 two separate resistance organizations had emerged, the larger linked to the London government in exile, the smaller to the Soviet Union. The Home Army (AK) numbered some two hundred thousand by 1944 and was united behind Sikorski until his death in a plane crash at Gibraltar in 1943. After that, the army split into two groups: The first, represented by the new premier and Polish Peasant Party (PSL) leader Mikolajczyk, sought accommodation with the USSR; the second, linked to commander in chief of Polish forces Sosnkowski, was virulently anti-Soviet. Yet a third approach emerged later when resistance leaders in Warsaw, such as Bór-Komorowski, put forward the thesis that Poles had to fight the Germans militarily but had to fight the Communists politically. These divisions proved fatal when the ill-conceived Warsaw uprising was launched in August 1944. It was not coordinated beforehand with either the Western Allies or the Soviet Union, and not even with the London government in exile! The only forces in a position to offer assistance to the besieged insurrectionists were troops of the Red Army, who had just penetrated the suburbs of Warsaw on the other side of the Vistula River. They made a feeble attempt to help, and when Western allies asked Stalin's permission to land behind Soviet lines while delivering assistance to the city, they were rebuffed. In spite of such divisions, the Polish resistance organization was perhaps the most effective of any established in a Nazi-occupied country. Some one hundred fifty thousand Germans were killed in occupied Poland, including top SS officials. Individual attacks on particularly brutal leaders and well-planned ambushes of military transport, payroll vehicles, and the like became commonplace as the occupation continued.

The other resistance force was the People's Guard (GL) whose membership numbered, at most, fifty thousand in 1944. This communist organization was less divided than the pro-Western resistance, and for this it was indebted to Stalin, who in 1937 and 1938 had killed off the leadership of the interwar Polish Communist Party (KPP) for alleged Trotskyite and fascist deviations. Those who survived, such as Gomulka and Ochab, had had the good fortune to be in a *sanacja* prison when Stalin summoned Polish Communists to Moscow for a squaring of accounts. They became only too well aware of the need to work closely with Moscow and, accordingly, set up the Polish Workers' Party (PPR) with Stalin's approval in January 1942. It gave birth, in turn, to a National Council of the Homeland (KRN) in December 1943, which took on all the appearances of a rival provisional government to the London one. In July 1944 the council was transformed into the Polish Committee of National Liberation (PKWN), based in the recently liberated city of Lublin, and at the end of the year it proclaimed itself the country's provisional government. On 5 January 1945, the USSR officially recognized this government, and twelve days later the Red Army entered Warsaw. Poland's postwar political configuration was effectively determined by these two events.

Those calling themselves realists believed no other solution was possible. After all, in Teheran in November 1943 Churchill, Roosevelt, and Stalin had agreed that the Curzon line would form Poland's eastern border and the Oder-Neisse rivers its western one, in this way transposing Poland 250 miles westward. The Yalta Conference of February 1945 produced further agreement on an interim government of national unity that would be composed of representatives from the two Polish governments. Mikolajczyk already had spurned an offer in 1944 to serve as premier in the PKWN because of his refusal to recognize the new eastern border and the distribution of seats in the committee (fourteen PKWN members, four London members). Churchill believed that the "free and unfettered elections" that were called for by the Yalta agreement would be enough to entice Mikolajczyk to return to Poland. When he did return in June 1945 to serve in a newly constituted provisional government, its composition was much more unfavorable to his party than the proposition he had rejected earlier. Moreover, instead of getting the premiership, he had to be satisfied with the posts of vice-premier and minister of agriculture. Within a month the United States and Britain extended diplomatic recognition to this government.

The last year of the war had provided a new generation of Poles with an old refresher course in history. Once again Poles were taught that insurrections (such as the Warsaw uprising) did not lead to national independence. The agreements made among the great powers determined how independent Poland could be.

NOTES

1. W.F. Reddaway et al. (eds.), *The Cambridge History of Poland*, vol. 1 (Cambridge: Cambridge University Press, 1950), p. 21.

2. T. Manteuffel, *The Formation of a Polish State* (Detroit, Mich.: Wayne State University Press, 1982), pp. 75–76.

3. Reddaway, *Cambridge History of Poland*, vol. 1, p. 57.

4. J.K. Fedorowicz (ed.), *A Republic of Nobles* (Cambridge: Cambridge University Press, 1982), p. 91.

5. Ibid., pp. 111–112.

6. N. Davies, *God's Playground*, vol. 1 (New York: Columbia University Press, 1984), p. 340.

7. Reddaway, *Cambridge History of Poland*, vol. 1, p. 439.

8. Davies, *God's Playground*, vol. 1, p. 487.

9. A. Gieysztor et al., *History of Poland* (Warsaw: Polish Scientific Publishers, 1968), p. 350.

10. Ibid., p. 323.

11. J.-J. Rousseau, *The Government of Poland* (New York: Bobbs-Merrill, 1972), pp. 2, 10.

12. Quoted in Davies, *God's Playground*, vol. 1, pp. 521, 523.

13. Gieysztor, *History of Poland*, p. 395.

14. Quoted in W.F. Reddaway et al. (eds.), *The Cambridge History of Poland*, vol. 2 (Cambridge: Cambridge University Press, 1950), p. 338.

15. N. Davies, *God's Playground*, vol. 2 (New York: Columbia University Press, 1984), p. 378.

16. R.F. Leslie, *The History of Poland since 1863* (Cambridge: Cambridge University Press, 1983), p. 221.

FURTHER READINGS

In addition to sources cited in the Notes, other important works on Polish history include:

N. Davies. *Heart of Europe*. Oxford: Oxford University Press, 1984.

M.K. Dziewanowski. *Poland in the Twentieth Century*. New York: Columbia University Press, 1977.

O. Halecki. *A History of Poland*. London: Routledge and Kegan Paul, 1978.

A. Polonsky. *Politics in Independent Poland 1921–1939*. Oxford: Oxford University Press, 1972.

A. Polonsky and B. Drukier (eds.). *The Beginnings of Communist Rule in Poland 1943–45*. London: Routledge and Kegan Paul, 1980.

P.S. Wandycz. *The Lands of Partitioned Poland, 1795–1918*. Seattle: University of Washington Press, 1974.

2

Politics in the People's Republic of Poland

The cornerstone of a Soviet-type socialist system is the Leninist principle that the Communist party plays the leading role in society. One way to view the turbulent events that have shaken postwar Poland at regular intervals is to consider them as a series of challenges to the party's hegemonic role. Initially, certain social groups, above all the less privileged ones, accepted and even welcomed the image the Communist party projected of itself—the vanguard of the pro-letariat, which was acclaimed as the leading class in society. But the steadily increasing series of aberrations from Marxist-Leninist ideas, the general incompetence of the leadership, and the economic disasters visited upon society that stemmed from the party's actual exercise of its leading role all contributed to the discrediting of the Leninist principle, the party performing it, and the entire political system in which it constituted an integrative part. In this chapter I examine political developments in the People's Republic of Poland that have caused the country to become the powderkeg of contemporary Europe. First, however, is a brief discussion of the major political institutions in the state.

THE POLITICAL INSTITUTIONS

The formal structures governing the political system today were first implanted in Poland immediately following World War II. These structures have their origin in the form of Bolshevik rule of Russia following the 1917 October Revolution. Figure 2.1 charts the principal institutions of the party and the governmental apparatus in Poland in the 1980s. At the outset I should emphasize that the various bodies have played different roles at different stages of socialist development. Few in Lenin's lifetime, for example, would have surmised that the

Figure 2.1 The structural framework of Poland's central authorities

Elected Party Organs   Elected Government Organs

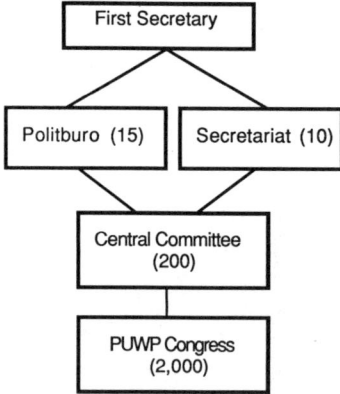

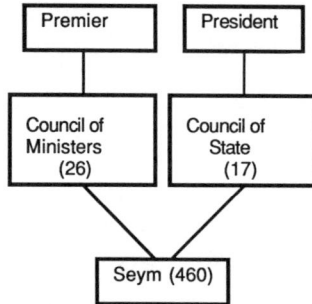

```
      First Secretary                Premier         President
        /      \                        |               |
  Politburo (15)  Secretariat (10)   Council of      Council of
        \      /                      Ministers        State
   Central Committee                    (26)           (17)
        (200)                            \             /
          |                               Seym (460)
    PUWP Congress
      (2,000)
```

Administrative State Apparatus
Ministries (26):

Agiculture, Forestry and Food Economy
Chemical and Light Industry
Commerce and Services
Communication
Construction, Housing and Local Economy
Culture and Art
Education and Socialization
Environmental Protection and Natural Resources
Finance
Foreign Affairs
Foreign Trade
Health and Social Welfare
Internal Affairs
Justice
Labor, Wages and Social Affairs
Metallurgy and Machine Industry
Mining and Energy
National Defense
Science and Higher Education
Supply and Fuel
Transportation
Office of the Council of Ministers
   (State Administration)
Office of Maritime Economy
Office of Physical Education, Sport and Tourism
Office of Religious Affairs
Office of Scientific-Technical Development
   and Implementation

Administrative Party Apparatus
Central Committee Departments (14):

Agriculture and Food
Cadres
Culture
Foreign Affairs
General Affairs
Ideology
Industry
Organization
Planning
Press, Radio, TV
Science & Education
Social-Legal
Social Organizations
Trade and Finance

position of general secretary of the party (held by a man regarded as the clerk of the organization, Stalin) would be transformed soon into an unassailable dictatorial post. Similarly, since the establishment of communist rule in Poland the role of the Seym has fluctuated sharply from one ruler to the next.

Table 2.1   Membership in Poland's Political Parties,
            1950-84

At end of	PUWP	ZSL	SD
1950	1,240,900	194,057	50,000
1960	1,154,672	258,700	39,100
1970	2,320,000	413,500	88,300
1980	3,091,900	478,600	113,700
1981	2,690,600	463,100	110,400
1983	2,185,700	470,900	100,900
1984	2,167,000	479,150	n.d.

Source: Rocznik Statystyczny. Warsaw: GUS,
          various years.

The relationship between party and government is crucial to an understanding of the actual operation of the system. Some observers have sought to encapsulate the relationship by imputing to the party responsibility for broad political policies and to the government responsibility for economic issues. Others have argued that party institutions are vested with real political power, whereas state organs simply carry out party policies and therefore have an executive character. Polish leaders themselves have often stated that the party ought to direct and the government govern. Nevertheless, scholars generally agree that the final say in any issue belongs to party leaders and party bodies.

Even under communist rule there are three legal political parties in Poland. In addition to the Polish United Workers' Party (PZPR), there are the United Peasants' Party (ZSL) and the Democratic Party (SD). Respective membership figures are given in Table 2.1. With only slight modifications, the distribution of Seym seats among the three parties remained the same from 1957 to the time of the 1985 elections—261 for the PZPR, 113 for the ZSL, and 37 for the SD. In the Parliament elected in October 1985 the PZPR's quota (its leadership ultimately determines the distribution of seats among political organizations) was reduced to 245, which still left it with an absolute majority in the 460-seat chamber. An insignificant change took place in the numbers of ZSL and SD deputies elected, but the number of independent deputies, that is, those not belonging to any political party, increased substantially from 49 to 75. The majority of nonparty deputies are drawn from the ranks of PZPR-approved mass organizations, such as youth and women's leagues. Among independent deputies, however, there were 21 (compared to the previous 16) representing the three Catholic groups—the party-inspired Pax bloc, the Christian Social Association, and the more independent Znak organization.

Although organizationally quite distinct, the ZSL and SD are de facto, institutionalized, special interest groups subordinated to the PZPR rather than full-blooded multi-issue parties. The ZSL's clientele consists of the nearly 15 million inhabitants living in the countryside, while the SD caters to white-collar workers in the state administration, schoolteachers, private artisans, small shopkeepers, and other sections of the growing petite bourgeoisie (which contradicts Lenin's view that the petite bourgeoisie would steadily disappear under a socialist regime).The influence of these two political organizations (the Polish word *partia* is studiously applied to the PZPR alone) on policy affecting their respective spheres is all too often underestimated, but this is quite understandable. Until 1982 an umbrella organization existed (the National Unity Front) that formally subordinated both the ZSL and the SD to the PZPR. As part of the reform drive following martial law, this front was disbanded and replaced with a broader institution—the Patriotic Movement for National Rebirth (PRON). The PZPR remains the undisputed wielder of power in the political system, however, and when we speak of the party we refer specifically to it.

The most powerful political official in People's Poland is the first secretary of the PZPR. This position was held by Gomulka until 1948, when he was displaced by Bierut, and he returned to it in 1956. Other first secretaries have included Edward Gierek (1970–1980) and General Wojciech Jaruzelski (since 1981), and two interregnum leaders, Ochab (in 1956) and Kania (in 1980–1981).

Officially, the first secretary is elected by the party's Central Committee. In practice, the latter body invariably approves the recommendation submitted to it by the Politburo, and the Kremlin leadership has also to ratify all such appointments. The Politburo, too, is chosen by the Central Committee to manage day-to-day political affairs of the country. It includes the fifteen or so most influential leaders in Poland and meets almost every week. One other body elected by the Central Committee is the Secretariat, which is responsible for overseeing the functioning of the elaborate administrative machinery of the party. An individual who is elected to both Politburo and Secretariat is truly in the inner sanctum of the leadership.

The role of the Central Committee is generally limited to choosing from among its members those persons who will be given stewardship over the party and the nation. But in Poland some of its sessions have in fact proven very turbulent, as documents from the Solidarity period (1980–1981) demonstrate. In contrast to the Communist Party of the Soviet Union (CPSU), the approximately two hundred members of the PZPR Central Committee do have some input in the policy-making process. Debates can be meaningful, especially in crisis periods, and unanimity of views is not assured.

The party's congress is usually held every five years unless a sudden political crisis necessitates an earlier convening. The extraordinary Ninth Congress, held in the midst of the 1981 political crisis, was an example of the latter case. The Tenth Congress, in summer 1986, marks a return to the regular schedule. The congress session is composed of delegates chosen by rank-and-file party members in factories, offices, villages, and military units throughout the country. Its most important task is to elect the Central Committee, and again, in practice, this election is manipulated by the incumbents of high office. Thus, the nominal chain of influence is from the bottom up; the real chain goes from the inner elite downward.

This practice is sanctioned by the Leninist principle of democratic centralism: In reality, democracy is circumscribed by centralism. Although freedom to discuss issues, criticize policy proposals, and elect leaders is countenanced by Communist party statutes, an overriding policy consideration is the need for unity and, as the practice has evolved, unanimity. Centralized power is the surest guarantee of such unity. Thus, Communist parties, perhaps above all Leninist-type parties, confirm the iron law of oligarchy: "Who says organization says oligarchy."

Democratic centralism also dictates relations between central and local party authorities. Local officials rarely have a chance to influence their higher level counterparts and more usually are required to carry out directives issued by central bodies. Looking at Figure 2.2, we can conclude that in every local party organization power is centralized in the hands of the first secretary and his executive committee. In turn, this local party leader receives his orders from higher up.

The government is organized along similar lines. Given, however, that it receives "instructions" from party institutions at all levels of the hierarchy, in the case of a local town council, such a body is effectively placed under triple subordination—to its chief executive officer or mayor; to its provincial counterpart; and to the local party organization.

At the central level, the premier, the Council of Ministers (which in 1985 was composed of twenty-six members), and the head of state

Figure 2.2   The structural framework of Poland's local authorities

ADMINISTRATIVE   **PARTY**   **LOCAL GOVERNMENT**
LEVEL

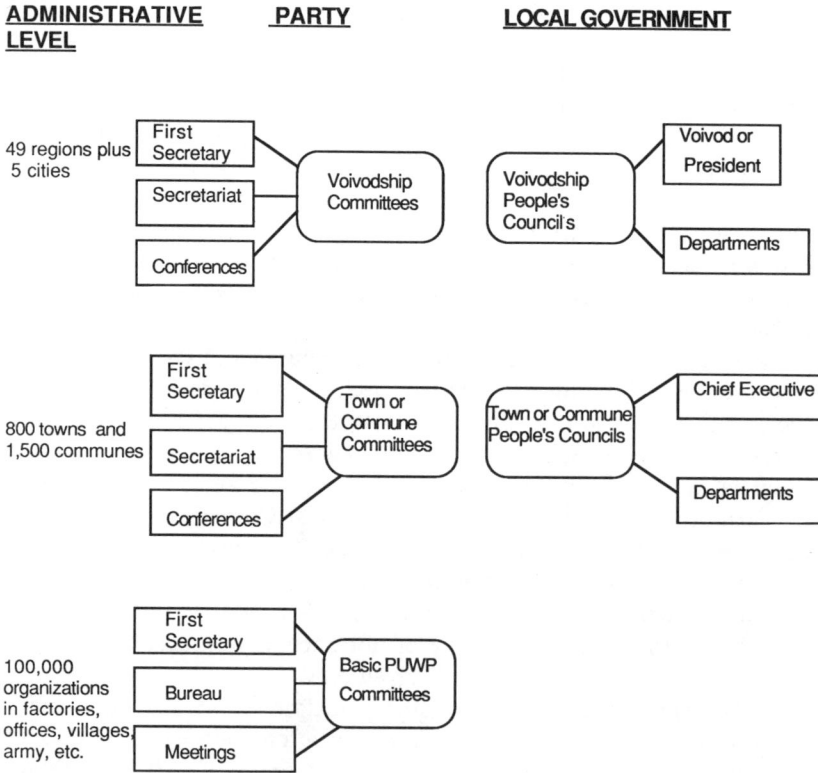

Note: Below voivodship level numbers are approximations.

(that is, the president of the Council of State—hitherto a largely ceremonious organ whose importance may increase since Jaruzelski assumed its headship in the fall of 1985) usually have been elected to the Seym in general elections that are held every five years. To be a Seym deputy is not a requirement for these higher offices, however. Of course, all are nominated to these positions by the dominant party in the Seym, the PZPR, and remain accountable to it.

The Seym's main function is to enact legislation. Most of this is inspired by the resolutions, programs, and drafts passed by the party, but the Seym has on occasion shown a mind of its own. The purpose of the Seym is also to represent the interests of society through a process of popular election of representatives. A relatively unknown fact about the Polish political system is that its legislature includes independent deputies not belonging to any political party. As previously noted, the PZPR decides how to apportion seats to these groups, and although it would certainly not permit the election of an outspoken critic of the regime, it does not require absolute subordination of all independent deputies to the party line in Seym voting. The decision to increase the size of the nonparty bloc in the 1985 elections should be seen as an effort by the regime to coopt into the political system skillful, credible, and prominent figures in Polish society who are both independent and convinced the system can best be reformed from within. They are willing to lend the authorities their good names in exchange for the opportunity to help influence policy.

A brief note on the most important changes in the composition of the Seym following the October 1985 elections is in order. First, the small proportion of deputies (less than 20 percent) who were reelected to the legislature was unprecedented in postwar history. What is more, of the 460 deputies taking their seats only 28 were concurrently members of the party's Central Committee; previously, the number was 99. From another perspective, this means that only 10 percent of Central Committee members (compared to 40 percent previously) had parliamentary mandates. This drastic reduction was intended to symbolize the policy of not encouraging accumulation of offices by members of the political elite.

Another demonstration of this principle (tried out on a more modest scale in earlier periods, such as after Gierek's accession to power) was the election to the Seym of only one-half of those holding a post on the party Politburo or Secretariat (11 of 23) and one-half of those serving as party first secretaries in the provincial apparatus (25 of 49). Previously, anyone in the party's top organs along with all provincial bosses were automatically elected to the legislature. Finally, the size of the apparatchik contingent in the Seym was cut by half: Whereas previously, 15 percent of parliamentary seats were held by full-time employees of the party apparatus, after the 1985 elections that figure was 7 percent. The significance of these elections goes beyond the issue, therefore, of how many electors boycotted the event. An overhauled Seym was returned, one based much less on party notables. This phenomenon, however, also suggests the very limited political experience of the new deputies, as symbolized by the election of a famous cyclist (Szurkowski) and an actor (Siemion) in the so-called national constituency (a bloc of 50 seats set aside to represent the country as a whole rather than the more traditional regional constituency). It appears unlikely the new Seym will be able

to challenge effectively the policies put forward by the inner elite—
a contrast to the more boisterous Seym of the Solidarity period.

With regard to leadership, in postwar Polish history two individuals have simultaneously held the offices of PZPR first secretary
and prime minister of the government: Bierut did so between 1952
and 1954 (he also occupied the ceremonial post of president of the
Republic until 1952), and Jaruzelski did so between 1981 and late
1985 (when he traded the prime ministership for the presidency).
Since the Stalin era, cumulation of offices at the very pinnacle of the
hierarchy has been discouraged, but it nevertheless occurs. Key
ministers, for example, of defense or internal affairs (responsible for
state security), are usually Politburo members, and at the lower level,
local government leaders are frequently party bosses, too. The party-
state dichotomy becomes difficult to maintain because of, among other
reasons, such multiple officeholding.

The final organizational legacy of the Polish-Stalinist and Russian-
Bolshevik systems is the administrative machinery. State administration
resembles that found in any major Western country with two possible
exceptions. The Ministry of Internal Affairs enjoys a special, elevated
status in communist countries. Even in the post-Stalinist period its
employees engaged in enforcing state security have acted at times
like a state within a state. In addition, the Ministry of Defense plays
a crucial political role, enhanced further since General Jaruzelski
acceded to party and government leadership. But this is a phenomenon
not unique to socialist states. The second peculiarity is the great
number of functior.al ministries concerned with industry—engineering,
metallurgy, mining, chemicals, construction, energy, and so on. This
pattern indicates the centrality of the heavy industrial sector to the
entire system.

One of the more perplexing facets of a communist regime is the
creation by the ruling party of an administrative apparatus that
replicates that of the state. So as not to be exclusively dependent on
the information and advice of public servants, and simultaneously to
inspire them with *partiinost*, or party spirit, the PZPR has its own
extensive bureaucratic apparatus divided into functional departments,
each of which is overseen by an individual member of the Secretariat.
The employees of these departments—the so-called party apparatchiks—generally possess formidable power and, like all bureaucrats,
tend to be a conservative force seeking to undermine reform measures.
Even in Lenin's time concern was voiced that party bureaucrats were
beginning to dominate elected party officials. In present-day Poland
it remains true that the surest career path to a high post in the party
(Politburo or Secretariat) is through full-time administrative work in

the Central Committee's functional departments. Whether through their control of policy implementation or through accession to elected party organs, the apparatchiks have indeed become a force to contend with.

To sum up, the constellation of political institutions in Poland has engendered oligarchic, centralist, and bureaucratic tendencies. This phenomenon is more regime-specific than nation-specific. Nevertheless, the Polish leadership has, due to a combination of conservatism, inertia, and lack of imagination, failed to undertake serious modifications of an essentially Leninist-Stalinist structural arrangement that other states have carried out (most notably Yugoslavia and Hungary). The result has been systemic petrification and, with it, a series of challenges emanating from a variety of sources to the political order. I have documented six separate cases in People's Poland.

THE FIRST CHALLENGE: CIVIL WAR 1944-1948

Any government Poland adopted after 1945—whatever its type—would have had to confront profound, objective difficulties in the war-devastated country, difficulties that would have made its bid for legitimacy, credibility, and popularity a gargantuan task. The country and its capital lay in ruins, Poland's industrial and agricultural base lay devastated, the nation's population had been decimated, and Polish society's moral fiber had been deeply shaken. Poland's intelligentsia had been all but wiped out by the virtual genocide of the Jewry, the Katyn atrocity, the systematic and summary Gestapo roundups and executions of intellectuals during the occupation, and the wartime flight of officers, leading government officials, and members of the cultural elite to Western Europe.

The country's borders were shifted westward by 150 miles, and large displaced eastern populations (numbering some 3 million), primarily from backward agrarian regions, had to be transferred to the industrial areas "regained" from Germany, such as Silesia (and its principal cities Katowice/Kattowitz and Wroclaw/Breslau) and western Pomerania (Szczecin/Stettin). Many ethnic Germans residing in the "regained" areas were forcibly expelled by the new Polish communist government. Others foresaw a bleak future and fled westward. Apart from the fear of retribution, the fact that 73 percent of the industrial capacity, 70 percent of agrarian land, and 54 percent of all buildings in the region had been devastated was reason enough for leaving the area. Ethnic tensions were also heightened in Galicia, where Ukrainian military organizations (the best known was the Ukrainian Insurrectionary Army—UPA) engaged in a sporadic war of attrition against the Polish militia. The Ukrainian forces were ruthlessly wiped out in 1947 during the course of Operation Vistula, when the Polish military evacuated and, in great part, devastated Ukrainian settlements, such as in the Bieszczady region.

The Polish peasantry was also restless. The new socialist government had promised to redistribute land shortly after taking power, yet it remained unclear whether the small-parceled farms created were intended to satisfy peasant land hunger or were just a prologue to collectivization. The large size of the rural population (approximately 70 percent of the total), coupled with its unpredictable attitude to the government, caused further tension in the country.

Not the least problem was that political differences between Poles were, in part, converted into an armed struggle. From 1944 to 1948 a sputtering civil war was fought between Polish security forces, who were headed by Communist party leaders, and disparate, isolated groups of anticommunists organized into loose "forest detachments." Some were linked to the wartime Home Army, others to the now-outlawed right-wing National Democrats; still others were newly constituted ultraright resistance groups, and communist rulers alleged others had ties with Mikolajczyk's Polish Peasant Party. According to the authorities some twenty-five thousand men organized in 150 separate armed underground units continued to operate in the country in late 1945. By the time security forces had completely eliminated them three years later, no fewer than twenty thousand Communists and security officials had been killed. No data were provided for partisan losses, but we can assume they were significantly higher. This tragic and rather senseless civil war was immortalized by film director Andrzej Wajda in his 1957 classic *Ashes and Diamonds*.

The provisional government established at the end of 1944 was a coalition of various political parties—the Polish Workers' Party (PPR), the Polish Socialist Party (PPS), the Polish Peasant Party (PSL), and the Democratic Party (SD). At the outset the pro-Moscow PPR, with only twenty thousand members, was one of the smallest parties, so it looked to "fellow travelers"for support. The establishment of a coalition government contained a further advantage in that it would offer the semblance of the political pluralism that had been envisaged in the Yalta agreement between the Allies.

But like its pro-Moscow counterparts elsewhere in Russian-liberated Eastern Europe (as well as in Tito's Yugoslavia), the PPR leadership set out to eliminate serious political opposition gradually, adopting the so-called "salami tactics" pursued by Hungarian communist rulers. Slice by slice the various types of opposition in the country would be cut off from the body politic. In early 1945 sixteen leading members of the Home Army were arrested by the Soviet liberation forces, taken to Moscow for a show trial, and sentenced to long terms in labor camps. The communist authorities then sought to influence the internal makeup of the prewar noncommunist parties by lending support to those leaders willing to collaborate with the PPR. Persistent pressure tactics paid off in the end. The last important opposition figure in Poland, Mikolajczyk, fled to the West in 1947, abandoning his Polish Peasant Party in the process. The PSL was thereupon purged, then amalgamated with a left-wing peasant grouping to form the United Peasants' Party (ZSL). In turn, the PPS was taken over by leftist politicians such as Cyrankiewicz. By late 1948 the PPS was formally merged with the now more powerful PPR to form the Polish United Workers' Party (PZPR), which remains Poland's hegemonic ruler to this day.

The postponement of the "free and unfettered elections" envisaged by the Yalta accord was a crucial element in the communist seizure of power. It is true that a general referendum was held in June 1946 in which the opposition participated, but it was neither free nor unfettered. An intimidation campaign was launched against the opposition in the run-up to the plebiscite, and ballot forms mysteriously disappeared following the voting. The very issues raised in the referendum provided the communist authorities with a "no-lose" situation: The electorate was asked to approve proposals for abolition of the Senate, the nationalization of industry and land reform, and recognition of Poland's new western frontier. The government urged the population to vote yes on all three issues. In order to mobilize those opposed to the authorities, Mikolajczyk exhorted a vote against the mainly technical first issue. It is significant that by this time all political parties had committed themselves to nationalization and agrarian reform (as included in the referendum's second point). Of course, no Polish organization could oppose the extension of the country's border westward, which partially compensated for lands lost in the east to the USSR.

The official results were contested by the opposition. According to the authorities, 68 percent of the electorate had voted in favor of the crucial issue of Senate abolition. However, the opposition claimed that in the fourteen provinces where ballot counting was open and poll boxes were not whisked away by the security forces, 83 percent had voted no on the first question. The official results were allowed to stand.

Flushed with this success the authorities called for general elections in January 1947. Similar campaign tactics were used: intimidation, arrests, raids on the headquarters of Mikolajczyk's party, invalidation of opposition candidatures, and disenfranchisement of more than 1 million citizens. This result, too, was a foregone conclusion. The democratic bloc made up of the PPR, Socialist, and Peasant parties obtained 80 percent of the vote and 394 of 444 parliamentary seats. Mikolajczyk's Polish Peasant Party, which by this time appealed to all forces, peasant or not, that opposed the communist authorities, received 10 percent of the vote and 28 seats. In October 1947 Mikolajczyk bowed to the inevitable and left the country, thereby providing one further stigma the rulers could attach to his name.

The piecemeal elimination of the noncommunist opposition was nearly complete. Throughout this process in Poland, as in the other Eastern European states, Soviet security forces oversaw the entire operation. Through this relationship the new government was able to realize its initial goal of consolidation of political power. But this Soviet connection proved a major dilemma in the long term. As the political scientist Bromke put it, "The less support Polish Communists had at home, the more they leaned on the Soviet Union; yet, the more heavily they relied on assistance from Russia, the less popularity they had in Poland."[1]. Not surprisingly, perceptive Poles began to equate the leading role of the Polish Communist Party with the leading role of the Soviet Union in Polish affairs.

The PZPR has consequently suffered from a crisis of legitimacy since 1948. This crisis grows from the inability of the PZPR to convince a significant portion of the public that existing political institutions and political arrangements are the most appropriate for Poland. The crisis of legitimacy affects not just the PZPR and its leaders but by extension the entire political system constructed upon the party's hegemonic role. There is very little "diffuse support" (a reservoir of favorable attitudes or good will within society that is not policy generated) for the authorities. But their ability to survive for forty years owes as much to periodic leadership changes and policy shifts— aimed at eliciting "specific support" (favorable attitudes stimulated by particular system outputs)—as to timely and selective mobilization of the apparatus of coercion. These methods of system maintenance are briefly examined in the following sections.

THE SECOND CHALLENGE: NATIONALISTS VERSUS STALINISTS

With prewar parties Bolshevized and anticommunist leaders removed from Polish politics, one final phase in what we may term, in the Polish context, "kielbasa tactics" remained to be put into effect so as to assure full Stalinization of the state. This phase was the elimination of the alleged "rightist-nationalist deviation" within the leadership of the workers' party. Again, in Poland as elsewhere in Eastern Europe, a factional struggle was played out between the more and the less trusted supporters of Stalin, that is to say, between those Communists who had spent most of the war years in Moscow (the Muscovite faction) and those who had taken part in resistance organizations located in their occupied countries (the nativists). Inconveniently for Stalin, the head of the Polish Communists was Gomulka, a member of the latter group. Of even greater concern to the Soviet dictator was Gomulka's clearly stated "Poland first" views, which by 1947 had crystallized into a program for a Polish road to socialism.

In 1947 and 1948, even before the schism between Tito and Stalin, Gomulka could not have done much more to antagonize the Kremlin strongman. In September 1947 he played host to a meeting of Eastern European communist leaders called to ratify the establishment of a new Moscow-controlled Communist International. While Tito's emissaries acquiesced, Gomulka voiced his strong dislike for the idea of the Cominform. At the same meeting he expressed his opposition to the Soviet model of collectivization of agriculture. Then in June 1948 he publicly praised the policies of Rosa Luxemburg's pre–World War I party, the SDKPiL, and those of the interwar Trotskyite Polish Communist Party. These organizations had criticized many of the policies followed by Lenin and Stalin respectively. It was not surprising that Gomulka's political position and his very life were put in peril by such beliefs.

His repeated defiance of Stalin helped strengthen the hand of the Muscovites. In September 1948 he was replaced as leader by Bierut and in the next two years stripped of remaining party and government posts. His "rightist-nationalist heresy" finally led to his arrest in July 1951, and a show trial was to be prepared in which he would figure as chief traitor. The trial was intended to produce the same results as in similar trials of nativist leaders in other Eastern European states.

It is ironic, therefore, that Gomulka escaped the fate of the excommunicated and executed Communists of Hungary (Rajk), Bulgaria (Kostov), Albania (Xoxe), Romania (Patrascanu), and Czechoslovakia (Slansky). As historian Nicholas Bethell put it, "The five who were dead had opposed Stalin hardly, if at all. But Gomulka *had* opposed him. He was the guilty one. . . . And yet he was the one who was still alive."[2]

That Gomulka survived was the result of a combination of the idiosyncrasies of the Polish political system, his own personality, and good fortune. Bierut never fully became the "little Stalin" that, for example, Rakosi in Hungary aspired to; consequently, he was less remorseless in rooting out class enemies. Gomulka's personal courage cannot be disputed given his challenges to Stalin in 1947 and 1948 and his unrepentant defense before the party's Central Committee in 1949. As a result, his "willingness" to cooperate in a show trial was by no means assured. Finally, the period of High Stalinism came to a sudden end in March 1953 when the long-serving Kremlin chief died. This event, more than anything else, assured Gomulka's physical safety.

The palace crisis of 1948—the ouster of Gomulka by the Stalinist wing of the party—although only involving infighting within the elite, left enduring marks on Polish communism as it developed in subsequent years. First, Gomulka was confirmed as a Polish patriot and staunch anti-Stalinist by these events. When, therefore, a more general political crisis broke out in 1956 that could only be resolved by dismantling the Stalinist order, it was Gomulka who was called upon to rescue Polish communism.

Second, the advancement of a program outlining a Polish road to socialism was rejected by Polish Stalinists in 1948 as a rightist-nationalist aberration, though in the following years many of its values were implemented in Yugoslavia. When the program was resuscitated during the 1956 Polish October, it was already tinged with ideas that went beyond crude anti-Stalinism. More specifically, between 1948 and 1956 the Polish road had evolved into a centrist platform that painstakingly avoided the undesirable features of both Soviet-type sectarianism and full-blooded Yugoslav revisionism. Although the program's more seasoned ideas could not have the mass appeal of the original ones, nevertheless, they allowed Polish rulers to avoid the political extremes toward which other Eastern European states occasionally gravitated, such as the revisionism of Hungary's Nagy in 1956 or Czechoslovakia's Dubček in 1968. These extremes were so intolerable to the Soviets that invasions were launched to suppress them. Likewise, Poland's centrist platform avoided the petrifying dogmatism of Czech leaders immediately preceding and following Dubček that drove a chasm between the rulers and the governed as happened nowhere else. In short, the eight-year interruption in Gomulka's tenure in power and in the program he advanced brought about a symbiotic relationship between Stalinism and the Polish road that was, at the same time, functional for the political system and erosive for its popular appeal.

The third impact of the 1948 factional struggle was entirely negative. According to some recent analyses of postwar Polish crises commissioned by Polish rulers themselves (in particular, the 1983

The Old Town Square in Warsaw, rebuilt from rubble after World War II

Kubiak Commission report), the wrong faction won that struggle and set Poland on a course that initiated a cycle of crises. All postwar crises originate in the 1948 power struggle, it is argued, including the ones that led to the formation of Solidarity in 1980 and the imposition of martial law in 1981. Bierut's takeover left a legacy of political institutions, processes, and methods that were never significantly modified afterward. Popular discontent with the system owes its origins to the structural defects that followed from the victory of the Muscovite faction.

In its defense, Polish Stalinism never ran totally amok as in other communist countries. The maverick dimension of pre–World War II Polish communism and its continuation by Gomulka up to 1948 helped moderate Stalinist excesses. This is not to suggest Polish Stalinism had an entirely human face. As in other Soviet-type societies the influence of the Kremlin *vozhd* was visible everywhere, from the architectural design of the Palace of Culture towering in the center of reconstructed Warsaw to the socialist realism of artists and writers of the period. In military and political terms the Soviet leadership left nothing to chance and assumed direct control of critical spheres of government. In 1949 Soviet marshal Rokossovsky was appointed Polish minister of defense, deputy chairman of the Council of Ministers (or government), and a member of the PZPR Politburo. The tenth department of the office of State Security (UB) was run by Soviet "advisers" who monitored the activities of the Polish leaders themselves. Moreover, as Bromke concluded, "the Soviet ambassador in Warsaw assumed a role of virtual overseer of the Polish Communists, freely intervening in the party and government affairs."[3]

Intimidation and terror were other distinctive features of the Stalinist system. Any Pole who had relations in the West was suspect and often assigned to an inferior job. Many members of the Home Army and of Polish forces that had fought abroad were arrested or persecuted. Polish socialists who had taken part in the Spanish Civil War on the Republican side were among thousands of members purged from the ranks of the PZPR in the late 1940s. Nineteen air force and navy officers were indicted on trumped-up charges of sabotage and executed between 1951 and 1953. In the latter year the primate of the Roman Catholic church, Cardinal Wyszyński, was placed under house arrest. Finally, the elaborate party, state, and security apparatus was fashioned in those years and in many ways reflected Stalin's paranoic and tyrannical mind.

THE THIRD CHALLENGE: DOGMATISTS
VERSUS REVISIONISTS

Many scholars of communist regimes believe that party leaders wait for cues from the Kremlin before embarking upon any reform drive in their own state. An example frequently invoked is the dismantling of the Stalinist system: Khrushchev's denunciation, in a secret speech to the Twentieth Congress of the Communist Party of the Soviet Union (CPSU) in February 1956, of the "errors and distortions" engendered by the cult of personality system supposedly triggered off comparable liberalization drives in neighboring Eastern Europe. In looking at the Polish case the cue may have been forthcoming earlier: In late 1953 Stalin's security chief, Beria, was liquidated in a conspiracy of Soviet Politburo members. This victory of the party over the security apparatus and the resultant collective leadership system that emerged was replicated in Poland (as well as Hungary) soon after. Thus, the de-Stalinization drive preceded the Polish October of 1956 by several years.

The New Course, announced by Soviet premier Malenkov in 1953 and soon adopted in much of Eastern Europe, was officially implemented by Bierut in October 1953. It may be viewed as the first stage of de-Stalinization, for it modified the basic assumption underlying the six-year economic plan (1950–1955) by shifting investment funds from heavy to light industry and agriculture. Its political dimension included Bierut's surrender in 1954 of the premiership to former PPS leader Cyrankiewicz. With uncanny political dexterity Cyrankiewicz was able to serve in this post under three party secretaries and between 1970 and 1972 in the post of head of state under a fourth. In Poland, de-Stalinization was given further impetus by the defection in 1953 of a high-ranking security official to the West. Colonel Swiatlo had been deputy head of the tenth department of the UB, responsible for monitoring the political reliability of top party cadres. After learning of Beria's execution the colonel fled to the West—not the last time, incidentally, that a high-ranking official badly compromised under a despised system, seeing his own political fortunes on the ebb, sought haven in the adversary capitalist system. Swiatlo's broadcasts to Poland on Radio Free Europe described in detail police methods that had been employed, direct Soviet involvement in Poland's internal affairs, and, most damagingly, the private lives of the "new class" in socialist Poland—the ruling red bourgeoisie. The security police was thoroughly discredited: In December 1954 the Department of Public Security was stripped of ministerial status, and most of its functions were transferred to the Ministry of Internal Affairs, which exercises them to the present day.[4]

On the surface the triumph of party reformers over die-hard Stalinists might have appeared inevitable at this juncture. But the period 1954–1956 was one of intense factional struggle within the PZPR leadership, and the hardliners (soon to develop into the so-called Natolin group) fought a successful rearguard action. Their political clout was reinforced by the removal from office in 1955 of the reformers in other socialist countries—Malenkov in the USSR and Nagy in Hungary. Despite the swell of grass-roots opinion within the party and throughout Polish society (especially among intellectuals) for meaningful liberalization, the drive was effectively thwarted until 1956. It was only renewed after large-scale protests had taken place that had to be put down with force.

It is a difficult task to establish linkage between factional struggles within the ruling elite and the eruption of mass protests on the streets. It is a fact that in June 1956 workers' strikes and demands for bread and liberty in Poznań coincided with the ongoing battle for power between Stalinist dogmatists who defended the existing system of rule, liberals and nationalists espousing the ideas of Gomulka (who had quietly been released from prison in late 1954), which earned them the title of revisionists, and an increasingly isolated centrist faction led by Ochab that, nevertheless, could be tarred with the Stalinist brush.

A similar pattern of events occurred in March 1968 when student demonstrations coincided with a bitter struggle in the Politburo between Gomulka and an aggressively nationalist, anti-Semitic faction centered on the person of General Moczar. In 1970 and 1980, too, social upheavals accompanied challenges to incumbent coalitions headed by Gomulka and Gierek respectively. It cannot be established with any degree of certainty whether in all these cases one faction within the party (presumably the nonruling one) adopted the perilous strategy of fomenting social unrest so as to provide justification for the call for a leadership change; or incipient social discontent served as a catalyst splitting the leadership about how best to resolve the crisis. Whichever the case—Marxian dialectics would offer the neat explanation that the two interact—in Poland in 1956 two uncontrollable events took place that forced an immediate political outcome.

First, Khrushchev's secret report on Stalin's sins found its way to Poland, was translated and distributed to leading officials, and caused incredulity and havoc. Second, Bierut died suddenly while on a visit to Moscow in March. One farfetched explanation for the cause of his death, offered by a Western scholar, was that "it is not improbable that the shock of reading the speech contributed to the heart attack from which he died."[5] Many Poles believed, however, that Bierut had been done in by less subtle communist methods. The power and ideological vacuums created within the PZPR by the Moscow events, followed by workers' protests in Poznań that left more than fifty dead and the industrial proletariat at obvious odds with the regime, proved to be indispensable preconditions for the return to power of Gomulka. Ironically, the manifest weaknesses of Polish communism gave rise to the second ascendancy of postwar Poland's most charismatic leader.

The limits to Soviet power in post-Stalinist Poland also became apparent in 1956. In the Central Committee's election of a new first secretary to succeed Bierut, Khrushchev's apparent favorite, Zenon Nowak, lost out to Edward Ochab. Later that year the latter was replaced by a figure even more unpalatable to the Soviets, Gomulka. Hundreds of thousands of Poles gathered in Warsaw in late October and demonstrated peacefully in favor of his election—perhaps the only case of a genuinely free and unfettered "election" held in a Soviet client state since Yalta. Compounded by mysterious movements of Polish army units to counter the sabre-rattling of Soviet divisions in the country and Gomulka's face-to-face confrontation with the most powerful members of the Soviet Politburo who had flown in unexpectedly one day at dawn, the nativist Polish Communists won this test of will. In Hungary a terrible tragedy began to unfold at exactly the same time.

The appointment of Gomulka had immediate repercussions. The Russian-born defense minister Rokossovsky was sent packing, Polish primate Wyszyński was released from house arrest, more than one hundred thousand Poles were repatriated from remote parts of the USSR where they had been exiled after the war, the Soviets cancelled more than half a billion dollars of debts Poland had incurred, and a bilateral treaty on the legal status of Soviet troops "temporarily" stationed in Poland was concluded (see Chapter 3). Collective farms were broken up and the collectivization drive halted, returning Poland's agricultural system to the family farm model. Censorship was eased, administrative and economic decentralization was instituted, multi-candidate electoral constituencies were created, socialist legality (due process) replaced arbitrary, class-based law, a more independent Catholic political group, Znak, was formed and allocated representation in the Seym, the Club of Catholic Intelligentsia (KIK) sprung up in five major cities, and, perhaps most significantly, factory employees established workers' councils to help manage their enterprises. The bloody crushing of the Hungarian revolution served as a grim reminder to the Polish leadership, however, of the parameters within which reform could be pursued.

A combination of international and domestic events in 1956 and 1957 convinced Gomulka there could be no "second stage" in the Polish October, no authentic political pluralism of the kind that liberals in the party and in intelligentsia circles were calling for. As in 1948, Gomulka was again vulnerable to charges of Titoism in the reform program he was implementing. Other Eastern European leaders' envy at his remarkable comeback and successes—a factor that cannot be underestimated in analyzing the notorious absence of a unified Eastern European "lobby" in dealing with the Kremlin—played an important part in curtailing radical political experimentation. Notions of political realism and *raison d'état* were advanced to explain the leadership's conservatism, a ploy repeated on several subsequent occasions. Threats of the extinction of the Polish state or at least of the loss of the regained territories were carefully diffused in Polish society in order to implore its understanding of the allegedly well-intentioned rulers' predicament.

It is questionable whether Gomulka himself would have desired greater political liberalization and democracy, international pressures aside. He was a veteran Communist no less autocratic than the Stalinists in whose company he had spent so many years. The influence of revisionists, or liberals, within the party and society had to be eradicated if the party's hegemonic role, and that of Gomulka's in the party, were to be preserved. Gomulka appreciated the natural strength that accrued to a political leader who occupied the political middle ground, and early in 1957 (scarcely months after the Polish

October) he began to attack with equal vigor Stalinist dogmatists and eclectic revisionists. As he put it: "Influenza, even in its most serious form, cannot be cured by contracting tuberculosis. Dogmatism cannot be cured by revisionism." In Gomulka's eyes despotic Stalinism could not be cured with political pluralism.

In Gomulka's defense it must be said that throughout his life austerity and a simple working-class lifestyle were values dear to him. He disdained equally the embourgeoisified workers and the unproductive intellectuals "who produce neither bread nor steel but only small talk." The fact that over time he perceived revisionism as the greatest danger to the party reflected his belief that it constituted the quintessential deviation of the intelligentsia, in the way that dogmatism was the deviation of the proletariat. In this context it is not surprising that Gomulka ultimately preferred to err on the side of the latter and that, predictably, his next political challenge was issued by the former.

THE FOURTH CHALLENGE: SOCIETY DISUNITED VERSUS THE PARTY

Gomulka's open disavowal of reformist ideas at the Third Congress of the PZPR, held in March 1959, signaled the beginning of a period known as the "little stabilization." In political, social, and economic spheres efforts were made to forge policies, administrative methods, and a general ethos or civic culture that would contrast favorably with those of the Stalin era. Gomulka's road to socialism increasingly came to mean, in the 1960s, a non-Stalinist road; hence, it was not specifically Polish nor easily distinguishable from similar processes taking place in the German Democratic Republic or the Soviet Union. Particularly characteristic of these processes was the primacy given to economic questions over political ones, though we should not therefore conclude that consumer-oriented policies now took precedence over industrial growth. The failure to pass on to a second economic stage of consumer growth probably was more crucial to Gomulka's eventual undoing than his decision not to move to a second political stage of the Polish October.

Behind the veneer of stabilization lay a series of unresolved problems that affected various groups in society. The first to offer resistance to the leadership's restorationist policy (a policy that sought to reinvigorate the party's leading role in society) was the intelligentsia, both from within and from outside of the PZPR. For many years Gomulka had talked of the creeping revisionism inherent in intellectual circles, and student riots in March 1968 confirmed these suspicions.

A decade earlier the rulers had undertaken a verification campaign of party members to weed out liberal intellectuals, and shortly after, a number of the intelligentsia's beloved liberal journals (the most famous being *Po Prostu*) were closed down. Gradually, censorship was reimposed and cultural life regimented anew. If during these years Gomulka had changed political course, he had considerable company. In order to demonstrate the nature and scope of the political zigzagging that socialist systems seem to engender, let us examine briefly the career paths of a number of leading intellectuals of that period.

Gomulka's main intellectual nemesis at that time was the archrevisionist philosopher Leszek Kolakowski. He belonged to that rare breed of party member who took his Marxism seriously. Sympathy for the utopian visions sketched in the writings of the young Marx soon turned Kolakowski into a devastating critic of what today is called the real existing socialism of Eastern Europe. His first polemical battle with party chiefs occurred in 1956, and in 1966 Kolakowski marked the tenth anniversary of the Polish October by indicting the status quo policies of the Gomulka regime. For his humanist Marxism he was expelled from the PZPR in 1966 and, in the aftermath of the 1968 events, dismissed from his post at the University of Warsaw. He subsequently left for England and the United States, and his views have since become virulently anti-Marxist.

Kolakowski's principal intellectual critic in the early years was another philosopher, Adam Schaff. Schaff had once praised Stalin's political ideas (as Kolakowski himself had done at the outset of his career) as a "shining beacon that lights our way," and in 1957 he took Kolakowski to task for alleged revisionism. But political fortunes in communist states are highly volatile, and ten years later Schaff found his own views being attacked by official ideologues as smacking of revisionism. His belief, stated in *Marxism and the Individual*, that alienation did not automatically vanish in a socialist system and his critique of the centrally planned economy led to a full-scale inquiry in the pages of the PZPR's theoretical journal *Nowe Drogi*. Following the March 1968 disturbances Schaff was implicated with a group of Jewish intellectuals that had allegedly masterminded the student protests, but he was not expelled from the party. For a while he retreated into academic philosophy (semiotics and semantics) and headed the Vienna-based European Center for Social Sciences. But his ideological attraction to Eurocommunism and his subsequent call (under martial law) for a reformed, authentic Polish Communist Party (issued, among other places, in books published in West Germany) brought charges of slander from the PZPR's disciplinary organ, the

Central Control Commission. Unrepentant, he was officially expelled from the PZPR in 1984.

The career paths of two liberal members of the 1956 intellectual establishment are just as wayward. The biting political satire of Jerzy Urban on the pages of the shortlived *Po Prostu* has often been viewed as the high point of intellectual creativity in the Polish October. The journal's closure created a vacuum that was partially filled by the sociocultural weekly *Polityka* under the editorship of Mieczyslaw Rakowski. During the next two decades, while Urban practiced his craft in a nonpolitical satirical magazine *Szpilki*, Rakowski's paper developed into an officially sanctioned organ of unorthodox views. The editor's own writings reflected a critical distance from the policies of the rulers.

When in 1980 Solidarity was formed by workers and then recognized by the authorities, Rakowski's liberalism propelled him into the inner political elite, which was seeking ways to deal with the maverick trade union. In 1981 he served as the government's "well-meaning" contact with Solidarity leaders, but personal animosity as well as profound political differences arose between him and Wałęsa and led to the breakdown of negotiations. When martial law was imposed at the end of the year Rakowski retained his position as vice-premier, and he undertook the unpleasant task of meeting with liberal intellectuals and informing them that the period of reform was over. Later Rakowski also visited the Lenin shipyards in Gdańsk (where Solidarity was born) and told workers that the independent trade union was dead and that workers would be given "no second chance" to establish such an institution. In November 1985, having fulfilled the often onerous duties imposed by the Jaruzelski administration, he was relieved of his vice-premiership and offered in return less influential posts.

Urban's *volte face* was more dramatic and extreme than Rakowski's. Although not a party member, in the martial law regime he surfaced as the official press spokesman of the government and was uncharitably described in the West as the "clown and court jester" of Jaruzelski's government. His hardhitting cynicism was directed at all liberal groups in society, and he engaged in regular ad hominem attacks on Wałęsa. Perhaps his most celebrated statement was that if the West imposed economic sanctions on Poland, the political leaders would always find something to eat even if the rest of society might not. Since 1982 Urban has focused upon his person (probably deliberately, as a lightning rod) the wrath of all society.

From this sketch of four prominent intellectuals of the Polish October and their subsequent careers we can conclude that a communist system seems often to produce bizarre effects in a thinking person. Former and present party members can shift with great ease from Marxist orthodoxy to revisionism and Eurocommunism or to anticommunism, and vice versa. Of course, political positions are relative: To cite one Polish social scientist, Karpiński, "Revisionism must be seen in contrast to the so-called party line. One is not revisionist in general, but only in relation to the current party line, which changes and is not always clear."[6]

The fact remains that for various reasons much of the intelligentsia was disappointed with Gomulka's course. In March 1964 the "letter of the 34," signed by well-known intellectuals, condemned policies stifling Polish culture. The following year two young historians, Kuroń and Modzelewski, issued an "open letter to the party" criticizing the growth of the central bureaucratic apparatus, which, they claimed, had transformed itself into a new class. Tension increased in the universities, and in March 1968 the closing of a play by the nineteenth century romantic poet Mickiewicz (certain anti-Russian lines of which were underscored in the production) was the spark that set off widespread student protests. Intellectuals had made no effort to gain the support of the working class, and the demonstrations were easily put down with force. Nevertheless, a nucleus of intellectual leaders emerged from this crisis and was to become the vanguard of struggles against the regime in the second half of the 1970s.

The church, too, ran into trouble with Gomulka shortly after his accession to power. In 1958 the church was told to remove all religious symbols from state schools—an issue that resurfaced in 1984. In 1959 it lost its tax exemption on clergy income and property and on churches and seminaries. In 1961 the church inevitably lost the battle about the right of religious instruction in state schools. Conflict between the country's two most powerful institutions heightened in 1965 when the ecclesiastical hierarchy dispatched a letter to German bishops proposing mutual forgiveness for wrongs committed by each nation against the other. The party regarded this as unprecedented meddling in foreign affairs. In December 1970, however, Gomulka followed the church's lead and signed a pact of reconciliation with West Germany. The celebrations marking Poland's millenium in 1966 also exacerbated the conflict: In its commemoration the church highlighted the nation's conversion to Christianity, while state festivities focused on the secular dimensions of nationhood. Cardinal Wyszyński's public statements at this time were remarkable for their anticommunist rhetoric, a style that was to change when church-state relations were normalized in the 1970s.

One other group figured in the conflict with the authorities but more as an object than an active participant in the struggle. Poland's Jewry had always played a prominent part in the socialist movement and in the 1920s had represented more than one-half of the KPP's membership. After the communist takeover of Poland in 1944 many in the party's Muscovite faction were Jewish: This was to be expected given that it would have been doubly dangerous to be a Jewish communist and to remain in Poland under the Nazi occupation. Leading Jewish figures included Berman, vice-premier and Politburo member responsible for the security apparatus; Minc, minister of industry and commerce and the most influential economist of the 1940s; and Zambrowski, Politburo member responsible for agricultural policy.

In contrast to other communist parties there was no witchhunt of Jewish members in the formative years of the PZPR. As Dziewanowski has written:

> The PZPR did not have in its annals either a cruel suppression of the Jewish cultural elite, like that conducted in the USSR in 1948–49, or, like its Czechoslovak counterpart, the Slansky trial—nor the slaughtering of many Hungarian Communists of Jewish extraction in 1949, or the brutal liquidation of the overwhelmingly Jewish Pauker-Georgescu-Luka faction in Rumania.[7]

The equivalent of an anti-Jewish campaign in the ranks of the PZPR came only in 1968. Even in this case Jewish Communists were more a pawn in a power struggle than a consensus target of the leadership. Early in the 1960s a nationalist faction within the PZPR had begun to coalesce around General Moczar, who became minister of internal affairs in 1964. Called the Partisans because of many members' associations with the wartime communist resistance network, the faction was in some respects both anti-Soviet and anti-Semitic. Prominent Polish Jews became politically vulnerable following Israel's victory over the Arab states in 1967, which led to the severing of diplomatic relations between much of the communist world and the Jewish state. Gomulka criticized Polish Jews who had taken pride in the Israeli victory but condemned both Zionism and anti-Semitism. The Partisans pressed him to take anti-Jewish sentiments further, especially when a number of university professors implicated in the March 1968 student riots were found to be Jewish. In the end many Jews both inside and outside the academic community lost their jobs or were pressured to resign, and the vast majority decided on emigration to the West.

Gomulka's role in this campaign was equivocal. Although acquiescing to the ouster of Jewish intellectuals, he continued to condemn the nefarious nature of anti-Semitism. By pursuing a Janus-faced policy he rode out the Partisans' offensive, survived the 1968 events, and turned for his support to the working class. The latter had remained passive in 1968, but when it rose two years later with its own set of grievances, Gomulka immediately fell from power.

In fact, throughout the 1960s the industrial proletariat had not joined in the sporadic and often amorphous opposition to Gomulka. The party boss interpreted this in the light of Hungarian leader Kádár's 1961 maxim—"who is not against us is for us." After 1968 Gomulka offered workers' representatives the vision of factory self-management, a concept that had been quietly abandoned after 1958. Perhaps the call served more to accelerate than to sublimate workers' political demands. In December 1970, in response to a government decision announced two weeks before Christmas to increase food prices, widespread strikes broke out in the Baltic ports of Gdańsk, Gdynia, and Szczecin and threatened to envelop the whole country.

This industrial strife was equated with an antiregime uprising, and the reaction of the central leadership as well as communist officials in the given localities was the reflex of those socialized in the Stalinist ethic—armed repression. Forty-five persons were killed and 2,000 injured (according to official totals) by security forces in several days of disturbances. Gomulka's position became untenable. He was held responsible for the shootings and, more importantly, for having caused the protests in the first place through misguided policies. He was replaced by Edward Gierek, the first secretary of Poland's most important industrial region, Silesia. More significantly, the 1970 crisis witnessed the reemergence of a confident and critical working class movement.

THE FIFTH CHALLENGE: SOCIETY UNITED VERSUS THE PARTY

Gierek ruled Poland for ten years and left an indelible mark on society, notwithstanding the post–1980 fashion among communist and Western scholars alike to minimize his achievements. The 1960s values of austerity and self-reliance were replaced by virtually unbridled materialist aspirations in the 1970s. Very early on in the decade it became clear that Poland was living above its means. In February 1971, only two months after Gierek's takeover, Rakowski, the editor of the influential weekly *Polityka*, warned that "we have to realize that as from this moment we are living on credit."[8] What he had in mind at the time were the sizable loans extended to Poland by the USSR to bail the country out of its immediate economic difficulties. But the small economic boom in the first part of the decade was financed primarily by easily available Western credits from governments and private banks alike, who displayed confidence in the new Polish ruler. The nation was to pay a high price for its short-lived prosperity.

Part of Gierek's political program was a "civilizing mission" in which Poland's political culture was to make the final break with Stalinism. According to this program, political culture had to be modern, it had to be modeled on advanced Western industrial societies, and it had to substitute repressive tolerance and popular consent for violent repression and coercion as the basis of rulers' legitimacy. In order to reinforce national integration, Gierek's program also assigned precedence to individual interests and incentives over collective ones.

Nonetheless, Gierek was viewed with considerable skepticism in the immediate aftermath of the December 1970 events. The public remembered how Gomulka had taken power in 1956 while enjoying greater credibility and charisma, and still his administration eventually ran aground. Gierek's much publicized political style was to seek out direct contacts with the workers. Hence, when a second wave of strikes took place in Poland in the first months of 1971 he personally addressed meetings convoked by workers' leaders and requested workers' help in solving the nation's problems. Over time Gierek's popularity grew, probably peaking in 1974. Had he resigned at the PZPR's Seventh Congress held the next year (as well-placed rumors had him contemplating), he would have earned a preeminent place in postwar Polish history. Communist party chiefs do not resign voluntarily, however, and Gierek quickly saw his popularity erode in the last half of the 1970s.

A concomitant of Gierek's unofficial slogan that "Poles never had it so good" was the notion that the new red bourgeoisie never had it so good either. In 1972 the notorious *nomenklatura* system was formalized by the Politburo, and the patronage system by which high-ranking party officials would dispense rights of appointment to lucrative political, administrative, economic, military, scientific, and social positions became clearly delineated. Even though the living standards of many groups in society were rising, the gap between them and this new class was continually widening. The exclusive stores, country cottages, Western cars and assorted gadgets, availability of passports for travel to the West, access to hard currency at ridiculously deflated exchange rates, and the virtual immunity of this caste from investigation for wrongdoing generated feelings of animosity and relative deprivation among both old guard Communists such as Gomulka and principled oppositionists such as the intellectuals who in 1976 formed the Committee for Workers' Self-Defense (KOR), whose name belies its broader concerns. When economic difficulties began to compound this animosity, it was simple for Polish society to conclude that the new class had embezzled the country's national wealth. When the opportunity presented itself in the halcyon Solidarity days of 1981 for a general reckoning with corrupt officials, some twelve thousand members of the *nomenklatura* were convicted of stealing or squandering public monies.

By the mid–1970s a number of specific issues produced conflict between the authorities and social groups. The most noteworthy involved revising the Stalinist constitution, a process that took place after much delay in the Soviet Union and other Eastern European states at this time. Poland's 1952 constitution had referred to the political system as a people's democracy; in the new version it was to be recognized as a full-fledged socialist state. More controversial (though less dubious) were three other proposed modifications: 1) to now give constitutional status to the PZPR as "the leading political force in society"; 2) to link rights of citizens to their fulfillment of duties to the state; and 3) to specify as the cornerstone of foreign policy the "unshakable fraternal bond" with the Soviet Union. Intellectuals railed against this constitutional ratification of the Sovietization of the country, and they dispatched a "letter of 101" to the Seym Commission examining the draft. In February 1976 the authorities retreated, and all three offensive passages were, though not deleted, toned down. For instance, the last point was reformulated to read Poland "strengthens its friendship and cooperation with the Soviet Union and other socialist states"—a far cry from the German Democratic Republic's constitutional acknowledgment of "eternal and inviolable ties with the USSR."

The constitutional issue was, in reality, an example of symbolic politics, for the party was always in firm control. The more profound crisis involving relations between state and society, however, had not been defused. In a statement made in May 1976, a prominent member of KOR, the economic historian Edward Lipiński, noted: "Socialism cannot be established by decree. It is created and can be created only within the framework of the free activities of free men. Fundamental changes must take place, or at least be initiated. Otherwise it will be impossible to prevent a tragedy, which could take the form of a violent revolt or a reversion to Stalinist methods."[9]

The very next month the more substantive battle he had warned about took place, involving violent clashes between workers and the authorities. The unpopular Premier Jaroszewicz announced a proposed increase in the price of meat and other food. In economic terms the higher prices were fully justified: Prices had been frozen since early in Gomulka's reign, while in the West galloping inflation had followed the Organization of Petroleum Exporting Countries' (OPEC) oil price increase in 1973. Polish workers were not consulted about the price increases, however, and they saw their living standards rising more slowly than those of other social groups. Industrial workers in three cities (Ursus near Warsaw, Radom, and Plock) called strikes and staged demonstrations. The leadership feared the disturbances would spread and the next day rescinded the price increases. At the same time, strike leaders were arrested and sentenced to lengthy prison terms.

On this occasion other groups organized in support of the workers. KOR was set up by Kuroń and other intellectuals to assist families of the imprisoned, and church leaders used their good offices to have the sentences commuted. In spite of the ominous emergence, from the rulers' perspective, of a unified protest movement cutting across class lines, Gierek's response was to beat a tactical retreat, ignore the symptoms of a deeper crisis, make no attempt to investigate the cause of the protests, continue to muddle through the aggravating economic morass, and disregard the burgeoning opposition movement of the late 1970s.

The rapidly deteriorating economy and an increasingly self-confident and unified polity gave birth to the independent social movement institutionalized in Solidarity in 1980. Gierek had been alerted to imminent danger earlier that year at the Eighth Congress when rank-and-file trade unionists complained openly of the unresponsiveness of the highly centralized, government-controlled unions. At the congress Gierek promised a new law to reform trade unions and, for good measure, dumped his premier who then became the scapegoat for the economic malaise. These measures were seen by many Poles as either inconsequential or a further sign of the regime's vulnerability to concerted action. In June, when the new premier announced a new proposal for a food price increase, it produced the old effect: Industrial strife rapidly engulfed many parts of the country.

By the time the hardened shipyard workers on the Baltic coast downed their tools, the original series of economic demands (principally abolition of price increases and implementation of wage hikes) had become converted into political ones. Participants now realized that no meaningful economic improvements could be expected unless sweeping political reforms accompanied them. Workers adopted new tactics, too, establishing interlocking strike committees to coordinate efforts nationally. Out of these structures emerged the independent, self-governing trade union Solidarity.

One of the strike leaders in the Lenin shipyards of Gdańsk became the new movement's head. Lech Wałęsa already had been involved in the clandestine activities of an embryonic independent union movement in 1977. Although neither a Marxist by belief nor a party member by choice, the charisma and revolutionary zeal of Wałęsa bear comparison to Lenin. Together with other worker leaders he aimed to transform the country into an authentic workers' state and to return to the proletariat the political power that had been usurped by the PZPR. Whether it was because of the democratic nature of Solidarity's original demands or because Solidarity represented a viable alternative to the proven incompetence, corruption, and authoritarianism of the party, many Poles who were not industrial workers joined the movement and swelled its ranks to nearly 10 million. A substantial proportion of these consisted of young people under thirty, born and educated in People's Poland but disillusioned with its development. One sociologist even called the younger generation the "detonator" of the independent social movement. Solidarity's membership also included 1 million individuals who belonged to the PZPR, that is to say, one-third of the latter's membership.

Solidarity existed for a brief sixteen months before being destroyed by the martial law regime. Viewed positively, it embodied the hopes of much of Polish society for a more liberal, responsive, and pluralist political system. The organizational skills it commanded and the tactical moves it subsequently pursued during a series of basically nonviolent confrontations with the authorities (the beating up of Solidarity activists in Bydgoszcz by local security officials in March 1981 was an exception) demonstrated uncanny political maturity, perhaps earning it the appellation of a "twenty-first-century–type social movement." If Solidarity's practical successes were few and easily revocable by the authorities, its major achievement was a moral and irreversible one. Solidarity kindled "a fire in the minds of men," to quote Dostoyevsky, where for several decades there had been none. A participant political culture came into being and florished where there had largely existed a subject and subjugated one. The creation of a "self-governing Republic," as the Solidarity Congress proclaimed in September 1981, had been actually (if not legally) achieved in those sixteen months, despite the authorities' chicanery. The objectives spelt out in the congress program had near universal support: justice, democracy, truth, legality, freedom of opinion. Solidarity proved itself to be a revolutionary and proletarian force in a conservative and bureaucratized state that was governed by an incompetent and opportunist party. It was a nationwide and Polish Kronstadt, that 1921 rebellion of a garrison of Soviet sailors and workers against the aberrations of socialism practiced by the Bolsheviks, a revolt crushed unmercifully by Trotsky.

It is also true that Solidarity sowed the seeds of its own destruction. In Solidarity's understandable desire to avoid the precedent set by the workers' party, it became overly democratic and decentralized, with regional branches of the union competing fiercely against each other for the coveted title of "most radical." Wałęsa's efforts to centralize decisionmaking earned him the opprobrium of the regional chieftains and his rivals in the national executive of the union—a fact conveniently set aside by those same rivals when he was awarded the Nobel Peace Prize in 1983. The movement was open and undisciplined, making it vulnerable to agents provocateurs and to the divisive tactics employed by the authorities. Finally, it could not resolve the problem of the correct distribution of power between its proletarian leadership and its team of advisers emanating from the ranks of the intelligentsia, especially the academic community. Solidarity was a catchall institution rather than a hard-nosed vanguard of the proletariat, and internal class tensions surfaced that weakened its overall unity. In short, although it would be wrong to depict the movement as counterrevolutionary in the way the authorities did, it certainly appeared to live up to another charge made against it— that of anarcho-syndicalism—a movement with minimal central direction that reflected grass-roots, spontaneous, workplace radicalism.

Within the party, factional struggle between liberals seeking a *modus vivendi* with Solidarity and hardliners harking for a return to the ancien régime initially undermined the leadership's resolve. By mid-1981 the struggle conveniently served as a pretext for a general policy of duplicity. Gierek had become expendable after the PZPR signed the August agreements recognizing the independence of the trade union, and he was replaced by the uninspiring Kania. The party's extraordinary Ninth Congress, convened in July 1981, was unprecedented in communist annals since Lenin's time in that 1) delegates to the session were elected democratically; 2) the congress itself elected the PZPR leaders democratically; and 3) the program approved by the meeting was committed to "socialist renewal" and other democratic objectives. But the Central Committee elected by the congress was inexperienced, weak, and easy prey for the apparatchiks who resented the reform thrust, and later for the inner ruling elite who chose to impose martial law.

While Solidarity was evolving steadily from a workers' movement into a political umbrella organization subsuming the interests of various special societal groups (writers, students, academics, clerical staff, shop assistants, peasants organized separately in Rural Solidarity), so the party underwent a process of disaggregation. Lower committees increasingly sought greater autonomy from central bodies while divisions within PZPR leaders and cadres at all levels deepened over the question of what to do about Solidarity. In the spring of 1981 in Toruń the first horizontalist structures were established that promoted interaction between party committees at the local level. Such a unique conception of party organization undermined the Leninist principle of democratic centralism by which lower committees were restricted in their functioning to carrying out the orders of vertically higher tiers, and horizontalism quickly spread throughout the country. Central party authorities were hard-pressed to discourage the horizontalists. In this way the existence of Solidarity not only posed a challenge to the top-heavy power distribution system of real existing socialism; it also served to accelerate the process of democratization within the party itself.

Although Solidarity did not entrust Wałęsa with much power, the PZPR began to search for a strong leader to lead it out of the enveloping crisis. Kania's commitment to renewal alienated hardliners in the leadership; at the same time he was accused of going too slowly on reform implementation by the liberal wing. Two alternative candidates appeared to replace the ineffectual if well-intentioned ex-security chief: the conservative Olszowski, former foreign minister and Politburo member, and the inscrutable minister of defense and, since February 1981 premier, Jaruzelski. With a stronger power base and a more ambiguous policy line the second man was preferred, and in October he was chosen by the Central Committee to replace Kania as first secretary. Two months later Jaruzelski became head of the Military Council of National Salvation that governed Poland under martial law. Preparations for the coup that suspended normal political processes and crushed Solidarity had undoubtedly anteceded the October Central Committee Plenum, but there is no evidence that a firm decision on imposing martial law had been taken prior to the general's assumption of the party stewardship.

In any event the correlation of forces had begun to shift in favor of the party by the fall of 1981. A flurry of wildcat strikes that Solidarity's central executive could not control, the ill-judged appeal to workers of other socialist states during the union's national congress in September–October (which particularly incensed the leadership of the USSR, East Germany, and Czechoslovakia), and the more uncompromising policies of the PZPR rulers (which included such "provocations" as increasing alcohol and tobacco prices without consulting the trade union) undermined the movement. But the real coup de grace to Solidarity was the same one that toppled the Gierek administration—the increasing gravity of the economic situation. Food became scarce, and by December 1981 the political crisis had severely affected industrial production, agriculture, the service sector, and the distribution network. Indispensable Western credits necessary to salvage the economy were harder to come by. Not without some grain of truth did Poles remark that "under Gomulka we had socialism, under Gierek we had capitalism, and under Kania we have kania-balism."

In addition to objective factors, a subjective aspect in Solidarity's demise needs to be mentioned. The movement's top leadership was guilty of an error of judgment in believing the authorities lacked the will, the capability, or the power base to undertake repressive action. Some of Wałęsa's advisers counseled deployment of contingency plans in case rulers resorted to force to destroy the movement. One year earlier, during the crisis precipitated by the authorities' unwillingness to register Solidarity as an official trade union, many workers had made preparations to defend and hold out in their factories should the security forces take action. But no Solidarity leaders seriously considered using force themselves as a way to seize power from the PZPR, as the martial law regime later imputed to the alleged extremists in Solidarity.

In short, Solidarity's leadership was repeating the mistake initially made by the party rulers in underestimating the strength of the adversary. There was a logical explanation for this miscalculation. One observer has concluded:

> It may be that the two sides underestimated each other's strength so drastically because they possessed different *kinds* of strength, and each side judged the other on the basis of its own kind: To the government the opposition looked weak because it lacked military and police power, while to the opposition the government looked weak because it lacked public support. According to the "realistic" laws of the government's existence, the Solidarity movement was an impossibility, but equally, according to the more "idealistic" laws of Solidarity's existence, martial law was impossible.[10]

The international context in which Solidarity existed was also very unfavorable to it. Much was made, understandably, of the constant military maneuvers held by Warsaw Pact countries around Poland's borders during this period. The Red Army brought up reservists and was poised for an invasion in December 1980, though finally Brezhnev held back.[11] Political pressure was continuously applied by Soviet leaders on their PZPR counterparts—for example, in the June 1981 letter condemning the vacillation of the Kania administration. Visits by Russian generals, such as the head of the Main Political Administration, Yepishev, and the commander in chief of the Warsaw Pact Forces, Kulikov, became more frequent and threatening. We should not lose sight of the fact, however, that Western governments, too, were concerned by the destabilizing impact on East-West relations produced by Solidarity's existence. They feared for the $22 billion worth of loans and interests that Poland owed them by 1980. Moreover, an independent and powerful trade union movement in whichever country it existed was ideologically alien to many of these governments. Even China, which could be expected to rejoice in the disunity caused to the Soviet bloc by the events in Poland, was concerned lest its proletariat should follow the Solidarity precedent. In short, the national interests of a variety of states mitigated against their lending meaningful support to Solidarity.

For a significant number of Poles the imposition of martial law elicited a mixture of relief from unbearable political tension, hope for a return to some economic stability, perplexity as to the real objectives of the militarized leadership, and a respite from the impractical system of "dual government" of the previous sixteen months. Certain industrial enterprises resisted the security forces sent in to bring about order. In the most ferocious resistance of this kind nine miners were killed in the Wujek colliery in Silesia in late December. Nevertheless, most Poles, contrary to national tradition, did not rise up. In their defense it can be asked whether, given past and present postures of Western states, such an insurrection made any sense.

THE SIXTH CHALLENGE: THE AUTHORITIES UNITED VERSUS SOCIETY?

In the view of dissident intellectuals, the declaration of martial law issued on 13 December 1981, constituted a declaration of war by the authorities against all society. The limited gains attained by Solidarity in liberalizing society were nullified, and the country seemed to be thrown back in time to the dark days of High Stalinism. Suspension of basic citizen rights, subjection of factories and offices to military rigor, internment without trial of thousands of people, and arrests and beatings were the most dramatic manifestations of the early months of martial law. Just as significant, though less tangible, was the psychological war conducted by the leadership: Militarization of the mass media, spot identity checks on the street, presence everywhere of soldiers and the reviled security forces (especially the riot police known as ZOMO—Motorized Units of the Citizens' Militia), and the general manipulation of public fear and hope created unpredictability. Thus, the nineteen months of martial law were a traumatic, bitter, and disillusioning experience for the generation born and raised in People's Poland.

At the same time, it should be stressed that Poland was a European country in which European values of human life prevailed. Accordingly, repression consisted of modern, technological, "civilized" methods rather than the crude murderous means employed in those same years in Lebanon, Iran, and Argentina. There was a significant difference between martial law, Polish style, and martial law, Chilean style, which we should not overlook. Although the special military tribunals set up to hand down verdicts on individuals charged with offenses under martial law represented the suspension of due legal process in the country, no summary executions of opposition leaders or unexplained *desaparecidos* ("disappearances") occurred. However, martial law and its aftermath did claim many victims: If we lend credence to a tally conducted by Radio Free Europe's Research Bureau, from the time a military government was established in December 1981 to the fall of 1985—that is, nearly four years of "normalization" of political life—some 118 Poles were killed, deliberately or as a result of police brutality, by various branches of the security forces.[12]

Initially, many observers felt that the recourse to martial law represented a defeat for Solidarity and the PZPR alike. Public opinion polls indicated that the prestige of both organizations declined markedly during 1981. Between May and November public confidence in Solidarity fell from 91 percent of respondents to 58 percent, while confidence in the party declined from 32 percent to 11 percent. Moreover, total PZPR membership fell by close to a half million by the end of 1981, only to decline by a further half million by the end of 1984 (Table 2.1). It has been argued that Solidarity's leaders enjoyed popular authority but lacked political power and sought to avoid political responsibility for helping manage the economy. Conversely, the PZPR possessed very little authority but was able in large part to retain its political power and was saddled with all the responsibility for the grave political and economic crises.

Given this deadlock, there was a certain inevitability in the emergence of the military under Jaruzelski as the dominant force in the country: It did have popular authority (its public confidence level in November was 87 percent, second only to the church with 89 percent), it possessed the necessary logistics to seize political power, and it was willing to accept responsibility for governing the country.

The political orientation of the military enhanced its mediating role. It threw its support behind the reformist policies of the Kania-Jaruzelski leadership and disassociated itself from the neo-Stalinist hardliners in the Politburo. The military's representatives continued to win the fully democratic, strongly contested elections that characterized the Solidarity period—first to the party congress, then to its Central Committee (Jaruzelski, though still only premier in Kania's administration, won a greater number of votes than any other Central Committee candidate). Accordingly, "the role of the military in Poland's present and future politics," argues Polish political scientist Jerzy Wiatr, "should be seen as both *system-stabilisers* and *system-reformers*."[13]

With hindsight it is clear that martial law was organized by military and party leaders together. The overall objective of martial law was to bolster the flagging PZPR so that it could rule another day, once its political opponents had been destroyed. The declaration of martial law was not a coup by the army, for the return to constitutional procedures followed relatively quickly (eighteen months). If the army has not fully returned to the barracks yet, it is because the general objective of martial law has not been realized.

In spite of repeated invocations of the ephemeral socialist renewal program by the military junta after 1981, no meaningful structural reform of the political system was undertaken. A supposedly spontaneous grass-roots "national unity" movement was established in the days after the martial law decree, and it was subsequently accorded constitutional status as the Patriotic Movement for National Rebirth (PRON). Many respected figures joined the organization: It was headed, for example, by the popular Catholic writer Jan Dobraczyński. But it has in no way diminished the party's hegemonic role in Polish society. Much the same applies to other organizations created after 1981 such as the Socioeconomic Committee, the National Commission on Culture, and the overhauled professional associations (such as those for journalists, writers, and actors). The new trade unions were declared to be independent of governmental or administrative interference, but they certainly were not free of party control. By mid–1985 total membership in them had barely reached half of those eligible.

However, I would be misrepresenting Polish society if I made no reference to sections of the population that have lent support to the authorities. Apart from PRON, various social strata have been willing to cooperate with the Jaruzelski leadership in the hope that constructive political and economic change will result. Parts of the intelligentsia (discussed more fully in Chapter 6), the peasantry, and, to a more limited extent, the "new," highly skilled working class have opted for participation in the post–1981 institutions. According to official figures 78 percent of the electorate voted in general elections to the Seym held in October 1985, despite calls by the Solidarity underground organization for a boycott. This represented only a 3 percent improvement on the turnout in the 1984 local elections and was still considerably below the 98 percent rate of the pre-Solidarity period. The highest turnout was in the rural regions, the lowest in working class constituencies such as Gdańsk and the Nowa Huta steelworks near Kraków. Although oppositionists disputed the results and Wałęsa claimed the figure was about 66 percent, even under such circumstances it is clear that profound divisions marked the political behavior of Polish society in the mid–1980s.

The major area in which radical reforms were introduced by the Jaruzelski administration was in the economy. Changes in the pricing system, in particular, the linking of commodity prices more closely to production costs, produced triple-digit inflation and de-moralized society even further. Given previous failures to bring about needed price reform, it may well have only been possible under conditions of martial law. Certain decentralization in the systems of planning and management was also introduced, but results in these spheres have been mixed.

In order to find out the public's reaction to government reform measures, surveys have been regularly conducted by the authorities, and the results have been published in the Polish press. Such results need to be approached with caution since various factors can skew the accuracy of surveys taken in communist states. But the findings, particularly of polls that are replicated at regular time intervals, can be indicative of the general character and attitudinal orientation of citizens. Let us look at poll results bearing on the issue of reform promoted by the Jaruzelski administration.

Surveys confirm the rather ambivalent attitude of Polish society toward the reform drive. Two polls, conducted in May 1983 and April 1985 by a government agency showed, for example, a slight increase in the proportion of respondents recognizing the need for economic reform (from 66 percent to 70 percent). But in the second survey opinion was divided as to whether Poland was emerging from the economic crisis (48 percent) or not (44 percent). Results from a different poll published in July 1985 also found that a significant majority of respondents (64 percent) thought present government policies did not present a chance for Poland to emerge from the economic crisis. The most criticized areas of government policy were price reforms, shortage of goods, and income levels; the most critical groups in the survey were industrial workers in large enterprises, highly skilled workers, and younger workers.

If there was little consensus among Poles on the specific question of reform, then there was general agreement that matters had improved in Poland during the past five years. A recurring question asked in annual surveys, carried out shortly after the new year, has been: "What was last year like for our country?" In the surveys reviewing the years 1980 and 1981 respondents expressed very negative views, but more recently, for example, for 1984 and 1985, they have given more positive assessments. Thus, the proportion saying 1980 and 1981 were good years was 8 percent and 2 percent respectively; the proportion saying they were bad years was 78 percent and 86 percent respectively. By contrast, 1984 and 1985 were seen as good by 26 percent and 39 percent of respondents respectively; the number saying these were bad years fell drastically, to 19 percent and 9 percent respectively (44 percent said 1984 and 1985 had been average years).

It is an open question whether such results, even if they are accurate, reflect growing public support for the Jaruzelski administration. Ardent Solidarity members may have perceived the two years Solidarity was in existence in a negative light because of the social tension and economic crisis that came to the surface. The years 1984 and 1985 may have been seen less negatively (the most common answer was, after all, an "average" year) because tension and crisis had been alleviated. Although it would be difficult to deny that a shift in public opinion took place between January 1981 and January 1986, this opinion may have been evaluating material, not political conditions.

Perhaps the most important question concerning economic changes is whether they can work at all without concomitant reform in the structure of political power. Here we observe a differentiated, if largely pessimistic, evaluation of the authorities' policies by Polish respondents. Nearly one-half (48 percent) of the sample in the July 1985 survey believed the authorities were not taking measures to prevent a recurrence of past crises, 26 percent said the actions were superficial, and another 13 percent held that old methods were still employed.

A poll of industrial workers carried out in late 1984 by the Polish underground reported that domestic political factors were largely blamed for the country's problems: Workers blamed a lack of democracy (68 percent), a lack of a proper role for trade unions and workers' self-management (64 percent), excessive party influence in political life (59 percent), and bad political leadership in the 1970s (92 percent) and at present (64 percent). If there was a consensus that the world should not model itself on the Polish brand of socialism (64 percent), the underground might have been surprised to discover that the remaining one-third of the sample did not object to such a tendency. When asked to assess the chances for improvements in Poland, 30 percent said they thought gradual improvements in the political system were possible. Finally, findings from a separate series of government-sponsored polls, made public in October 1985, found a recurring 5 percent of respondents in 1984 and 1985 asserting the need for an overhaul of the existing system or, at the least, in the system of governing. By contrast, one-quarter claimed the present system was good and needed no modifications, and a further 27 percent thought it was good in principle, although in need of some changes.

Another contentious issue that poll findings can help clarify is popular attitudes to public ownership in a communist state. According to the Solidarity underground survey, a majority of the sample (58 percent) favored social ownership of the means of production and a planned economy, while 42 percent supported free competition. Paradoxically, however, a government-sponsored study reported in December 1985 found a different, although not contradictory, tendency: 82 percent of respondents favored the introduction of market laws and competition, and 61 percent wanted to see an increase in private sector activity. But many advocates of market socialism also wished to preserve the chief benefit offered by the socialist economy—full employment. Fifty-seven percent of respondents opposed creating a pool of unemployed. Another apparent contradiction uncovered by the December 1985 poll was that although 55 percent wanted an increase in the autonomy of enterprise directors, 77 percent desired an increase in the influence of worker self-management bodies. In both cases, of course, the power of central authorities would be eroded.[14]

From such disparate data sets we can infer that the political culture of Poland in the 1980s is characterized by heterogeneity, inconsistencies, and even antagonisms. Although there exists a hard-core group strongly opposed to the political system, a somewhat larger part of society has, for a multitude of reasons (opportunism, realism, perhaps even genuine ideological commitment), accepted the system in its present form. There is a third group that we should not ignore: It consists of citizens who are uninterested in politics, either because of personal taste or as a result of disillusionment. In all likelihood, this category is the largest: A mid–1985 poll found, for example, that a small fraction of respondents following politics "keenly" (3 percent) or "fairly keenly" (13 percent), with more than half asserting they had "no interest in political life."[15] Neither the political leadership nor its undergound counterpart can take comfort

from the mix of responses—proregime, antiregime, or apathetic—
compiled by such attitudinal surveys.

The issue of political and economic reform has produced internal
divisions within the leadership as well. As united as the military and
party authorities might have been in imposing the political order
entailed by martial law, profound differences subsequently arose
between hardliners and liberals about the extent to which the new
polity should reflect the dominant mechanisms of the pre–August
1980 and the sixteen-month Solidarity eras respectively. The hardliners
hoped to exploit martial law to eliminate all forms of opposition,
whether centered in Solidarity or the Catholic church, in intellectual
circles, or within the party. Their conception was to impose the Soviet
model en bloc on Poland, eliminating all national idiosyncrasies. By
contrast, the liberals may originally have entertained the idea of
resurrecting an independent social movement in another guise, perhaps
as a loyal opposition to the PZPR. They envisaged a reformed electoral
system that resulted in controlled but contested elections, and they
expected the legislature to serve as an early warning system of crises
for the authorities.

In late 1984 it appeared as if the first group was ascendant.
The brutal murder of Father Jerzy Popieluszko, a pro-Solidarity priest,
in October 1984 by officers of the security forces was the most visible
sign of this ascendance, but there were many other manifestations
as well—the clamping down on the academic community, more
frequent press attacks on the church, and the arrest of certain opposition
figures after amnesty had been granted.

The catch-22 in the Polish situation was that a repeat of the
social ferment that occurred in the summer of 1980 could well play
into the hands of the hardliners. They continued to identify as Gierek's
greatest sin his refusal to use force against strikers. The hardliners
would, in all certainty, if they seized power, not repeat that mistake.
But Poland was generally tranquil in the year that followed, and
Jaruzelski could point to limited successes at home (the holding of
parliamentary elections after a three-year delay and the continued
prestige enjoyed by the army) and abroad (personal visits to the
United Nations and France in late 1985). Perhaps most importantly,
succession in the Kremlin in March of that year brought to power a
man who projected pragmatism and reform-mindedness and who
was an age cohort of Jaruzelski. It seems plausible that the emergence
of Gorbachov signaled a decline in the fortunes of PZPR hardliners.
By late 1985, for example, the most prominent representative of this
faction, Stefan Olszowski, had been forced to resign his seat on the
Politburo and his position as Polish foreign minister.

Although 1985 was a year of setbacks for the neo-Stalinists, it remained an open question whether dissonance between the rulers and the ruled decreased. It did appear that a much-loved motto of Polish politicians, the need for political realism, had gained support. In the longer term a less amorphous and more institutionalized solution to the cycle of state-society clashes in Poland is required. The leadership must give attention to two major matters: setting up a reliable early warning system of impending crises, one grounded in a modicum of political pluralism that would be more responsive to societal interests; and employing prophylactic methods when crisis symptoms appear—in other words, adjusting socioeconomic policies to meet citizen needs.

Given the complexity of the Polish situation it is not without reason that world leaders have often expressed bafflement or dismay at events in this country. Franklin Roosevelt once remarked that "Poland was the headache of the West," and his Soviet contempory, Stalin, added, not without foundation, that "communism fits Poland like a saddle fits a cow." Ultimately, the course pursued in Poland is contingent upon internal developments in the Soviet Union. A more pragmatic leader in the Kremlin has more ability to bring about an improvement in state-society relations in Poland than the periodic exhortations of Wałęsa, the moderating efforts of the Catholic church, or the activities of Solidarity's dwindling underground network. The problem, as the Poles see it, is that Soviet leaders have hardly ever sponsored reform or liberalization measures in Eastern Europe. Gorbachov, like Gierek in the early 1970s, offered a new and welcome political style to communist leadership. But whether there was to be a matching substance to it remains to be seen. The key questions of Poland's relations with the USSR, and its international politics generally, form the subject of the next chapter.

NOTES

1. A. Bromke, *Poland's Politics: Idealism vs. Realism* (Cambridge, Mass.: Harvard University Press, 1967), p. 55.

2. N. Bethell, *Gomulka* (Harmondsworth, Middlesex: Penguin Books, 1972), p. 191.

3. Bromke, *Poland's Politics*, p. 69.

4. For an account of the security apparatus, see M. Checinski, *Poland: Communism, Nationalism, Anti-Semitism* (New York: Karz-Cohl, 1982).

5. R.F. Leslie (ed.), *The History of Poland Since 1863* (Cambridge: Cambridge University Press, 1983), p. 345.

6. J. Karpiński, *Countdown* (New York: Karz-Cohl, 1982), p. 108.

7. M.K. Dziewanowski, *The Communist Party of Poland* (Cambridge, Mass.: Harvard University Press, 1976), p. 298.
8. M. Rakowski, *Polityka* (20 February 1971).
9. *Le Nouvel Observateur* (16 May 1976).
10. J. Schell, "Reflections: A Better Today," *New Yorker* (3 February 1986):61.
11. For an intriguing analysis of Brezhnev's purge of prointerventionist military officers, see R.D. Anderson, Jr., "Soviet Decision-Making and Poland," *Problems of Communism* 31, no. 2 (March-April 1982):22–36.
12. See J. Bugajski, "The Dead Victims of Martial Law and Its Aftermath," *Radio Free Europe Research*, BR/100 (9 September 1985):1–23.
13. J.J. Wiatr, "Professional Soldiers and Politics in Poland." Paper presented at the Inter-University Seminar on the Armed Forces and Society, Chicago, 18–20 October 1985.
14. Sources for the opinion poll results are presented in the order discussed in the text: The May 1983 and April 1985 polls were reported in *Zycie Warszawy* (23 August 1985). The July 1985 results were found in *Polityka* (27 July 1985 and 10 August 1985). Data for the annual "good year, bad year" poll were taken from *Zycie Warszawy* (5 February 1986). The underground survey came from the underground journal *Obecność*, no. 10 (Summer 1985). Results from the government polls reported in October 1985 were found in *Zycie Warszawy* (30 October 1985). Finally, the December 1985 survey was taken from *Polityka* (14 December 1985).
15. Reported in *Przegląd Tygodniowy* (8 September 1985).

FURTHER READINGS

N.G. Andrews. *Poland 1980–81*. Washington, D.C.: National Defense University Press, 1985.
N. Ascherson. *The Polish August*. Harmondsworth, Middlesex: Penguin Books, 1981.
J. Bielasiak and M. Simon (eds.). *Contemporary Polish Politics*. New York: Praeger, 1984.
G. Blażyński. *Flashpoint Poland*. New York: Pergamon, 1979.
A. Bromke and J.W. Strong (eds.). *Gierek's Poland*. New York: Praeger, 1973.
A. Brumberg (ed.). *Poland: Genesis of a Revolution*. New York: Vintage Books, 1983.
L. Labedz (ed.). *Poland Under Jaruzelski*. New York: Charles Scribners, 1984.
B. Misztal (ed.). *Poland After Solidarity*. Rutgers, N.J.: Transaction Books, 1985.
P. Raina. *Political Opposition in Poland 1954–1977*. London: Poets and Painters Press, 1978.
J. Staniszkis. *Poland's Self-Limiting Revolution*. Princeton, N.J.: Princeton University Press, 1984.
R. Taras. *Ideology in a Socialist State: Poland 1956–1983*. Cambridge: Cambridge University Press, 1984.

J. de Weydenthal. *The Communists of Poland*. Stanford, Calif.: Hoover Institution Press, 1978.

J. de Weydenthal, B.D. Porter, and K. Devlin (eds.). *The Polish Drama 1980–1982*. Lexington, Mass.: Lexington Books, 1983.

J. Woodall (ed.). *Policy and Politics in Contemporary Poland*. London: Frances Pinter, 1982.

3

International Politics— Between East and West

An examination of Poland's thousand-year history and its contemporary political situation reveals a dilemma common to a number of other states in the region (such as Czechoslovakia, Hungary and the German Democratic Republic): Although geographically it lies in the heart of Europe and historically it is linked more closely to the Roman Christian tradition of Western Europe than to the Byzantine system of Russia, Poland finds itself, since 1945, subsumed within the politically defined conception of Eastern Europe. Critics of the Yalta order have argued the case for the eventual establishment of either a unified Europe, as scholar and statesman Brzezinski has outlined,[1] or a distinct Central European entity that would cut across present borders in the region, as the Czech writer Kundera has eloquently urged.[2] In his 1985 encyclical entitled *Slavorum Apostoli,* Pope John Paul II also focused on the need to overcome misunderstanding between Eastern and Western Europe. A different international status for Poland was put forward by Polish intelligentsia circles during the Solidarity period. This conception called for the Finlandization of Poland—that is, giving the country the right to choose its socioeconomic system, permitting a measure of political contestation, but maintaining a foreign policy closely aligned to the USSR. By looking in this chapter at Poland's international politics, past and present, we may be better able to judge whether such propositions are feasible and realistic.

SHIFTING BOUNDARIES, CHANGING DEPENDENCIES

In Chapter 1 I described how Poland, even at the time of its founder, Mieszko I, was confronted with an unhappy fact of international life that derived from its geopolitical position: It was squeezed

between the two great nations of Russia and Germany. In the second
half of the tenth century Poland was involved in wars with both
nations; in the mid-twentieth century the country emerged broken
from fresh conflicts with both states. One can perhaps only com-
miserate with a nation located in such an international context and
paraphrase the lament of a Mexican statesman referring to his country's
position vis-à-vis the United States: "Poor Poland, so far from God,
so near Russia and Germany." In Poland's case the first part of the
statement may, perhaps, be off the mark.

A further trick of history is that after radical shifts of borders
throughout the medieval period and the complete disappearance of
borders in the late eighteenth century, the lands presently occupied
by Poles are uncannily congruous with those originally inhabited by
the Polanie settlers. During the Piast dynasty (966–1370) Poland's
primary political concern was containment of Teutonic expansion—
in other words, securing the country's western and northern frontiers.
Piast Poland was also a relatively homogeneous state ethnically. By
contrast, the Jagiellonian kings (1385–1572) brought about considerable
expansion eastward, in large part at the expense of Muscovy and
tsarist Russia, and incorporated many non-Polish peoples into the
Republic. The analogous dichotomy between Pilsudski's interwar
Second Republic, an ethnically heterogeneous state concerned foremost
with the menace posed by Bolshevik Russia, and the postwar People's
Republic, a fundamentally Polish state searching continuously for
manifestations of German revanchism, is striking.

Since Poland has come within the Soviet orbit, official histories
have naturally emphasized the supposedly superior wisdom of Piast
as opposed to Jagiellonian foreign policy. There is another fundamental
difference, going beyond simple directional orientations, between Piast-
communist and Jagiellonian-Pilsudskite approaches. In the interwar
period (as under the last Jagiellonians) excessive independence in
foreign affairs and an unwillingness to forge meaningful international
alliances produced mortal danger to the country. Conversely, since
1945 Poland's quasi-total dependence on the Soviet Union has proved
troublesome, both in generating legitimacy problems for the leadership
and in involving the country in international tensions not of its own
making. Significant examples of Polish involvements in these international tensions include participation in the Warsaw Pact invasion
of neighboring Czechoslovakia in 1968, bellicosity (up to the early
1980s, at least) toward China and Israel, official policy support for
Soviet moves into parts of Africa and then Afghanistan, and logistical
support for the strengthening of the Soviet military bloc. Analysis

of Poland's international politics ought to begin, therefore, with its postwar relations with the USSR.

THE CENTRALITY OF RELATIONS WITH THE USSR

Even before the Red Army's liberation of Poland from Nazi occupation, much of the Polish population and many of its leaders suffered acutely from Russophobia. A verse contained in the poetic drama *Forefathers' Eve* (Part Three), written in 1832 by Poland's national poet Mickiewicz, might accurately have expressed the sentiments of a majority of Poles at the end of World War II:

> Yet I also know what it is to be free by the mercy of a Muscovite,
> The scoundrels will remove the chains from my hands and feet
> But will seize my soul—I shall be exiled!

Soviet power in Eastern Europe was consolidated through a series of devices. In August 1945 the pro-Moscow Polish government, like others in the region, signed a Treaty of Friendship and Mutual Assistance with the USSR. Through such bilateral pacts the Kremlin was able to create a bloc of states dependent on it. The more specific purpose of the Polish-Soviet agreement was to formalize the boundary changes that followed from the Red Army's territorial conquests in 1939. In late 1947 the establishment of the Cominform effectively sanctioned the leading role of the CPSU in determining the policies of Eastern European Communist parties. In addition, the 1936 Soviet constitution became the model for constitutions adopted in the period 1946–1949 by the USSR's client states. Poland was somewhat recalcitrant in this respect: Ratification of its constitution didn't occur until 1952.

Any measure of economic independence for Eastern Europe was quickly quashed when Stalin forbade the Poles, Hungarians, and Czechs from taking part in the 1947 Paris talks that approved the Marshall Aid Plan. Initially all three countries had expressed interest in participation. Prior to the creation of a communist Common Market, termed the Council for Mutual Economic Assistance (CMEA), in 1949, the USSR had already become Poland's principal trading partner and supplier of capital and machinery in return for coal purchased at $1.25 per ton—a price ridiculously below world market prices.

Prior to 1956 the Soviets never admitted the inequality of such economic agreements. Faced with a mounting desire on Poland's part for greater national autonomy in Eastern Europe following Khrushchev's de-Stalinization, the Soviets now ventured a clever explanation for the unequal agreement with Poland. According to foreign minister Molotov, the total economic value of the eastern territories annexed by the Soviet Union from Poland was $3.5 billion; the total value of the western territories Poland "regained" from Germany was $9.5 billion. For the Poles, therefore, the geographic shift westward supposedly represented a stupendous economic gain. On closer examination this claim becomes highly debatable: Officials in the Third Reich viewed these lands—which accounted for 21 percent of interwar German territory but only 12 percent of its population and 7 percent of its industrial production—as backward. Even if the area was richer in resources than the eastern *kresy* Poland lost, the inference Molotov drew from this was specious. The least the new regime could do, he suggested, was to share some of its Silesian coal bounty with the country's liberators.[3]

When Khrushchev had finally recognized the validity of national roads to socialism and Gomulka had taken power for a second time, at the top of the agenda for both new leaders was renegotiation of the countries' political and economic agreements. In the end Khrushchev acknowledged that the Soviets had obtained the better deal, and he agreed to cancel Polish debts to the USSR of $626 million incurred in the period 1949–1956. Reportedly that figure only represented half of Gomulka's claims on Poland's eastern neighbor.

Khrushchev's remaining years in office (until October 1964) were noteworthy for the polycentrism that evolved in the world communist movement. The USSR's break with China became irreversible, the independence of Yugoslavia was grudgingly recognized, Red Army divisions stationed in Romania were successfully persuaded to go home in 1958, and Albania ceased to play any part in the Warsaw Pact—the Soviet military alliance established in 1955—after 1961. Gomulka's much touted Polish road to socialism paled in comparison to the assertive foreign policies of these formerly compliant clients of the Soviet Union.

While Poland obtained a modicum of redress in its terms of trade with the Soviets, there were two other indications of a more autonomous Polish foreign policy line. The first involved essentially nonpolitical matters: In the years 1957 and 1958 Gomulka was able to obtain two U.S. loans, each worth close to $100 million. At the same time, he fostered improved cultural ties between the two countries, such as scientific exchanges and tourism. Given the size of the Polish community in the United States (according to the 1980 census 8.2 million U.S. citizens are of Polish descent; by contrast only 1.1 million Soviet citizens in the same year were officially listed as of Polish origin), this policy was and remains a natural one to pursue. In the 1970s under Gierek, U.S. loans and Polish cultural contacts with the United States grew by leaps and bounds, and they played a significant part in producing economic crisis and political instability by the end of the decade. The attitude of Soviet leaders in 1956 and 1957 and in the 1970s was one of suspicion about Poland's special cultural bonds with the United States, coupled with a measure of relief that capitalism was helping prop up a weak socialist economy.

The second sign of a more autonomous Polish foreign policy line within the Soviet-led bloc was on the question of relations with West Germany. Poland insisted that the latter recognize the Oder-Neisse border as final before relations could be resumed. The Soviet position was initially more conciliatory to Adenauer's Germany, but it hardened in alignment with Gomulka's unyielding demand.

In terms of international diplomacy, a superficial image of Poland striking out on its own was projected after 1956. In 1957 foreign minister Rapacki submitted a proposal before the United Nations calling for a ban on all nuclear weapons in Central Europe, that is, in Poland, Czechoslovakia, and the two German states. The plan doubtlessly coincided with Soviet security interests and may even have been inspired by the Kremlin; nonetheless, its acceptance by the West would have strengthened Poland's international status in Europe. It would have reversed the trend toward establishment of rival military political and economic blocs in Europe. Moreover, West Germany had begun the process of remilitarization, and the Adenauer government had continued to insist on a revision of Poland's western border running along the Oder-Neisse rivers. U.S. acceptance of the Rapacki plan would have permitted Poland to improve political relations with the West and might have decreased its isolation in and dependence on the Soviet camp, though in a more modest way than had occurred with Yugoslavia.

For the West the problem with the Rapacki plan was that it would have greatly enhanced the Soviets' strategic position if Central Europe were to be defended by conventional forces alone; the USSR had significant military superiority in that regard. Accordingly, the United States and West Germany rejected this plan as well as a subsequent modified version of it, labelled the Gomulka plan.

Increasing polycentrism in the communist world had little impact on Polish foreign policy. Gomulka gradually evolved into one of the Soviet leadership's most reliable allies, and by 1965, when the Polish-Soviet Friendship Treaty was renewed, Brezhnev was able to herald the bilateral links as "a relationship of a new type." As the second most important military power in the Warsaw Pact and the third

most populous communist-ruled country in the world, Poland clearly
became the Soviet Union's most important bloc ally after the defection
of China. Gomulka seemed to take pride in this dubious status, as
evidenced by his zeal for the campaign against "international Zionism"
following the 1967 Arab-Israeli war and his enthusiasm for the 1968
invasion of Czechoslovakia so as to eradicate Dubček's dangerous
heresy of "socialism with a human face."

In looking at bilateral Polish-Soviet relations we should not
overlook an important agreement concluded in late 1956 that regulated
the "legal status of Soviet troops temporarily stationed in Poland."
Article 1 of this so-called status-of-forces accord declared that the
presence of Soviet troops in the country could not infringe upon
Polish sovereignty nor lead to interference in its internal affairs. Article
2 stated that the respective governments would determine the size
and location of the Soviet military contingent.

Although these provisions presaged similar bilateral security
pacts signed by the Soviets with other states in the bloc in 1957,
implicitly greater respect for Poland's autonomy was signaled by the
inclusion of a clause whereby Soviet troop movements outside their
bases required the express permission of the Polish authorities. Un-
questionably, this qualification stemmed from Soviet troop movements
in the country during the Polish October, which, as noted in the
previous chapter, were countered by Polish army movements intended
to defend major cities. It is significant that in the sixteen tumultuous
months of Solidarity's existence in 1980 and 1981, the Soviets applied
military pressure on Poland from outside its borders (through mobilization of reservists, Warsaw Pact maneuvers, and naval exercises
off the Baltic coast). The two Soviet armored divisions in the country
(more than twenty-five thousand men)—one at Legnica in Silesia,
which constitutes the Soviets' main supply and communications base,
the other at Drawsko Pomorskie near Szczecin, which guards nearby
airfields serving the 400 Soviet tactical aircraft stationed in Poland—
maintained very low visibility throughout the crisis.

In virtually all countries of Europe, of course, the stationing of
foreign (U.S. and Soviet) troops and firepower is now taken for
granted. In this context Poland hosts fewer foreign military forces
than the two Germanies, Czechoslovakia, or Britain. However, in
Western Europe the justification given for U.S. bases is national
security. In Eastern Europe, in addition to national security, a more
ephemeral reason is also provided—*raison d'état*—which implies that
the national regime may be too weak internally to survive without
the stationing of Soviet troops. In the case of Poland, Soviet and
Polish leaders also advance a pragmatic explanation for their security

arrangements—the need for the USSR to maintain communication and logistical links with its massive forces located in the German Democratic Republic.

We see, therefore, that as in the case of its internal political system, Poland's relations with the Soviet Union have been shaped primarily by arrangements first established after the war, then redefined in the de-Stalinization era. The degree to which foreign policymakers could demonstrate initiative, although broader after 1956, has nevertheless been meticulously controlled by Kremlin leaders. When the Polish government showed signs of responding positively to West German Chancellor Brandt's *Ostpolitik* in 1969, the Soviets insisted that they be the first to sign a treaty before their client states could go ahead. In August 1970 Brezhnev and Brandt ratified a pact mutually renouncing the use of force, and in December Gomulka was finally able to conclude his own agreement, which contained the Federal Republic's recognition of Poland's western frontier. This treaty is Gomulka's most significant foreign policy legacy. Two weeks later he suffered his most humiliating defeat when shipyard workers toppled his administration.

In the 1970s a close relationship was forged between Gierek and Brezhnev. They met very frequently (at least twice a year) and shared a desire to modernize their economies through importing Western technology, capital, and know-how. In their political style the two leaders had in common a patronizing approach, one based on largesse and magnanimity toward clients and adversaries alike. Both gave particular attention to relations with West Germany, which soon became their most important trading partner in the West. Just as Brezhnev met regularly with U.S. presidents—with Nixon twice, Ford, and Carter—so Gierek played host to U.S. leaders (Nixon in 1972, Ford in 1975, and Carter in 1977), and he embarked on the first postwar official visit by a Polish leader to Washington—meeting with Ford in 1974. Other prominent visitors to Warsaw during this decade included such Kremlin favorites as President Valéry Giscard d'Estaing of France, Chancellor Helmut Schmidt of West Germany, and the shah of Iran. Even the duke of Edinburgh made two unofficial trips to Poland in this period. Outside of his U.S. visit, the most important foreign trip by Gierek was to the Vatican to see Pope Paul VI in 1977, a visit that dovetailed with the normalization of church-state relations at home. Although it may be claimed that at least this contact represented an initiative of the Polish regime, we should not lose sight of the fact that Soviet foreign minister Gromyko had already met twice with Pope Paul VI, in 1970 and 1975.

It is highly improbable, therefore, that this flurry of diplomatic activity at the summit level would have been possible and, more importantly, enormous Western credits obtained, had the Kremlin not been seeking improved East-West relations at that time. The signing of the Helsinki agreement in 1975 was the culmination of these relations. Although for Brezhnev it represented both tremendous propaganda and a personal victory, the agreement brought Gierek recognition of Poland's western border by all European countries and by the United States.

When East-West relations began to deteriorate toward the end of the Carter administration, Poland was both a victim and a factor in that deterioration. At the beginning of the 1980s, in particular, the intransigence of both the Kremlin and the Reagan administration was exacerbated by the imposition of martial law in Poland, which in turn severely curtailed the room for maneuver available to Jaruzelski. Symbolically, the only heads of state to visit Poland under martial law were Muammar Khadafy of Libya and Pope John Paul II; in turn, Jaruzelski did not venture further afield than the Soviet bloc capitals. But by the mid–1980s Poland's international isolation had largely been broken. The traditional contacts with Western Europe resumed (the first important visitors to Warsaw after martial law was lifted included premiers Papandreou of Greece and Craxi of Italy), and Jaruzelski made important visits to India and the United Nations. Economic relations with China began to flourish, and rumors circulated about the possible restoration of diplomatic ties with Israel (both phenomena were linked to initial Soviet overtures). At the same time, exchanges of visits between Polish and Soviet leaders remained frequent. In fact, Gorbachov's first foreign visit as party chief was to Warsaw in April 1985 to renew the Warsaw Treaty Organization (WTO) for another twenty years.

This brief look at Polish diplomatic activity underscores how fully the country's foreign policy is enmeshed with that of the Soviet Union. As a result, Poland's relations with the USSR are not only crucial in themselves: Since 1945 they have essentially determined the global policies of successive Polish leaders.

THE WARSAW TREATY ORGANIZATION

The cornerstone of Poland's international security system is the Warsaw Treaty Organization, or Warsaw Pact, which was founded in 1955 but became operational in the early 1960s. From its inception the pact's command structure has been dominated by the Soviet military leadership: In the pact's thirty-year history the commander in chief has always been a marshal of the Soviet Armed Forces. Military doctrine, too, has been designed to serve Soviet strategic interests. The concept of coalition warfare foresees "rapid offensive mobile military operations against NATO" by joint Soviet and Eastern European forces. By opening an "external front" against enemy forces on their territory, the Polish interpretation of this doctrine states that it would be possible to "thwart their invasion of the territory of the socialist countries."[4] Over time, however, the intrabloc policing function of the pact has grown in significance. The pact invasion of Czechoslovakia in 1968 and its remorseless pressure through joint military exercises around Polish borders in 1980 and 1981 each produced the desired result—the elimination of political pluralism in a member country.

Odd as it may seem, direct Soviet control of the Polish armed forces has actually loosened since the pact became operational. In the 1950s Soviet officers occupied such crucial Polish military posts as minister of defense, chief of the general staff, commander of the ground forces, heads of all service branches, and commanders of all four military districts. By contrast, "direct controls were totally absent in the 1970s in Poland [and] direct Soviet military representation in Warsaw itself was reportedly limited to about a dozen Soviet officers."[5]

The Soviet military is confident, however, that sufficient alternative mechanisms are now in place to ensure Polish military dependence on the USSR. One Western expert on the WTO, Christopher Jones, has identified five interlocking control mechanisms that deny pact members such as Poland the ability to rely on their own forces for defense. These are 1) the unified command of the WTO; 2) the common arsenal of Soviet weapons; 3) shared military doctrine; 4) an integrated network of political (that is, party) administrative control of the military forces; and 5) an integrated system of officer education.[6]

Soviet-designed standardization of men and materiel guarantees that the Polish military is only effective when it is used in conjunction with Soviet objectives. Put another way, the Polish army is less a national than a communist army, or "the Polish contingent of a larger Soviet-controlled force."[7] Perhaps Soviet confidence in the ability to control the Polish military is most clearly manifested in the delivery to Polish forces of nuclear-capable surface-to-surface delivery vehicles, including two navy missile corvettes. Polish personnel have also been trained in their use. It goes without saying that the actual warheads remain under Soviet control and are likely kept on Soviet territory.

Poland, together with Czechoslovakia and East Germany, makes up the powerful Northern Tier of the Warsaw Pact. Table 3.1 presents recent data on Polish military manpower and defense expenditure.

Table 3.1 Polish Military Forces and Expenditures, 1985

Army	210,000
Navy	19,000
Air Force	90,000
Total: Regular Forces	319,000
Reserves: All Services	501,000
Para-Military Forces *	218,000
Citizens Militia	350,000
League for National Defense+	200,000

Total Defense Expenditure (1983): $5,766,000,000
Percentage of Gross Domestic Product: 2.7% (1983)

* includes border troops and internal defense forces

+ citizen support group

Source: The International Institute for Strategic
           Studies, The Military Balance 1985-86.
           London: IISS, 1985, pp. 34-35, 170.

The size of the regular forces is one-third greater than the next most powerful WTO member (Czechoslovakia) and is generally comparable to that of British forces. During the period 1975–1982 no member of either the WTO (including the USSR) or the North Atlantic Treaty Organization—NATO (including the United States) increased its defense expenditures at the rate that Poland did. During these eight years Polish defense spending rose by 49 percent. What is more, according to The Military Balance, a yearbook put out by the London-based International Institute for Strategic Studies, Poland undertook a further sharp increase in military outlays from 1982 to 1984, by about 36 percent.[8] This growth seems much more than was warranted to carry out the task of restoring order to the country under martial law. It ought to be viewed within the dual context of a general militarization of Polish society in which the armed forces took on a leading role and the further deterioration of East-West relations, which provoked a military buildup by states in the two military pacts. We should also keep in mind that Poland's increased defense spending came during a period of severe economic recession for the country. When, by 1985, the threat of civil disturbances within Poland had receded and relations between the two superpowers had improved slightly, defense spending in Poland fell for the first time in five years. Of course, it would be naive not to recognize the priorities of Soviet leaders and the needs of the WTO as two determinants of Poland's defense expenditure levels.

When we examine defense spending as a proportion of Gross Domestic Product (GDP)—that is, the total value of goods and services produced within a country—we find that Poland is as defense-conscious as either West Germany or France, though not as much as the USSR, the United States, or Britain. During the early 1980s the defense share of the total state budget was officially reported to be close to 9 percent. In contrast, U.S. analysts estimated Poland's defense spending in these years as closer to 20 percent of the state budget. The overall impression of the Polish military obtained from these figures is that it ranks among the most powerful of the European middle powers and that it is a linchpin of the Warsaw Pact.

The issue of the reliability of the WTO's various national contingents inevitably comes up in an analysis of military capabilities. In his study of this issue Daniel Nelson concluded that the reliability of Poland's forces was enhanced by the way the country was systematically well integrated into the Soviet alliance system: Joint military maneuvers with the USSR and extensive bilateral trade were the most important methods of such integration. In addition, Poland's military preparedness was, as I have suggested, considerable. Given the nation's propensity toward political turbulence, we can agree with Nelson that "Poland's systemic integration and military potential, however, are countered by highly negative political and socioeconomic conditions."[9]

Other factors must be taken into account in evaluating the reliability of the Polish military within the WTO. These include the combat scenario (location and objective) and conflict duration. In the final analysis the sheer military assets and potential of the Polish armed forces must at once boost the Kremlin's confidence in the Warsaw Pact and produce occasional disquiet. The key to reliability remains, therefore, the maintenance of a loyal officer corps.

SYSTEMIC INTEGRATION AND
TERRITORIAL INVIOLABILITY

I have now discussed factors that brought about Poland's political and military integration into the Soviet alliance system. In the next chapter I look at corresponding forms of economic integration, which are also extensive. Two related questions arise from this analysis: Given the level of integration into the Soviet bloc, how is it that

Poles have regularly managed to stage protests against shortcomings in the Soviet-type socialism in operation in their country? Why has the Soviet Union not acted directly to suppress such protests?

The first question was largely answered in the preceding chapters. Regardless of the political system governing the nation, Poles appear to have a propensity to rebel. Their history and political culture are characterized by insurgence, and the cyclical protests in People's Poland must be seen in this more general context. Furthermore, systemic integration into the Soviet bloc at the present time subsumes the all-important spheres of foreign policy, international security, and modal political system. Areas remain in which the Polish authorities enjoy discretionary powers. These include, for example, the *modus vivendi* with the powerful Catholic church, respect for the private agricultural sector, and the point at which forces of repression are used against oppositionist movements. Given the greater threshold of tolerance of popular protest that exists in Poland compared to the USSR, the public has been able regularly to vent its frustrations against the regime. Growing self-confidence, political experience, skilled leadership, organizational foundations, and a sense of political efficacy have contributed in the past to the magnitude of public challenges to the authorities.

Under such circumstances we might expect the Soviet leadership to seek to intervene directly in Poland. Why, then, has the USSR not put Poland's house in order once and for all, as in the cases of Hungary in 1956 and Czechoslovakia in 1968? First, a number of geopolitical reasons for Soviet reticence must be advanced. As noted earlier, Poland's population is the largest and its surface area is the greatest of all Eastern European states. Second, the Soviet leadership is to a certain degree constrained by the history of Russian-Polish relations. If proletarian internationalism of the Soviet variety is to mean anything at all, if it is to be distinguished in any way from the previous two hundred years of interaction between these two nations, then past solutions should not be adopted to resolve present problems. Third, the Polish insurrectionary tradition may possibly act as a deterrent. The Brezhnev doctrine may well have spelled out that instability in one socialist country is a matter of concern to the entire socialist commonwealth. But like the rest of Soviet ideological and doctrinal thought, the idea is sufficiently elastic to take into account various national idiosyncrasies.

One distinctive national attribute of the Poles is insurrection against foreign dominion. Whether they would actively and protract-edly resist a Soviet-led invasion today is highly questionable. Poland's neighbor is now a global power and has attained strategic equivalence with its major world adversary. Resistance against Soviet military forces would be even more futile than cavalry charges against tanks, as a Polish unit undertook against invading Germans at the outset of World War II. Nevertheless, there might be a lingering feeling among Kremlin leaders that such bravado among the Poles cannot be ruled out. As a result, the Polish insurrectionary tradition may live on in mythical form.

A final reason why Poland, the most rebellious nation in the Soviet bloc, has not been invaded lies in the nature of its political leadership. Since 1945 the country has not spawned any utopian Communists. Postwar Polish communism has followed in the Dzeržyński tradition, that is, the crude and pragmatic style of Lenin's Polish-born security chief. The more intellectual and utopian Luxemburgist tradition seems to have been abandoned. Perhaps Marxist idealists are driven to work outside the framework of the PZPR machine. A Polish Dubček, for example, might inexorably be drawn to critical leftist groups such as Experience and the Future (DiP), the Club of Catholic Intelligentsia (KIK), or even the Committee for Workers' Self-Defense (KOR). Whatever the exact explanation, Polish rulers during the years have proven politically unimaginative and unexpectedly servile to the Kremlin, more so than their counterparts in Hungary or Romania. It was the Polish political-military elite, after all, who solved a Kremlin headache by imposing martial law in 1981. Thus, I suggest that although the Polish population has been revolting, its leadership has been conforming. Given these conditions, Soviet intervention has proven unnecessary.

The Kremlin has all the leverage it requires, therefore, to control the tempestuous Poles through a process of osmosis. A reliable ruling elite, buttressed by a broader social class—the red bourgeoisie—who owes its relative influence and affluence to the Soviet-style system, serve as secure pillars of the political order. It is an undeniable fact that significant sections of the population have done well by the present system. This situation led one embittered Polish intellectual to comment about the martial law regime: "If nothing else it taught us how many swine there are in this country." Although such a remark is extremely jaundiced, it does point to the existence of a certain unfavorable phenomenon: In contemporary Poland what could be termed prematerialist values (the romantic insurrectionary tradition) as well as postmaterialist ones (described by Inglehart as "cognitive mobilization," that is, demands to participate in the political process[10]) are strongly rivalled by petite bourgeois ones (materialism and *asekuranctwo*, or self-interested security). The latter are, ironically, to the

Soviets' liking, and direct Soviet intervention in Polish internal affairs has accordingly assumed the form chiefly of economic assistance.

But it is necessary to end this section on a cautious note: It would be dangerous to assume (as some groups in society did during the Solidarity period) that the factors mitigating against Soviet military intervention in Poland will always deter the Kremlin leadership from launching such an enterprise. Invasion of a Poland about to break away from the bloc might be a worst-case scenario for the Kremlin, but it will remain a Soviet crisis-resolution option for the forseeable future.

SATELLITE OR MAVERICK?

In the late 1970s Poland appeared to have successfully carried out osmosis tactics of its own, at least as far as relations with the West were concerned: All types of contacts (economic, cultural, political) with the United States and Western Europe had rapidly increased. There was a symbolic dimension to these relations as well. At that time many a Pole could well say: "We have our man in Washington [Zbigniew Brzezinski, President Carter's national security adviser], our man in the Vatican [Pope John Paul II], and our man in Tel Aviv [Prime Minister Menachem Begin, who was born and raised in Warsaw]. The problem is—who is our man in Warsaw?"

Indeed, for a variety of reasons many Poles have always been more attached to the West than to the Soviet bloc, which, in their perception, was made up almost entirely of nations traditionally hostile to the country (a notable exception is Hungary, with whom the Poles share, significantly, neither a common border nor a mutually comprehensible language). During the halcyon days of détente close governmental relations with Western countries were welcomed, not least because it made possible travel and even work as a *Gastarbeiter* ("guest worker")—for precious hard currency—in countries such as Sweden, Austria, West Germany, England, and the United States. But the Poles' quasi-uncritical fascination with the United States, in particular, goes beyond the economic and cultural dimensions of greenbacks, pop music, U.S. movies, and contemporary literature. Results of one survey carried out in 1981 among Poles traveling in Western Europe showed that in a major conflict between the Soviet Union and the United States, 64 percent of respondents said they would side with the latter and only 9 percent with the former.[11] Political scientist Adam Bromke concluded in a similar vein: "The Soviets have overestimated the linguistic and cultural affinities that they share with the Poles. In fact, in terms of history and political

culture, the Poles are westerners."[12] Clearly, then, Poland's political
and military security arrangements are at odds with the political and
cultural attitudes of its population. It may be a gross oversimplification
to view the cycle of postwar popular protests in the country as a
manifestation of such anti-Sovietism, but it would be an oversight
to see no anti-Soviet, pro-Western bias in them.

Some observers have regarded Gierek's *Westpolitik* foreign policy
of the 1970s as an effort to reduce the dissonance between bloc status
and popular orientations. By establishing closer ties with Western
states having strong economies, such as West Germany, France, and
the United States, Poland's leverage with Moscow was arguably
enhanced. A linkage was said to exist between the amount of trade
with the West and the extent of liberalization at home. Gierek, too,
had lived for a number of years in Belgium and France, returning
only in 1948, which made him Poland's most Westernized leader.
Increase in contact with the West was, in short, seen as the product
of a number of coalescing factors that served several important political
purposes at home and abroad.

Perhaps out of fear that closer ties between the United States
and Poland would upset the process of détente with Moscow, in 1975
Helmut Sonnenfeldt, Henry Kissinger's spokesman, sought to put a
damper on such relations. He asserted that Eastern Europe was within
the Soviet "scope and area of national interest." Furthermore, the
United States would promote an "organic relationship" (signifying
more structural Soviet controls) between that region and the USSR.
According to the Sonnenfeldt doctrine, the United States should
encourage the "clearly visible aspirations in Eastern Europe for a
more autonomous existence within the context of a strong geopolitical
influence." He added: "This has worked in Poland. The Poles have
been able to overcome their romantic political inclinations which led
to their disasters in the past."[13] If for the next few years economic
and cultural contacts between Poland and the United States continued
to expand, the Polish authorities had been reminded nevertheless of
the political limits of U.S. cooperation. Washington was not about
to renege on the Yalta agreement.

Similar U.S. realism was in evidence during the rise of the
Solidarity movement in 1980 and 1981. In spite of Soviet charges of
Western inspiration of and assistance to the independent trade union,
official U.S. policy was restricted to warning that irreparable damage
to East-West relations would be caused by a Soviet invasion. Economic
aid, especially agricultural assistance, continued to be furnished. Carter
provided $670 million in credits to the Polish government while
seeking to dissuade the AFL-CIO from giving financial help to

Solidarity. By contrast, the Reagan administration granted Poland only $50 million in commodity credits in 1981. The extent and nature of covert activity in Poland by U.S. intelligence agencies and the KGB at this time remains, of course, a moot question. When martial law was imposed the Reagan administration imposed economic sanctions against the military government and, above all, suspended Poland's most-favored-nation (MFN) status, stopped Export-Import Bank credits, and blocked Poland's application for membership in the International Monetary Fund (IMF). The U.S. ambassador was recalled from Warsaw, and hostile propaganda attacks were launched against the Jaruzelski regime.

In contrast to the Hungarian rebellion of 1956, however, the United States did not exhort the Poles to rise up against the regime. Reporting by Radio Free Europe and Voice of America to Poland was not emotive, making it all the more effective. The problem was, as Sovietologist Jerry Hough concluded, that the U.S. administration faced difficult choices with respect to Poland, none of them satisfactory. The most important consideration was that "the extent to which the Polish people will be able to live a freer life will largely depend on developments in the Soviet Union. . . . Insofar as the United States has an influence on Polish developments, it is likely to be through its policy towards the Soviet Union and the Communist world in general."[14] In examining Poland's relations with the West we see, therefore, how we are soon taken back to our starting point, the centrality of Poland's relations with the USSR.

If successive Polish governments have not truly been communist mavericks in the pursuit of improved relations with the West, then neither have the Western states, especially the United States, acted as mavericks by seeking to lure Poland from the Soviet orbit. We should consider the soundness, therefore, of historian Piotr Wandycz's analysis of prospective U.S. policy towards Poland: "It must avoid holding out unrealistic expectations or, inversely, exhibiting a willingness to sacrifice the Poles for the sake of the superpowers' cooperation."[15] Bromke has argued the case more forcefully for encouraging communist polycentrism—the taking of separate roads to socialism by Eastern European states—as a constructive foreign policy option. While putting at ease Soviet security concerns in the region,

> the West should repeatedly keep reminding the USSR that the tightening of its controls over Eastern Europe would result in the worsening of East-West relations; and, conversely, that the advance of polycentrism in the region, by bringing Communism in the various countries there

closer to the popular aspirations, would be conducive to the progress of détente.[16]

In a period of renewed tension between East and West there is a third policy, too, that is highly undesirable—to sacrifice the Poles for the precise purpose of heightening such tension. With the unfortunate coincidence at the outset of the 1980s of the breakdown in détente and domestic upheaval in Poland, this third policy has appeared the most threatening. It has inadvertently pushed the country further into the Soviet camp than at any time since 1956. Likewise, it has severely reduced foreign policy options available to the present Polish leadership. For the forseeable future Poland will remain squeezed between East and West. But we should remember that dependence on either bloc can shift incrementally from one end of the continuum to the other, and Poland's international relations, like those of all smaller powers, will be influenced by judicious foreign policy conducted by Washington as well as Moscow.

NOTES

1. Z. Brzezinski, "The Future of Yalta," *Foreign Affairs* 63, no. 2 (Winter 1984–85):279–302.
2. M. Kundera, "The Tragedy of Central Europe," *New York Review of Books* 31, no. 7 (26 April 1984):33–38.
3. A.R. Rachwald, *Poland Between the Superpowers* (Boulder, Colo.: Westview Press, 1983), p. 11.
4. A.R. Johnson, "The Warsaw Pact: Soviet Military Policy in Eastern Europe," in S. Meikeljohn Terry (ed.), *Soviet Policy in Eastern Europe* (New Haven, Conn.: Yale University Press, 1984), pp. 262, 266.
5. Ibid., pp. 258fn., 267.
6. C. Jones, *Soviet Influence in Eastern Europe* (New York: Praeger, 1981), pp. 230–231.
7. Cited by R. Rand, "The Relationship between the Soviet and Eastern European Armed Forces," *Radio Liberty Research* RL 21/84 (11 January 1984):2.
8. The International Institute for Strategic Studies, *The Military Balance 1984–85* (London: IISS, 1984), p. 158.
9. D.N. Nelson (ed.), *Soviet Allies* (Boulder, Colo.: Westview Press, 1984), p. 36.
10. R. Inglehart, *The Silent Revolution* (Princeton, N.J.: Princeton University Press, 1977).
11. Cited by Nelson, *Soviet Allies*, p. 25.
12. A. Bromke, *Poland—the Last Decade* (Oakville, Ontario: Mosaic Press, 1981), p. 174.
13. "State Department Summary of Remarks by Sonnenfeldt," *New York Times* (6 April 1976).

14. J. Hough, *The Polish Crisis: American Policy Options* (Washington, D.C.: The Brookings Institution, 1982), pp. 71–72.

15. P.S. Wandycz, *The United States and Poland* (Cambridge, Mass.: Harvard University Press, 1980), p. 424.

16. A. Bromke, *Eastern Europe in the Aftermath of Solidarity* (Boulder, Colo.: Eastern European Monographs, 1985), p. 114.

FURTHER READINGS

J. Karski. *The Great Powers and Poland 1919–45*. Lanham, Md.: University Press of America, 1985.

J. Korbel. *Poland between East and West*. Princeton, N.J.: Princeton University Press, 1963.

R. Lucas. *Bitter Legacy: Polish-American Relations in the Wake of World War II*. Lexington: University Press of Kentucky, 1982.

M. Rakowski. *The Foreign Policy of the Polish People's Republic*. Warsaw: Interpress, 1975.

D. Singer. *The Road to Gdansk: Poland and the USSR*. New York: Monthly Review Press, 1982.

S. M. Terry. *Poland's Place in Europe*. Princeton, N.J.: Princeton University Press, 1983.

P.S. Wandycz. *The United States and Poland*. Cambridge, Mass.: Harvard University Press, 1980.

4

Economic Planning, Reform, and Development

One of the best-known axioms of Marxism is that the economic base of a society—the prevailing mode of production and the relations of its forces—determines "in the last instance" the political, institutional, and ideological superstructure of that society. Such economic determinism, whether actually intended by Marx or not, has served Polish communist leaders well as an explanatory model of postwar political crises. Challenges to the system are conveniently interpreted as dissatisfaction not with socialism but with the functioning of the economy of People's Poland. Political crises, by this reasoning, are economic in origin; reform of the economic base can, by itself, improve the performance of unreformed political, institutional, and ideological structures.

Economic difficulties that have arisen in postwar Poland—and they are legion—are said to stem from a variety of sources. These include imbalances produced by the legacy of the country's interwar capitalist economy, reconstruction imperatives following the ravages of World War II, industrialization imperatives in the 1950s and 1960s that sought to transform Poland from a rural agrarian society into a modern industrial nation, dislocations generated by an overcentralized economic management system (the so-called command economy), and the erroneous policies of past leaders on such issues as agriculture, investment, planning, and trade. A neo-Marxist might also invoke Marx's forecast that at a certain stage of social formation further development of the forces of production (technology and know-how) becomes blocked by prevailing but outmoded and inappropriate property relations (Marx had in mind capitalist relations). In countries of real existing socialism, the neo-Marxist would conclude, concentrated state ownership has been responsible for curbing technological development and, with it, economic growth.

In this chapter I explore Poland's economic development since 1945, looking at the impact of several kinds of factors: objective (land, natural resources, past history), institutional (the Soviet-style command economy and its elaborate appendages), and spontaneous (voluntarist policies of individual leaders, the second economy). I describe the regular efforts made to reform the economy and the benefits and costs of economic interdependence with both the socialist and capitalist worlds; I also evaluate the often overlooked achievements of Poland's postwar economy, while simultaneously gauging the extent to which its notorious economic failures have originated in factors either beyond the control of the rulers or of their own making.

BACKGROUND

In the Introduction I considered the principal natural resources found in Poland and the production levels attained in the 1980s. The picture that emerged of Poland's natural and especially energy resources ought to breed optimism about the country's economic prospects. As one economist put it, "Among the nations of Europe Poland is outstandingly well endowed in primary energy. Only Britain and Western Germany take precedence of her in total energy-wealth; and only the latter in energy *per capita*."[1] Yet, paradoxically, as other industrial nations showed signs in the 1980s of emerging from the energy-induced world recession, Poland's economic crisis continued to deepen.

In addition to natural wealth, the country's postwar economy was shaped by previous economic structures. The partition period was one of foreign exploitation, which in turn taught Poles how not to toil for their oppressors. In the interwar years, too, a large proportion of industry (40 percent in 1937) was owned by foreign concerns. In petroleum foreign ownership reached 88 percent, in chemicals, 60 percent, and in mining and foundry, 52 percent. Private indigenous capital was in especially short supply, and the state became heavily involved in certain branches of industry, for example, owning 100 percent of aircraft and automobile factories, 55 percent of foundries (though less of mining), and 30 percent of machine tool plants.

The pattern of ownership according to ethnic origin also revealed significant differences. Of private Polish owners of corporations 51 percent were Catholic and 40 percent Jewish, but in wholesale trade the pattern was reversed (53 percent Jewish and 28 percent Catholic). As a result, Jews, especially Jewish shopkeepers and craftsmen, were more visible in the urban areas where commerce thrived, and they invited invidious comparisons with poorer Polish Catholics employed in factory work or living in the countryside. The pattern of economic activity by ethnic group had regional variations. Thus, in the textile city of Łódź, ownership of the large mills was evenly distributed among Polish Catholics, Polish Jews, and Germans. But the highly feminized work force was drawn almost exclusively from the Catholic section. An ethnic portrait of this industrial city, and its attendant tensions, is found in Wajda's film *The Promised Land*. In the eastern territories the local population was described by one scholar in this way: "In general, the more well-to-do classes were Polish and Catholic; the peasants were Ukrainian and Orthodox; and much of the local business and commerce was in the hands of Jews, who usually spoke Yiddish."[2] Some reasons for these distinct ethnic orientations are offered in Chapter 5.

In the interwar period there were disparities in patterns of economic activity from one industry and region to another. Fully three-fifths of industrial employment was concentrated in foundry, metal, and textile works. The major industrial centers were located in Silesia, Poznań, Warsaw, and Łódź, and other areas remained undeveloped. This problem was compounded by the transportation system: Under the partitions road and railway networks were designed to cater to the individual needs of the respective empires, so that individual Polish cities were better linked with Berlin, Budapest, Vienna, Moscow and Leningrad than with each other.

Poland's chief interwar trading partners were Western countries—Germany (a 24 percent share), Britain (15 percent), and the United States (10 percent). The economy was predominantly agrarian. Agriculture accounted for 45 percent and industry 30 percent of total national production; only 39 percent of the 1931 population was employed outside of agriculture. Furthermore, as a result of land reforms undertaken after 1919 this agrarian sector became "atomized": Soon two-thirds of all farms measured less than 12.5 acres, and only 11 percent were more than 25 acres. The family farm was, therefore, of very modest size. By contrast, in 1935 the 15,000 largest farms in the country encompassed 26 percent of the land and more than one-half the forested area. A prosperous and highly concentrated landed class was another feature of the rural landscape.

To summarize, the interwar Polish economy was to a large degree foreign controlled and Western oriented. Industrial development was unbalanced and the agrarian sector enormous but parceled. The labor force was, by and large, unskilled and ethnically and linguistically heterogeneous. For an incoming regime whose avowed objectives were gross capital formation, nationalization, integration into the socialist bloc, industrialization, balanced development, technical advancement and agricultural collectivization, the dichotomy between inherited structures and future policies could hardly be greater.)

Added to this were the ravages of war. Close to 20 percent of the population had been killed, several millions were forced to migrate westward, and 40 percent of national wealth was destroyed. In 1945 industrial production was 70 percent of the 1939 level, agricultural production was 47 percent, exports were 33 percent lower, and imports were 57 percent higher. Of these imports 80 percent constituted United Nations Relief and Rehabilitation Administration (UNRRA) aid, especially food and raw materials. The only inheritance that the communist authorities might have welcomed was the earlier economic etatism, that is, the major role played by the state in the economy. The new rulers were to expand on it and take over both the commanding heights and the more banal levels of the post–1945 economy.

THE COMMAND ECONOMY

The distinctive feature of a socialist economy is public ownership of the means of production. In Soviet and Eastern European practice this has meant that the state takes ownership of all important production enterprises, banking and financial institutions, foreign trade, and most of the service sector. In contrast, agriculture can be either collectivized (transferred to communal ownership) or etatized (run directly by the state).

There has been considerable debate among economists in socialist and capitalist countries alike about the meaning of public ownership. Some distinguish state ownership (nationalization) from socialized ownership and contend that although the first has been achieved in Soviet-type economies, the second is still far off. Certain critics decry state ownership as state capitalism while others view it as the system furthest from capitalism. More orthodox socialist economists argue, in turn, that so long as parts of the service and agricultural sectors are run by private citizens, full public ownership has not been attained. Such polarized views make us aware of fundamental disagreements concerning the essence of a socialist economy.

Perhaps as important a feature of Soviet-type economies as public ownership, whichever way it is defined, is central planning. The annual, quinquennial, and prospective (long-term) plans drawn up by state administrators have no real counterpart in capitalist economies. Growth rates of all sectors, investment and accumulation levels, production targets and methods, article assortment, and price structures are all fixed by the state and have the force of law. Apart from planning the whole economy, the state also undertakes close administrative scrutiny of plan implementation. Central directives, regulations, and indicators are set by individual ministries and handed down by fiat to industrial corporations, individual enterprises, and local plants. Central control over coefficients of material and labor inputs is a primary characteristic of the command economy. We can define such an economy, therefore, as the combination of state ownership of, planning for, and administrative controls on all significant production enterprises.

In an agrarian society such as Poland was prior to World War II, the Stalinist model of rapid and forced economic development had considerable appeal. Nationalization would ensure state direction, forcible transfer of labor from agriculture to industry would provide necessary manpower and absorb the surplus agricultural population, and capital would be used to promote a high rate of industrial investment, with priority being given to production of producer rather than consumer goods. Economic growth would, in these ways, be institutionalized through the state.

Nevertheless, in the first years after the war the Stalinist developmental strategy underwent serious questioning in Poland. The regime's foremost economist, Hilary Minc, recommended in 1946 that 40 percent of the industrial labor force continue to be employed in the private sector. However, nationalization of all enterprises having more than fifty employees occurred in 1945, and by 1947 the private sector employed only 11 percent of industrial labor. There was also disagreement on the balance to be struck between industrial and agricultural growth and between investment and current consumption. While PPR leaders assigned priority to industry and investment, Polish Socialist Party representatives argued that the relative scarcity of capital combined with the abundance of labor begged development of labor-intensive industries, especially light industry that would manufacture consumer goods.

The main goals of the three-year plan for the period 1947–1949 were to rebuild the country's productive capacity while raising the population's general standard of living. The process of accelerated industrialization was put on hold, and the respective shares of producer and consumer goods in total industrial output were still not grossly disproportionate—in 1949, 59 percent to 41 percent. It should be noted, however, that this plan was by design indicative (forecasting) rather than imperative (command). Perhaps for this very reason it proved to be highly successful: Gross industrial production targets were overfulfilled by 9 percent and exceeded the level attained in 1938 by 48 percent, while gross agricultural production had by 1949 reached 86 percent of the prewar figure in spite of the loss of 20 percent of Poland's arable land to the Soviet Union. The judicious implementation of nationalization measures, encouragement of continued private investments and small-type entrepreneurship, especially in the regained territories, and availability of foreign aid were primarily responsible for the three-year plan's achievements.[3]

The full-scale application of the Stalinist developmental strategy came on the heels of this rare postwar Polish economic success. In 1948 the six-year plan was drafted to subsume the 1950–1955 period, and it was made binding rather than indicative. The prime strategic targets of this plan (which was revised several times) were a high growth rate in the production of producer goods, collectivization of agriculture, and restrictions on private economic activities. It was wildly ambitious in planning for increases in both per capita consumption and real wages and in levels of investment and accumulation (that part of the national income that is produced but not consumed in a given year). In practical terms the high levels of accumulation set in the six-year plan signified the sacrifice of current living standards for future ones and the buildup of the defense industry in response to the Cold War and the Korean conflict (for example, in 1951 Poland began manufacturing tanks for the first time).

The balance between investment outlays in heavy and light industry was shattered; 85 percent went to the former, mostly into metallurgy, machine building, fuel, and chemicals. Food rationing, which had been virtually eliminated by early 1949, was reintroduced in 1952. Although Stalin's death and the ensuing New Course allocated greater resources to current consumption, the real wages of the majority of the labor force did not rise because wage hikes could not keep up with retail price increases. Agricultural production barely matched demographic growth despite (more probably, because of) the introduction in 1951 of a system of compulsory deliveries from peasants. State and private disinvestment from this sector along with the destabilizing effects of collectivization further weakened Polish agriculture.

Finally, the six-year plan discouraged both an import and export strategy and preferred autarkic development. Limited foreign trade was subsumed within the newly established Council for Mutual Economic Assistance. By 1955, 64 percent of total turnover in foreign trade was with socialist countries (of which one-half was now with the USSR, compared to a miniscule 1 percent in 1937) and only 29 percent with developed capitalist states.

The strategy of "pure extensive growth" generated a modest increase of 8.6 percent in Poland's Net Material Product for 1950–

1955 (compared to the more impressive 12 percent plus in Romania, East Germany, and Bulgaria). This figure was to be exceeded by only one other plan, that for 1971–1975, when enormous inputs of Western machinery, equipment, and capital permitted an increase in industrial investment. In comparing these two plans that were twenty years apart, we see that inspite of differences they did help create first an industrial base, then rapid modernization of the Polish economy. We should also bear in mind, however, that both were followed by political crises engendered by the frustrated expectations of large sections of the population. Both the 1950s "iron and steel" and the 1970s "petrochemicals and cars" orientations of the plans appeared to fetishize "production for productions' sake," as Kuroń and Modzelewski wrote in their "open letter to the party." Leadership in both decades did not foresee how the misconceived economic priorities served as catalysts for political crisis.

REFORM EFFORTS

It can be argued that Polish leaders have in fact demonstrated acute sensitivity to the part played by economic factors in molding general political conditions. When we observe how frequently economic reform programs are put forward as a panacea for sociopolitical crises, we could conclude that the entire system must surely have been overhauled since 1945. Let us examine the various reform efforts undertaken.

After 1956, Poland, like other Eastern European states, was caught up in a process labeled "economic revisionism." Two major reform proposals were advanced by Gomulka's specially appointed Economic Council. The first was reorganization of the system of economic management so that the individual economic enterprise, not some central ministry, would serve as the basic economic unit. The second was gradual introduction of quasi-market relations founded on the idea that the price and output of a given commodity ought to be determined by demand. Responsiveness to market factors not only would improve planning, production, and pricing mechanisms but would also boost wages. The influence of Yugoslav ideas of self-management was visible in this reform effort. Due largely to the resistance of dogmatists in the political hierarchy and in the economic bureaucracy, by 1958 the reform drive was thwarted, and a return to the methods of direct central controls ensued.

The fundamental ideas underlying the first reform proposal continued to resurface in various guises during the next three decades. In 1964 a series of fragmentary reforms was introduced that sought to enhance the economic effectiveness of individual enterprises. Management was encouraged to promote maximum profitability, and, to this end, directors were henceforth to be appointed on the basis of economic qualifications rather than political criteria. The scientific bases of planning were supposed to be deepened, cost accounting of production units improved, more flexibility in setting output targets given to the enterprise, and increased adaptation to changing demand patterns ensured.

Again, however, the proposed changes were aborted. As one economist, Gamarnikow, succinctly noted, "the terms 'economic effectiveness', 'profitability', or 'optimal production' have a completely different meaning for the members of the ruling party establishment than for people like professor Oscar Lange [chairman of the 1956 Economic Council and a highly-respected economist], or other protagonists of pragmatic reforms." [The ultimate objectives of the two groups differ: "The basic aim of the party establishment is to introduce a greater degree of efficiency and rationality into the existing economic system while retaining full-scale control." By contrast, the authentic economic reformers "want to change the system itself, so that it would eventually operate on the basis of purely objective economic considerations."[4]

The latter group was also committed to the notion that genuine economic change presupposed reform of the structure of macroeconomic decisionmaking. In turn, this reform necessitated novel political conceptions, methods, and institutions. For Wlodzimierz Brus, the country's leading advocate of economic reform during the 1960s, the unmodified Stalinist steering system was no longer appropriate for the stage of economic development the country had reached in that decade. State preferences—more precisely, those of the bureaucratic elite—were at odds with public preferences. Only a democratized political system could make possible societal control over the means of production. For Brus the state should retain crucial economic functions such as fixing overall investment ratios between productive and nonproductive sectors, guaranteeing full employment, determining income policies, and monitoring other areas where socially desirable goals took precedence over market-determined individual preferences. Such a regulated market economy, he contended, would combine the best features of directive central planning, macroeconomic rationality, and efficiency with decentralized market socialism, microeconomic flexibility, and profitability. Brus's outline of economic reform, elaborated in his numerous books on the socialist economy (see Further Readings to this chapter) had many similarities with the model conceived by Ota Sik that emerged during the 1968 Prague Spring.

The actual changes proposed by the leadership in its third effort at reform, in 1968, hardly reflected such ideas, however. The ossified Gomulka administration sought only to improve the methods by which central objectives were reconciled with decentralized implementation. The central economic authorities were to continue defining the strategic growth targets. Thus, for the approaching 1971–1975 quinquennium, growth was to be more intensive and selective than before. Individual economic enterprises as well as 121 *zjednoczenia*—or conglomerates of enterprises—that had been created in 1958 and revived in 1966, were to become "profit centers," governed by cost effectiveness, profitability, and a new material incentive system that rewarded productive directors and workers. Before this package had been implemented, however, Gomulka was ousted from power by workers on the Baltic coast. Brus's fate, ironically, was hardly different: He was pressured by the authorities to leave the country in the wake of the 1968 student protests.

The new party chief, Gierek, adopted a very different approach to economic reform. He reinforced the role of the central plan in determining strategic growth targets while at the same time seeking what he called an "optimal combination of social interests with those of every working person." The crux of the new reform thrust was the establishment of an intermediary institution between central economic authorities and basic production units—the so-called "large industrial associations" (for which the Polish acronym is WOG). In contrast to Gomulka's *zjednoczenia*, the WOGs were given far-ranging powers in matters of employment, wages, and investment earmarked for replacement and modernization (developmental investment remained under central control). A WOG's investment projects were to be financed through bank credits it managed to acquire—not through the more secure route of central budgetary allocations. A strong concentration of material resources and manpower in such "socialist corporations" was thought to offer two distinct advantages over the previous system: State planning and management would be streamlined by reducing the number of institutions subordinated to central authorities (the reform "from above"), and large-scale production entities would be utilized to raise output and efficiency (the reform "from below"). In 1973, accordingly, the first 27 socialist corporations were formed having a 20 percent share in total national industrial output, and by the end of 1975 the number had grown to 110, having a 65 percent share in total industrial output.

Gierek's reform signified rationalization of the traditional system rather than a new conception of socialist planning and management. The reform substituted organizational concentration and limited devolution for genuine decentralization and enterprise autonomy, and it reinvigorated central control by introducing indirect methods to complement direct ones. This reform, like its predecessors, proved short-lived. By 1975 the ministries had reverted to familiar controls, setting restrictions on all WOG investment decisions, on their use of retained profits, and on their ability to obtain physical allocation orders for materials and equipment. Although the WOG organizational framework remained intact, the modified rules of economic planning and steering had all but disappeared.

There were other facets to Gierek's economic reform program. Incomes policy was to play a more important role in generating overall economic growth. During the previous decade the rates of increase of both wages and productivity had stagnated, and Gierek's concern for linking increases in personal incomes (real wages rose by an astounding 10 percent annually during 1971–1975) and expanded social benefits to greater productivity (industrial production as well as national income produced registered a 10 percent average annual increase in those years) was essentially a sound policy.

Moreover, as Brus pointed out, "the gains in consumption were not to be achieved at the expense of investment." Gierek's strategic maneuver consisted of "import-induced growth" by which modern equipment, know-how, and production licenses were to be purchased on credit from the West. Two sets of figures underscore the extent of change from Gomulka's to Gierek's conceptions of international economic interdependence. For the entire 1960–1970 period Poland's foreign trade deficit with Western industrialized countries (the Organization for Economic Cooperation and Development, or OECD) amounted to $284 million. But Gomulka's "unimaginative 'prudent householder behavior' meant forfeiting all the advantages of wise use of credits." More disastrously, as matters turned out, Gierek's team "inherited a fairly clean bill of health which they could exploit."[5] In Gierek's first five years in office imports were up 24 percent and exports 19 percent, while the total value of credits obtained from nonsocialist countries between 1971 and 1980 was a staggering $38.6 billion.

Gierek's unwise use of credits, his overexpansionary domestic policies, and the deterioration in Poland's terms of trade resulted by December 1980 in indebtedness to Western countries of $23.5 billion. Of this total, $15.2 billion was produced by the cumulative 1973–1980 trade deficit, the remainder by the interest burden. By the end of 1981 the external debt had reached approximately $26 billion, most of it to sixteen Western countries (including a little more than $3 billion to the United States). Approximately two-thirds was government and government-guaranteed debt, the remainder private unguaranteed debt. Since 1981 regular negotiations have taken place in Paris between the Polish government and Western creditors to agree on formulae for debt rescheduling. In April 1984 the country signed an agreement with Western commercial banks by which it received a five-year grace period in repaying 95 percent of the installments on its principal that fall due between 1984 and 1987.

The "Gierek deficit" was exacerbated by the policy of decentralized decisionmaking in foreign trade. Industrial ministries and the conglomerates could now set up their own foreign trade enterprises rather than go through the hitherto monopolist in this area, the Ministry of Foreign Trade. But if they became unbridled in their trading relations with Western counterparts, it was due largely to the example set by the government.

Why did Gierek's "new development strategy" fail so miserably? Most of his planners believed that only extensive Western credits and the transfer of Western technology could help modernize the Polish economy and make it capable of producing the type and quality of manufactured goods that would, in turn, find an export market in the West. According to Zbigniew Fallenbuhl, a leading specialist on the Polish economy, the impact by the mid–1970s of world stagflation, an unjustifiably broad investment front, excessive imports of capital goods, and policies that ploughed investment into nonprofit generating sectors of industry ruined the strategem. As world export markets shrank, depriving Poland of foreign currency earnings and plunging the country into greater indebtedness, so the import intensity of industrial production continued to increase. In short, "the central planning and management system . . . was unable to expand profitable exports of modern manufactured goods to discriminating Western markets, especially at a time of brisk international competition," and "the main burden of earning hard currency had, therefore, to be placed on the traditional export branches," in particular coal, whose world price was also falling. Like Brus, Fallenbuhl espoused more far-reaching and comprehensive economic reform than the timorous experimentation under Gierek.[6]

It was the stopgap, improvised nature of Gierek's reform efforts that spelled their undoing. According to Brus, "The measures taken were halfhearted, slow and subject to withdrawal at the first hurdle," and a clear illustration of this came in June 1976 when the government announced a food price increase averaging out to 39 percent (for meat, 69 percent). After six years of pegged prices at a time when Western European countries suffered from double-digit inflation, the measure was an economic necessity. Nevertheless, in the face of worker protests the hike was rescinded, and the 1976–1980 five-year plan was redrafted. The investment drive was halted, and distribution of national income was shifted in favor of consumption. The structure of supply foresaw an increase in the share of industrial consumer goods, in particular because agricultural production had fallen off. Although agricultural production recorded an average annual increase of 3.6 percent in the previous quinquennium, it decreased by a startling 2.6 percent in 1975, then registered a negligible annual increase of 0.7 percent during 1976–1979. The revised plan also helped hold wage increases down to an annual actual rise of 1.2 percent in those years.

By 1980 three phenomena had become obvious. First, Poland's material potential had increased significantly in the preceding decade, and the country now ranked close to, if not actually in (as Gierek claimed), the world's top ten industrial powers. Second, Brus's observation was fundamentally correct; that is, "the five years 1971–75 constituted an exception in an otherwise not very distinguished record for a system which takes long-run growth as its main claim to superiority." Third, the most striking feature was not Poland's economic difficulties in themselves (which country did not have them in the mid–1970s?) but, following the same author, "the apparent inability to combat them with purposeful, longer lasting, consistent policies of the type one would expect to find in a centrally planned economy."[7]

Whatever else one might say of the martial law regime, it did dedicate itself to purposeful and drastic economic reform. In looking at the selected economic indicators given in Table 4.1, we are confronted with results that suggest shock treatment had been applied. After more than three decades of increases in national income, industrial and agricultural production, and real income, a significant decline in all these categories other than agricultural production was noted during the 1980s. Likewise, a gradual increase during the 1950s, 1960s, and 1970s in retail and food prices and the general cost of living was followed in the 1980s by drastic increases. But the economic record of the Jaruzelski administration is not necessarily as disastrous as data from Table 4.1 suggest. When national income for 1985 is compared with that for 1979, there is indeed a negative growth rate of 10 percent. However, when 1985 national income is contrasted with 1982 national income, a 15 percent positive growth rate took place. These results underscore both the economic deterioration that occurred between 1979 and 1982 and the solid improvement that was recorded thereafter.

Before we examine the economic changes that were proposed during the Solidarity period—when the economic crisis was at its

Table 4.1 Selected Economic Indicators 1946-83

On December 31	1946	1950	1960	1970	1980	1981	1982	1983
National income produced	27	48	100	180	305	268	253	269
Global industrial production	13	32	100	223	461	411	402	428
Global agricultural production	35	74	93	117	129	134	130	134
Average monthly real income in socialized sector	–	–	100	120	188	192	144	146
Real income of private farmers	–	–	100	112	147	209	154	145
State retail prices of consumer goods	–	57	100	110	168	199	417	508
Food prices	–	48	100	108	154	176	464	524
Cost of living	–	–	100	120	188	234	472	581

Notes: 1960 = 100 (except agricultural production 1961-65 = 100); measures are in constant prices; - denotes no data.

Source: Rocznik Statystyczny 1984. Warsaw: GUS, 1984, passim.

worst—and those that were implemented during and after martial law—when improvement began—let us look at a problem that plagued the Gierek administration and has still not been eradicated today. This is the existence of a burgeoning black market, or second economy, which mushroomed as a result of Gierek's "enrich yourselves" policies of the early 1970s and contributed to the moral and social malaise that underlay the 1980 crisis.

THE SECOND ECONOMY

The conditions that seem most propitious for the evolution of illegal economic activity are the combination of sizable disposable incomes chasing relatively scarce consumer goods. This was the situation in the second half of the 1970s after wage rises had outstripped cost-of-living increases. Political considerations had induced the authorities to maintain prices of many nondurable goods below production costs, and this led to excess demand pressures. Gierek sought to attain a domestic market equilibrium by allocating a larger proportion of national income to consumption. But by continuing to import consumer goods he upset the external equilibrium. Even such measures as he did initiate only partially absorbed the excess money supply, and the black market became a more viable outlet. In brief, consumers who had the money but could not find desired goods in the state shops sought to obtain them in other places.

One source for highly desirable goods was the government's own network of foreign currency shops, called Pewex. Here it was possible to purchase both Western manufactured goods and Polish goods hard to obtain in normal stores. The catch was that the customer paid in a convertible currency (usually dollars). The demand for *waluta* (or Western currency) was stimulated, therefore, by the Pewex chain, and Pewex indirectly spawned an extensive network of money changers in Warsaw and other localities. Although buying dollars privately from foreigners (at up to four or five times the bank-set exchange rate) was illegal, the Polish authorities tolerated the practice on the premise that 90 percent of all foreign currency in the country would, sooner or later, be spent in a Pewex shop. The abuses fostered by this system, together with the inequalities in purchasing power created between *waluta* holders and zloty (the Polish currency) earners, were one of Solidarity's principal grievances in 1980 and 1981.

In addition to Pewex, a second retail chain was created under Gierek to serve as a supplier of goods to the privileged. This consisted of the so-called commercial shops that sold meat at prices well above those in regular state outlets. Predictably, these were better stocked, and the queues were not as long, but they became a source of acute relative deprivation, too. Just as importantly, the example set by the state of creating an official second economy was soon emulated by full-blooded black marketeers whose operations differed little from the Pewex or commercial shop chains. In this way the inspiration for the black market originated in the state itself.

Those individuals—branded by the authorities as speculators— who serviced this lucrative black market frequently obtained their stock by buying up quantities destined for state shops. A bribe or other favor would often persuade the shop assistant, and often its manager, to redirect commodities from intended clients to the spec- ulator. Other individuals selling on the black market obtained goods in short supply through massive purchases in better stocked nearby countries (Hungary, East and West Germany, Austria) or through the network of Poles traveling frequently abroad (merchant seamen, airline crews, diplomatic personnel, businessmen, tourists, students, and unofficial full-time *commis-voyageurs*).

(The second economy served important functions both in relieving "monetary overhang" and satisfying consumer demands. Estimates of the total value of transactions concluded in it are difficult to calculate, but a figure of about 10 percent of GDP may be advanced. The existence of this economy produced several dysfunctional effects, however. Insofar as this second economy siphoned off production of the socialized sector, it served to aggravate the number and extent of so-called deficit goods. At the same time, it encouraged theft of state property and moonlighting in a second job. These were effective ways by which employees' nominally low incomes could be supplemented without the state having to contribute, and largely for this reason such operations were unofficially countenanced by the authorities)

But this economy also gave rise to a new petite bourgeoisie that often leapfrogged employees of the state sector in terms of living standards and material wealth. It often placed barter arrangements (exchange of favors, services, or goods) and more infrequently hard currency (dollars) at the center of transactions, thereby demeaning the worth of Polish currency, which was, after all, what everyone employed in the regular economy was paid with. [In short, the second economy drove home the advantages of economic wheeling and dealing over conscientious work, in this way heightening the sense of relative deprivation among those who remained outside the workings of the second economy, such as most of the industrial proletariat.] Although the emergence of an independent social movement in 1980 was undoubtedly a product of widespread discontent with methods of political rule and with the new ruling class, it also represented a backlash against socioeconomic inequalities and injustices and against the new economic class.

ECONOMIC REFORM IN THE 1980s

Many of the reform ideas advanced during the Solidarity period bear a striking resemblance to those put forward earlier by economists such as Lange, Kalecki, and Brus. (What is more unexpected is that a number of these ideas were subsequently put into operation by the Jaruzelski administration.) A special Commission on Economic Reform was even appointed to develop and coordinate the reform program. In one sense, the government's zealousness in sponsoring reform measures was self-defeating; the basis for government action ought to have rested in spontaneous, market factors rather than in administrative decrees. Nonetheless, the objectives and strategies of the economic reform program of the 1980s are the best evidence we have yet that Solidarity's practical impact on many questions was more lasting than its autonomous organizational life. Conversely, these reforms suggest that the post–1981 leadership has, in the economic sphere at least, shown more reform-mindedness than many credit it with. Let us consider the most recent reform efforts.

The most general principle advocated by reformers associated with Solidarity was the so-called "3-S" idea of the self-contained (or independent), self-financed, and self-managed economic enterprise. There was to be greater managerial independence in matters of employment and output, and more active participation by the work force in determining the size and use of the social fund and, to a lesser extent, output, pricing, and employment issues. The Jaruzelski administration implemented a modified version of the "3-S" concept. Less-detailed central planning was introduced, limiting the central economic authorities' ability to influence enterprises indirectly through credit and interest policies, price and income, and import and export controls. More responsiveness to social preferences was urged, and consultation with the general public (through polls, phone-ins, and the like) and specialized groups (trade unions, professional associations, experts) became common practice.

Finally, market disequilibrium was to be offset by the application of greater price flexibility and enhanced financial discipline. Three types of prices were introduced, which resembled those created under Hungary's New Economic Mechanism of the late 1960s: 1) state-fixed prices on politically sensitive products, such as staple foodstuffs, and on commodities playing a crucial part in the economy, such as raw materials; 2) state-regulated prices on potential inflation-starters such as investment goods; and 3) free or floating prices on many durable goods where the supply-demand balance could quickly reach an equilibrium. In practice the state retains the prerogative to freeze or otherwise peg all prices, and it has made use of this prerogative. Critics argue, therefore, that price reform and management reform exist on paper alone, and that the state has sabotaged their effective operationalization.

With regard to financial discipline the theory behind the reform program is that plant bankruptcies and labor unemployment should now occur when economic efficiency and rationality dictate this. Here, too, the central authorities have been reluctant to see such "unsocialist" phenomena take place, and in the 1980s many firms have been kept alive and unemployment staved off through the intervention of the state.[8]

The most recent reform efforts have highlighted once again the social and political limits on economic reform and the inherent etatist tendency in the Polish economy. At the same time we should not lose sight of certain distinctive features of the present reform package. In contrast to preceding administrations, the Jaruzelski leadership has addressed the fundamental problems of the Polish economy and has looked for practical and rational solutions. Given the incalculable economic difficulties Jaruzelski's administration inherited, we should for the present reserve judgment on its record.)

We can note, however, that the average Pole has suffered a significant drop in living standards in the 1980s, reaching the level recorded in 1972—hardly surprising with a cost-of-living increase of more than 250 percent between 1981 and 1984. Some of the inflationary pressure stemmed from a series of devaluations of the Polish currency between 1982 and 1984, beginning with a 57 percent devaluation of the much overvalued zloty a month after martial law was declared. It may well be that such measures and their consequences were inevitable the moment that rational economic criteria came to be substituted for irrational political ones.(The irony is, of course, that the previous political criteria served the interests of the citizen more than the prevailing rational ones.)

(Thus, in the 1980s Polish socialist leaders have for the first time admitted that poverty has become a serious problem in the country. There may have existed pockets of poverty before, but these were never acknowledged and by the mid–1970s appeared to be dwindling in numbers. It was all the more surprising, therefore, when 1982 government estimates indicated that close to one-third of the entire population was living below the "social minimum," or poverty line. The worst off were peasant families working small private farms and old-age pensioners, 50 percent of whom had incomes below the social minimum and one-third of whom were reported to be at the hunger threshold.) The hunger threshold was defined as a fixed monthly income of 4,000 to 6,000 zlotys, or $30 to $45 (although in terms of purchasing power 4,000 zlotys in Poland represented a larger sum of money than $30 in the United States). Economic inequalities between city and countryside persisted, if they did not in fact widen. For example, a detailed study published in the spring of 1985 found that with a base earnings index of 100 as the Polish average, the urban industrial conglomeration of Katowice province scored 135 while poor farming provinces (Przemyskie and Lomżyńskie) scored 85. When other quality-of-life criteria were introduced (car and television ownership, infant mortality, housing, savings accounts), the big cities (Warsaw, Poznań, and Wroclaw in that order) ranked highest and the rural backward regions (led by Nowosądeckie province) lowest.[9]

From the beginning of the 1980s Poland sought admission to the International Monetary Fund (IMF) in order to obtain loans. Admission means that austerity measures have to be imposed so as to satisfy IMF conditions for credit-worthiness. Such measures, as Latin American states have discovered, would aggravate the plight of the poor even further. Poland's socialist economy is challenged once again, therefore, as in 1945, with the task of coming to the aid of the growing ranks of destitute and immiserized persons.

AGRICULTURAL POLICIES

Poland's distinctiveness in the Soviet bloc owes as much to the persistence of private forms of farming as to the role played by the Catholic church in society. Of Eastern European countries only Yugoslavia also has an extensive private agricultural sector. I noted in Chapter 2 that as early as 1948—before Tito made clear his disagreement with collectivization—Gomulka publicly opposed Stalin's program of collectivization of the Eastern European countryside. Even after Gomulka was removed, party authorities continued to drag their feet on carrying out this policy by setting as a maximum target for 1949, for example, collectivization of 1 percent of the nation's individual farms. This was hardly the Stalinist way to achieve results.

From late 1949 to the fall of 1956 some 10,600 cooperative farms were established. But agricultural results were so poor that in 1951 and 1952 the state had to set compulsory deliveries from the peasants of, in succession, grain, meat, milk, and potatoes. Between 1949 and 1955 total agricultural production increased by only 13 percent. The authorities found no support among the poor and medium peasants for an antikulak (rich peasant) drive and, furthermore, ran into the stubborn opposition of the church whose backbone of support rested in the countryside. Divisions within the leadership and the introduction of the New Course in other bloc countries after Stalin's death ensured that the collectivization drive had been spent by the time Gomulka returned to power.

In the aftermath of the Polish October Gomulka presided over the reverse process of decollectivization. By mid-November of that year 85 percent of existing cooperatives had been disbanded. Gomulka's 1957 New Agrarian Policy drastically reduced compulsory deliveries, doubled prices paid by the state for agricultural produce, and reduced the tax burden on peasants. A contract system was instituted by which the peasant had, in the state, an assured market for all surplus production. In turn, the state could, by offering higher prices and fringe benefits for certain produce, continue to shape the structure

Table 4.2 Distribution of Agricultural Land by Sector

In 000s of acres	1970	1980	1983
Private	36,282	32,693	33,471
State	7,459	9,134	8,689
Cooperatives and Circles	687	2,337	1,919

Source: Rocznik Statystyczny 1984. Warsaw: GUS, 1984,
         Table 4, p. 275.

of agricultural output. Thus, more elasticity in peasant-state relations was introduced.

Gomulka continued to pay lip service to the ultimate objective of socialization of agriculture. In 1957 he established the agricultural circles, which were to serve as collective machinery centers, and in 1959 the Agricultural Development Fund, by which such machinery could be purchased. He was clearly aware of how modest these measures were: As he stated in the latter year, "The transformation of production relations in agriculture . . . lies at present in the common ownership of machines. There is no other way."

Gierek shifted emphasis back toward socialized agriculture. The amount of land cultivated by the state sector increased, and land cultivated by private farmers decreased, but private farming remained the backbone of Polish agriculture (Table 4.2). More than one-half of all agricultural machinery stock was owned by the state. The role of the state in agricultural marketing, the circles, and cooperatives was strengthened, and the State Land Fund was set up to acquire farms from retiring peasants in return for granting of state pensions. The share of investment credit disbursed to private agriculture fell dramatically from 88 percent in 1970 to 27 percent in 1980, while total agricultural investment in cooperative and state farms increased sharply. But the Gierek administration also adopted a number of measures that improved the position of the private farmer. Chief among these were the complete elimination of mandatory deliveries to the state, hefty increases in procurement prices, more abundant supplies of machinery and fertilizers, extensive credits to so-called "specialist" (qualified and full-time) farmers, and, just as significantly, the introduction of free state medical care for private farmers. In these ways the private farmer was brought into the mainstream of Polish society and granted first-class citizenship—a position private farmers had not previously enjoyed. By 1980 three-quarters of agricultural land remained in private hands, and although down from 81 percent a decade earlier, the decrease was due primarily to biological attrition.

The economic results of Gierek's agricultural policies were little different from those under earlier administrations. Although total production crept upward, it was the private sector that remained most successful. During 1976–1980 its net marketed production per acre was 23 percent higher than that of the socialized sector (it was 14 percent higher during 1971–1975). Gierek's assumption that more extensive socialization of land represented the logical solution to structural problems of agriculture was not borne out by these figures.

Some major agrarian reform measures were adopted in the Solidarity period and continued to be implemented under Jaruzelski. According to the 1981 Rzeszów agreement, first, the state was to guarantee the right of ownership and inheritance for private farmers. A subsequent amendment to the Polish constitution, in 1983, duly recognized the permanence of private family farms. Second, private farmers were to have priority in purchasing farmland from the State Land Fund. This was reflected in data on the private sector's share of land, which recorded an increase between 1981 and 1984. In the latter year there was a total of 2,843,500 individual farms comprising 40 million acres, up markedly from 1980. Third, access to credit was to be equalized for all sectors of agriculture. Although the crisis conditions produced a 30 percent drop in overall agricultural investment in 1981–1982 compared to the preceding quinquennium, 59 percent went to the private sector, compared to just 31 percent in 1978. Finally, private farmers were to be assured of profitability, living standards were to equal those of urban workers, and social benefits were to be further expanded.

A 1983 law on farmer pensions went some way toward these objectives when for the first time spouses were declared eligible to participate; it also foresaw a minimum pension equivalent to that for industrial workers by 1986. But real income of farmers fell by 23 percent, a rate higher than for workers. Moreover, the on-again, off-again agricultural fund, which the church was to administer and which would entail an influx of Western capital, had not, by 1986, gotten off the ground. Although the fund augured no structural change, it held out promise of a practical kind: More than one-half of its financial resources was earmarked for the purchase of tractors and farm machinery for the peasant. This is significant in light of the fact that 57 percent of all individual farms in 1985 had neither tractor nor plowhorse and thereby were dependent on the state-

In a provincial town, where horse-drawn carts are a common sight

controlled agricultural circles. Church authorities announced they had collected pledges worth some $28 million from Western sources, but the political authorities continued to hedge on a scheme that would sanction the bypassing of the party. Instead, they began their own negotiations (purportedly with the Rockefeller trust) on funding Polish agriculture.

Two other problems facing the agrarian sector have remained unsolved. One is the fragmented structure of Polish farming, similar in some respects to that of France. In 1970 the average farmholding in Poland (excluding minifarms under 5 acres) measured 15.6 acres. By 1982 it had registered an insignificant increase to 16.5 acres. In 1984, 45 percent of individual farms were of medium size, measuring 25–35 acres. Experts believe that about 35 acres are required for a farm to be as economically effective as other sectors of the economy, and the government's long-term development plan is to double the number of farms of more than 25 acres. But how this will be accomplished without antagonizing the small-scale farmer remains unclear.

The other problem is the continued poor performance of state-managed farms, which are three times more numerous than coop-eratives. The July 1981 reform of state farms granted considerable autonomy to their managers, and in the first year of the reform, a 22 billion zloty deficit had been turned into a 28 billion zloty profit.

But one-quarter of the farms continued to operate at a loss and had to be bailed out with government grants, thereby blunting the incentive effect of the reform. Poor management combined with low productivity of hired agricultural laborers—produced in turn by inaccurate indexation of wages to output—continue to characterize the workings of the socialized agricultural sector.[10] Prospects for a breakthrough are as dim as they were forty years ago.

Polish agriculture has been the Achilles heel of the economy. This situation may not be appreciably different from conditions in other socialist states (especially the USSR), and some of the causes (a low index of mechanization, insufficient investment, erratic government policies) are the same. But given the distinctive configuration of Poland's model, parcelization of holdings rather than peasant antipathy to state interference represents the most serious obstacle. Nevertheless, the private sector is likely to remain at the center of the agrarian economy for a long time to come.

POLAND AND COMECON

The vision of an integrated socialist world economy is one that Marx himself drew. The effort to put this idea into practice is more recent, and the problems it has encountered suggest the limits of economic cooperation between socialist states. The Council for Mutual Economic Assistance (CMEA or Comecon) was officially founded in Moscow in January 1949, but like its West European counterpart, the Common Market (or European Economic Community—the EEC), it took time to get going. In the early years long-term bilateral trade agreements were reached between socialist states under the auspices of the CMEA, and only in 1955 were questions of coordinated planning and specialization of production addressed. Until then the "Soviet embassy system"—that is, directives issued by the USSR to its client states by way of local embassies—had specified the long-range plans of the bloc and its commodity specialization.

In 1962 Khrushchev proposed that a supranational planning agency be established for CMEA. It was successfully opposed by Romania. Then in 1969 Brezhnev drew up a program for an advanced multilateral division of labor in the bloc. Again Romania vetoed the idea. Gomulka's position at this time was close to that of the Soviets: Poland stood to gain from greater transnational plan coordination and closer integration with the more developed economies of East Germany and Czechoslovakia. Such intensified cooperation could also serve, Gomulka believed, as a substitute for domestic reform. The creation in May 1970 of the CMEA's International Investment Bank owed much to Gomulka's enthusiastic support.

At that year's CMEA summit, however, the concept of "planned integration" of member countries' economies was rejected and the more abstract notion of transnational plan coordination approved. In response, Gomulka made an overture to West Germany. From then on the pattern of Polish foreign trade was reversed. Between 1956 and 1970 trade with Comecon countries had quadrupled while trade with the West had tripled; between 1971 and 1980 CMEA trade tripled and Western trade quadrupled. As Korbonski concluded, "The rapid expansion of trade with the West coupled with Poland's success in obtaining Western credits made CMEA less important and attractive as a source of investment goods and credits. The main attraction of the CMEA was its role as supplier of raw materials and market for manufactures."[11] The pattern of Poland's foreign trade since 1970 is presented in Table 4.3.

By July 1971, when a comprehensive program for cooperation and socialist economic integration had been concluded by the CMEA, most of its members had established diplomatic and trade relations with West Germany—then the dominant economic power in the EEC—and had adopted policies of economic interdependence with the West. Food riots had brought about Gomulka's overthrow and underscored the need for more investment in consumption, for which Western credits were desirable. The comprehensive program was a doctrinal attempt to reconcile the CMEA with economic realities. Support for integration of member states' markets through currency convertibility and direct trade between enterprises (as the Hungarians had been urging) had waned; the Polish case for plan integration was even more of a lost cause.

The modest achievements of the comprehensive program were the introduction of improved mechanisms of plan coordination, especially in current output, and CMEA collaboration on long-term target programs. Still, the "interested party principle" signified that each member could confine participation to CMEA projects in which it had a specific interest. A major change in this policy came with the June 1975 decision to pursue a cooperative strategy for investment projects of "common interest," all to be located in the USSR. Although East Germany and, of course, Romania had reservations about the scheme, Gierek favored it because it would increase Poland's energy supply. Of the seven CMEA ventures planned for the 1976–1980 period the largest was the Orenburg (Soyuz) project to construct a natural gas complex in Western Siberia and link it to Eastern Europe by way of a 1,800-mile pipeline. The project cost $6 billion and

Table 4.3   Pattern of Poland's Foreign Trade (in Current Prices)

Imports: % of total according to origin

	1970	1978	1981	1983
Socialist countries	68.6	54.1	55.0	64.1
of which CMEA	65.9	51.9	51.8	59.7
of which USSR	37.7	29.9	34.4	36.8
Developed capitalist	25.8	40.5	37.1	28.9
of which EEC	16.9	22.3	20.4	16.8
of which U.S.	1.6	4.4	6.1	1.4
Developing countries	5.7	5.3	7.9	7.0

Exports: % of total according to destination

	1970	1978	1981	1983
Socialist countries	63.9	61.1	48.5	54.7
of which CMEA	60.6	58.0	45.7	51.3
of which USSR	35.3	33.9	26.1	31.2
Developed capitalist	28.4	31.3	37.0	32.5
of which EEC	17.4	19.6	23.2	22.3
of which U.S.	2.6	3.3	3.1	1.7
Developing countries	7.7	7.6	14.5	12.8

Source: Rocznik Statystyczny 1984. Warsaw: GUS, 1984. Tables 6-8,
         pp. 355-7.

represented half the total value of all CMEA projects. Yet Gierek's efforts to interest the CMEA in helping exploit significant brown coal deposits discovered near Belchatów in 1960 were fruitless.

In the mid–1970s Comecon proposed to the Common Market arrangements for reciprocal most-favored-nation status and reduced mutual trade barriers, but the protectionist-minded EEC rejected the idea. By the late 1970s growing indebtedness forced Poland and other CMEA countries to curb imports from the West and place greater reliance once again on intra-CMEA trade and investment. Deteriorating East-West political relations hastened this process. Due to a shortage of funds no major new multilateral investment projects were undertaken by Comecon in the 1980s, but Poland's dependency on the bloc increased anyway after President Reagan imposed economic sanctions in early 1982 following the declaration of martial law.

Although Polish authorities have made it known unofficially that such sanctions only drive the country further into the bear's grip and are consequently not in the best interests of the United States, it is also true that the Soviets have no desire to be saddled with responsibility for Poland's enormous debt and prefer that Poland continue to follow a policy of economic interdependence with the West. This policy line also helps soothe the grievances of other CMEA members who would view Soviet economic assistance for a badly mismanaged client state as unwarranted preferential treatment.

The question inevitably arises as to whether Poland's economic interdependence with Comecon and above all the USSR—which accounts for 70 percent of the bloc's Net Material Product and industrial production—represents an asset or a liability. Put in traditional Soviet terminology, *kto kovo* (who exploits whom)? It goes without saying that in the Stalinist period the Soviets had the better of trade relations (witness the previously described great coal robbery), though it is worth noting that Poland did not suffer the kind of exploitation other Eastern European states did in having to agree to "joint companies" with the USSR. Nevertheless, current popular perceptions of the inequity of trade relations with the Soviet Union are in large part a carryover from Stalinist exploitation.

There was, however, a period in which Poland and the rest of the CMEA derived considerable advantages from economic interdependence with the USSR. High-quality manufactured goods were exported to the West while inferior ones were dumped on the vast, undiscriminating Soviet domestic market. Moreover, the price of energy inputs (such as crude oil and natural gas) from the USSR was well below the world market until five-year moving average prices were established in 1976. For fear of causing domestic political instability in Poland and elsewhere, the Soviets were therefore unable to maximize their benefits in the aftermath of the 1973 OPEC price hike. Put another way, what was in the Soviet economic interest was not in its best political interests.

In the 1970s Poland was relatively immune to Soviet energy leverage. Coal exports to the West assured an energy trade balance. But as demand for coal fell and oil prices rose, the country had become by 1979 a net energy importer and has remained so to the present. An even more damaging development was the Soviet announcement in 1982 of 10 percent cuts in deliveries of crude and petroleum products to Eastern Europe. This was an effort to limit its "implicit subsidies" to the region. Because Poland annually purchased

12.7 million tons of imported crude from the USSR compared to just 1.3 million tons from other countries requiring payment in convertible currency, this was a serious economic blow. The leveling up of Soviet oil prices to the world market further reduced Soviet trade costs with Poland and its neighbors. The relatively small trade credits granted Poland since 1981 suggest that the Kremlin leaders, like many Soviet citizens, felt that it was time to stop coming to the rescue of a nation that was both more affluent than and incorrigibly rebellious toward the USSR.

Poland could also no longer count on its hitherto advantageous structure of commodity trade with its eastern neighbor. Up to now the Soviets have run up trading surpluses with Poland, but only by exporting primary products (raw materials and fuels) in return for manufactures (machinery and durable goods). The once sheltered Soviet domestic market for manufactures may be harder for Polish industry to penetrate in the future as Western manufactures may increasingly be preferred. Likewise, in striving for export markets in the West, Poland might find itself competing with the USSR. Finally, if the use of the transferable ruble as an accounting unit in intra-CMEA trade and the transshipping to the Soviet Union of goods purchased by Poland for hard currency in the West (for example, navigational equipment for Polish-built ships) strongly improve Soviet terms of trade at the expense of Poland—as is almost universally believed in the latter country—then the *kto kovo* question has a straightforward answer.

But Kremlin leaders are aware that the maintenance of a viable political-military bloc has its economic price, and Poland has in fact been the recipient of meaningful Soviet assistance in recent years. Thus, the Soviet-Polish economic agreement signed in October 1985 guaranteed, at 1985 prices, a continued supply to Poland of crude oil and petroproducts for the period 1986–1990. In a move that was similar to actions taken by Western creditors, the Soviets agreed to reschedule Poland's foreign debt to the USSR of more than 5 billion rubles. In addition, so as to keep the Polish consumer satisfied, Soviet exports of highly desired goods such as refrigerators, automatic washing machines, and color television sets were to increase by close to 50 percent on existing totals. Clearly, trading arrangements between the two sides do often bring mutually beneficial effects, though the average citizen on both sides of the border sees them in a more jaundiced way. Whatever the exact truth in this complex matter, it has become obvious that both the Soviet Union and Western countries approach trading relations with Poland with greater caution than they did a decade ago.

NOTES

1. A. Zauberman, *Industrial Progress in Poland, Czechoslovakia, and East Germany 1937-62* (London: Oxford University Press, 1964), p. 129.

2. N.J.G. Pounds, *Poland between East and West* (Princeton, N.J.: Van Nostrand, 1964), p. 99.

3. See G.R. Feiwel, *Poland's Industrialization Policy* (New York: Praeger, 1971), pp. 229-236.

4. M. Gamarnikow, *Economic Reforms in Eastern Europe* (Detroit, Mich.: Wayne State University Press, 1968), pp. 32-33.

5. W. Brus, "Aims, Methods and Political Determinants of the Economic Policy of Poland 1970-1980," in A. Nove et al. (eds.), *The Eastern European Economies in the 1970s* (London: Butterworths, 1982), pp. 92-93, 102.

6. Z. Fallenbuhl, *East-West Technology Transfer: Study of Poland 1971-80* (Paris: OECD, 1983), pp. 17, 21-22.

7. Brus, "Aims, Methods and Political Determinants," pp. 94, 133-134.

8. Much of this account is taken from S. Gomulka and J. Rostowski, "The Reformed Polish Economic System 1982-1983," *Soviet Studies* 36, no. 3 (July 1984):386-405.

9. See the three-part study by Zygmunt Szeliga in *Polityka* (20 and 27 April, 25 May 1985).

10. Part of this analysis is based on E. Cook, "Agricultural Reform in Poland: Background and Prospects," *Soviet Studies* 36, no. 3 (July 1984): 406-426.

11. A. Korbonski, "Poland and the CMEA: Problems and Prospects," in P. Marer and J.M. Montias (eds.), *Eastern European Integration and East-West Trade* (Bloomington: Indiana University Press, 1980), p. 373.

FURTHER READINGS

W. Brus. *The Economics and Politics of Socialism.* London: Routledge and Kegan Paul, 1973.

———. *The Market in a Socialist Economy.* London: Routledge and Kegan Paul, 1972.

———. *Socialist Ownership and Political Systems.* London: Routledge and Kegan Paul, 1975.

J. Drewnowski (ed.). *Crisis in the Eastern European Economy: The Spread of the Polish Disease.* New York: St. Martin's Press, 1982.

G.R. Feiwel. *Problems in Polish Economic Planning.*New York: Praeger, 1971.

A. Korbonski. *The Politics of Socialist Agriculture in Poland: 1945-60.* New York: Columbia University Press, 1965.

J. Krejci. *National Income and Outlay in Czechoslovakia, Poland and Yugoslavia.* New York: St. Martin's Press, 1982.

Z. Landau and J. Tomaszewski. *The Polish Economy in the Twentieth Century.* New York: St. Martin's Press, 1985.

P. Marer and E. Tabaczynski (eds.). *Polish-United States Industrial Cooperation in the 1980s*. Bloomington: Indiana University Press, 1981.

J. Woodall. *The Socialist Corporation and Technocratic Power*. Cambridge: Cambridge University Press, 1982.

J.G. Zielinski. *Economic Reforms in Polish Industry*. New York: Oxford University Press, 1973.

5

Diversity in Polish Society

In preceding chapters I have alluded to the position of various classes in Polish society: the political power of the industrial working class, the assertiveness of the intelligentsia, the emergence of a petite bourgeoisie, the status of the peasantry, and the rise of a new ruling class. I have also mentioned the role played by particular social institutions and groups: the influence of the Catholic church, the disaffection of youth, the disappearance of the national minorities. So far I have tended to stress the similarities that cut across Polish society, depicting it as a relatively homogeneous organism that possesses common values and attitudes and is in equal measure affected by government policies.

In practice, of course, important differences persist from one social class and group to another. The communist authorities speak in more equivocal terms about the classless society they originally set out to create, and in some respects, they have made good use of class differences to divide and rule. In this chapter I break down Polish society by its principal component parts. I will examine the country's social structure (workers, peasants, intelligentsia), important groups and institutions (women, youth, the small Jewish minority, the church), and general social values and social pathologies. Such an approach should enable us to understand better the complex set of interrelationships that characterize Polish society.

SOCIAL STRUCTURE

In terms of its theoretical, methodological, and empirical contributions, Polish sociology has earned a reputation as one of the pioneering schools. As a result, we have available a comprehensive body of literature and research that sheds light on diverse aspects of Polish society. The following analysis of social classes makes use of the available data and focuses in particular on four components— political power, economic position, social prestige, and value system.

124

Table 5.1   Patterns of Employment in the Socialized Economy

	1950	1960	1970	1980	1983
Industry and construction	26%	33	36	38	36
Agriculture	54	43	34	30	30
Transport and communications	5	6	6	7	6
Trade and commerce	5	6	7	8	8
Other (education, science, culture, administration, health, etc.)	10	12	17	17	20

Source: Rocznik Statystyczny 1984.   Warsaw: GUS, 1984, Table 1, p. xxxv.

Workers

Formal political power in a socialist state resides in the working class. The Polish constitution refers to it as the dominant force in society, and its institutional embodiment, the PZPR, plays the leading role in political life. Since Gomulka's overthrow, however, the privileged position of the industrial proletariat has been eroded as rulers have increasingly spoken of Poland as a state encompassing all working people, thereby subsuming nonmanual occupations under one concept of a workers' state. Further dilution of the formal power of blue-collar workers has followed increasing government emphasis on the worker-peasant alliance (*smyczka*) and the worker-intelligentsia coalition as the cornerstones of the political system.

In short, the concept of a workers' state is now identified with an amalgam of social classes and strata standing apart from the traditional proletariat. Although this is not the type of workers' state Marx had in mind, it is the natural outgrowth of the stage of societal development that a country like Poland has attained. If, as Marx wrote in the *Communist Manifesto*, "the proletariat is the special and essential product of modern industry," so the worker-employee-administrator configuration seems the quintessential product of the modern tertiary-sector economy. In such a society the proletariat ceases to enjoy economic domination; that is, it does not control the means of production, the labor process, and its product. Nor is its productive role so crucial to overall economic performance. As we see from the data in Table 5.1, the proportion of the labor force employed in industry and construction has held steady in Poland since the early 1970s while real growth has been registered by the tertiary sector.

The complexity of modern government also makes the existence of a specialized group of party-state leaders to carry on direct government a functional necessity. More often than not this group is composed of a majority of nonproletarians. The emergence of this group led the Yugoslav critic Djilas to write in 1953 of the new ruling class under socialism, and "new class" theories have been popular ever since. These theories argue that by controlling (if not owning) the means of production, the political managers have substituted themselves for the workers as the wielders of power.

In order to mask this development as well as for reasons of ideology and legitimacy, the leadership still heralds the proletariat as Poland's ruling class. It points out, for instance, that workers have 40 percent representation in the composition of party membership. Top party officials refer post facto to instances in which workers have assumed direct political power, as in 1956, 1970, and 1980, though they neglect to mention that the authorities opposed and sought to crush such movements at the time. It might be more accurate to see such temporary proletarian political influence as evidence of a "king-maker" role. In the extended periods between workers' direct political involvement, an informal "social compact"—as political scientist Alex Pravda has termed it—is reached between the working class and the regime. In economic terms this compact translates into the motto "You pretend to pay us and we pretend to work." In political terms, according to Pravda, "workers' support for the system may be seen as being conditional on its provision of these welfare benefits and rights." Thus quiescence and depoliticization are exchanged for material welfare benefits.[1]

As in all modern industrial states, Poland's working class is sharply differentiated internally. There are highly skilled workers (in the shipyards), highly paid workers (at the coalface), semiskilled and unskilled workers (in the factories), and peasant workers (taking on their first nonagricultural employment). When we speak of workers' power we invariably refer to the first category; these workers have achieved acute political consciousness, skills, and efficacy. They serve as the vanguard of the entire working class, as the Solidarity experience bears out.

The economic position of manual workers further underscores the heterogeneity of this class. The coalface worker forms part of the labor aristocracy, earning (with bonuses) at least 50 percent more than the directors of an industrial enterprise (Table 5.2). Partly for this reason miners have displayed less militancy than other sections

Table 5.2 Average Monthly Wages in 1983 in Selected Occupations

(In Zlotys; Bonuses Included)

1.	Coalface worker	48,773	11.	Doctor	16,226
2.	Enterprise director	31,647	12.	Bricklayer	14,880
3.	Blast-furnace worker	25,911	13.	Tractor driver	14,427
4.	University professor	20,937	14.	Agricultural	
5.	Bus driver	19,254		laborer (crops)	12,375
6.	Welder	18,542	15.	Tailor	11,933
7.	Master foreman	18,405	16.	Technical engineer	11,896
8.	Agricultural laborer	17,797	17.	Medical specialist	11,579
	(livestock)		18.	Economist	10,914
9.	Assemblyline baker	17,666	19.	Senior shop	
10.	Rolling mill operator			assistant	10,520
	(chemical industry)	16,242	20.	Teacher	9,125

Source: Rocznik Statystyczny 1984. Warsaw: GUS, 1984, Tables 5 and 9, pp. 156-63.

Table 5.3   Selected Income and Consumption Indicators by Social Class (For 1983)

	Blue collar	White collar	Peasant
Monthly per capita income	8,594	10,254	10,537
Monthly expenditure on food	3,354	3,650	3,757
on alcohol	299	273	471
on culture, leisure, education	547	1,025	304
on clothing	952	1,148	1,015
Cars per 100 households	18.9	39.4	19.0

Source: Rocznik Statystyczny 1984. Warsaw: GUS, 1984, Table 15, p. 124.

of the industrial proletariat, though Solidarity radicalized them as it did other segments of society. Skilled manual workers (welders, blast-furnace metallugists) earn about twice as much as the average blue-collar worker. The unskilled are, of course, at the bottom of the economic ladder.

The large size of the unskilled group depresses average earnings for all blue-collar workers. As a result, blue-collar workers rank below both white-collar workers and peasants overall. From Table 5.3 we also observe that blue-collar workers spend least on food and clothing and have the lowest rate of car ownership. In economic terms, therefore, we conclude that Marx's chosen group, the manual workers, do not do well by the workers' state.

It should be emphasized that until now the most important advantage offered by the socialist system to the blue-collar worker was the opportunity to leave this group through professional advancement. In the first two decades after the war fathers could count on their sons attaining higher socio-occupational status. Such intergenerational mobility was afforded by structural factors because economic modernization created a changing demand for various types of jobs and qualifications. Children of peasants took factory jobs, those of unskilled laborers obtained the training and qualifications needed to become skilled workers, and persons who already came from the skilled worker stratum were able to find employment as technicians, administrators, and in other white-collar positions. In general the more education individuals obtained the higher they advanced in the occupational structure, though other factors sometimes intervened (father's socio-occupational status, starting position, period of first employment, place of birth, party membership, sex).

More recently, structural mobility in all socialist states has constricted as the economic strategy shifted from extensive to intensive growth; in the case of Poland, structural mobility has even stopped growing. The result is that intraclass mobility has become the more common form of intergenerational advancement. Although some sociologists contend that this situation will lead to a growth in social frustrations, the socioeconomic makeup of the working class is, as I have noted, differentiated enough to provide opportunities for significant upward mobility on the part of the lesser skilled. Furthermore, socio-occupational mobility does not always translate into economic advancement. Earnings in certain occupational categories of the working class are significantly greater than in nonmanual positions, so that individuals guided by economic self-interest alone are unlikely to push for entry into that stratum. Other factors (the nature of work performed, work responsibility, social prestige) may encourage mobility, but given the general economic slowdown, it is likely to result in the interchange of individuals between socio-occupational categories. That is, those individuals failing to maintain the required qualifications will be replaced by persons of other social origins who have obtained such qualifications for the first time. In this way the economy can enforce stricter labor discipline, not through the creation of a pool of unemployed but by increasing the number of individuals threatened with occupational degradation and downward mobility. Such a threat is not limited, of course, to just the working class.

When we turn to social prestige we find a rather unexpected pecking order in Poland. Studies conducted by sociologists such as Wesolowski, Slomczyński, and Sarapata indicate that the intelligentsia

Table 5.4   Hierarchy of Socio-Occupational Groups According to
            Material Benefit (Income) and Social Prestige

Material Benefit	Social Prestige
1. private service sector	1. intelligentsia
2. intelligentsia	2. skilled workers
3. skilled workers	3. private service sector
4. non-manual employees	4. non-manual employees
5. unskilled workers	5. unskilled workers

Source: W. Wesolowski, Class, Strata and Power. London:
        Routledge and Kegan Paul, 1979, p. 118. Reprinted
        by permission.

enjoys greatest social status (Table 5.4). The three most prestigious occupations listed by respondents were university professor, doctor, and teacher. Skilled workers ranked second, ahead of both the high earners in the private sector and white-collar employees. The low status of white-collar employees in Poland differs significantly from the higher status such employees enjoy in Western countries. Thus, the two occupations held in least prestige in Poland in 1975 were, in descending order, typist and office clerk. It appears that the privileged position assigned by Marxist ideology to the proletariat has permitted skilled manual workers in Poland to leapfrog nonmanual workers in occupational prestige ranking. Predictably, though, in Poland as elsewhere unskilled workers were regarded as having lowest occupational prestige; among the five occupations with lowest status were unskilled construction laborers, office cleaners, and unskilled agricultural laborers.

The asymmetry between economic position and social prestige may have functional or dysfunctional consequences, depending on one's perspective. On the one hand, it may seem to many individuals in various occupational categories that the general distribution of socioeconomic rewards "evens out" particular inequalities. Someone low on the income ladder, for example, may earn greater "social" rewards (doctor or teacher) and vice versa (private shopkeeper). On the other hand, such a dissynchronized system of social differentiation may produce discontent. The teacher or private entrepreneur may ponder the soundness of a system in which economic position and social status are incongruent. As for the white-collar employee and the unskilled worker, they take little consolation from the fact that their social and economic positions do overlap. Ranked at the bottom of the totem pole, persons in these categories may be most inclined to take vengeance on the system by means of time theft and theft of state property, black marketeering, on-the-job alcoholism, and absenteeism.

We have sketched the power, affluence, and status of Poland's differentiated working class. What, then, are the social values that it most esteems? In research conducted in the past two decades the ideals that most frequently have been espoused by workers are social justice and egalitarianism.[2] If these have a familiar socialist ring to them it suggests once again that the Polish political cliche of workers' protests being aimed at the aberrations of socialism—not socialism per se—is justified. The most serious of the aberrations perceived by the industrial proletariat were unwarranted social inequities and economic inequalities, stemming primarily from the privileges wrested by the new ruling class and its appendages (the security police, the bureaucrats, and the entrepreneurial suppliers of goods and services who can claim the honorific status of "by appointment to the Communist elite"). Workers have not indicated a desire for crude economic equality or leveling (*uravnilovka*); justified wage differentiation set within certain limits and connected with productivity and quality of work is regarded as compatible with economic egalitarianism. Likewise, workers do not view the elevated socioeconomic position of rulers through the utopian prism of the Paris Commune or Lenin's *State and Revolution* and expect that all state employees should enjoy parity across the board. The workers' sense that inequalities have been both unjustified and growing has been the crux of their grievances. Consequently, as Pravda has concluded, "should Communist regimes allow the current *embourgeoisiement* and growth of privilege to continue, they may find themselves confronted with ideological backlash of the most ironic type—workers pressing for implementation of principles of equality and the dignity of labor that they have 'salvaged' from Marxism-Leninism."[3] In this respect we can even speak of the "purer" Marxism of a workers' movement such as Solidarity, than of the party.

Peasants

The other half of the class alliance upon which the Polish political system is supposedly based is the peasantry. This class has been traditionally much less politicized than the working class, and the peasantry's declining numbers have also contributed to the relative marginality of this class. While the urban population has steadily increased from 8 million in 1946 to 14.4 million in 1960 and to 21.9 million in 1983, corresponding figures for the rural population are 15.6, 15.4, and 14.8 million.

However, peasants left on the farms have assumed an enhanced importance in overall agricultural production. Moreover, these peasants are generally better educated and economically more astute than earlier generations. Until the creation of Rural Solidarity in May 1981, private farmers lacked an effective institutional base from which they could exert influence. For example, less than 10 percent of PZPR members were drawn from this social class, while the satellite United Peasants' Party was always subordinated to it. Furthermore, because individual farmers were treated as landowners rather than employees, they were denied the right to establish labor unions. In any event, during the major confrontations between the authorities and society in the 1960s and 1970s the peasantry stood on the sidelines and exuded little interest in questions of "high politics"—democracy, political freedoms, political participation.

Largely in order to head off politicization of this class, the party leadership strongly opposed the establishment of Rural Solidarity, which was intended to be a trade union for individual peasants, and might have been able to stymie its growth had not the Catholic church and Wałęsa's Solidarity thrown their considerable weight behind the movement. The major goals the new organization—headed by Jan Kulaj, a twenty-three-year old peasant from southeastern Poland—set for itself were guaranteeing the permanence of private farms in Poland and obtaining equal treatment by the state for all agricultural sectors. In contrast to workers' Solidarity, the rural organization did not hesitate to recognize the PZPR's leading role in society, and it also more explicitly rejected a political role for itself. It claimed to have about 3 million members in mid–1981, that is, a figure exceeding the total number of private farms. Sources closer to the government asserted that only 15 percent of the peasants had joined Rural Solidarity.

Relations between the two unions mirrored the general social distance between the two classes. While the workers were more assertive and political in their demands, peasants remained less radical. Three factors may have shaped the political profile of Rural Solidarity: 1) the influence of the church over it, making the movement more conservative and cautious; 2) the seemingly effective divide-and-conquer tactics employed by the Kania and Jaruzelski administrations— in the countryside the authorities attributed responsibility for the country's catastrophic economic situation to the political games being played by the working class; in urban areas, by contrast, blame was put on the affluent peasantry (in Stalinist language, the kulaks) for creating a shortage of food; and 3) the leadership's genuine concern for improving agricultural performance and its concessions to the central issues raised by the peasants (discussed in Chapter 4), thereby in large measure gaining the confidence of this class. On his release from internment in 1982, for example, Kulaj praised the military government's agrarian policies in an interview on state television!

A Western specialist on Polish agriculture, Andrzej Korbonski, has incisively concluded that "the peasant must be treated as a *homo economicus*, capable of making rational economic calculations."[4] In the 1980s the authorities have stringently followed this dictum with the end result that peasant class consciousness remains fixed on economic rather than political matters.

With regard to the peasant's economic position we find that despite a drastic fall in living standards recorded in the 1980s (Table 4.1), peasants' average monthly income is marginally higher than white-collar employees and significantly greater than blue-collar workers (Table 5.3). Of the three groups, peasants spent most on food and, inevitably, on vodka, and spent least on cultural amenities. Even in the socialized sector of agriculture the hired laborer is paid a relatively high wage (Table 5.2).

In terms of social prestige the private farmer was ranked nineteenth of twenty-nine occupations in a 1961 study, twentieth of thirty occupations in a 1978 study, and has made few inroads in the 1980s toward achieving greater social status. The surest route to higher status was and remains abandoning the countryside for a job in the city. The number of peasant-workers—small-scale farmers who hold a factory job in town but also continue to work their land—has increased substantially since the 1970s. But the rate of permanent migration into urban areas has slowed markedly in the past ten years, and it seems likely that improved material standards and social benefits together with greater security and availability of farm credits in the 1980s will override any status grudges the private farmer class may hold.

Finally, we have already alluded to some of the values esteemed by the peasantry—private ownership of land, political conservatism, the preeminence of economic interests, and devotion to the Catholic church. There is one fundamental contradiction in the peasant's position, however, that needs to be underscored. As anthropologist C. M. Hann has written, "The aspiration to prosper on one's own land, and then pass this on to one's children, is extremely strong. But equally rooted in peasant traditions is the desire to escape from the monotony of the old peasant labor process."[5] Oddly, therefore, the future of private farming appears to be threatened most by this "pull in two directions" the peasant feels and not by a state takeover bid. The seeming solution to this is for the authorities to encourage modern commercial farming on a widespread basis, as has occurred in China recently. Until now Polish rulers have feared enhancing the already unique status of the peasant further.

We should add that a privatized way of thinking about many questions continues to characterize persons of peasant origin who have found work in the cities in state and economic administration. Job responsibilities are seen as the exclusive personal ballywick of these individuals, with all the attendant difficulties (refusal to delegate, arbitrariness, mutually ingratiating patron-client relations). Put simply, a strong sense of individualism—as opposed to collectivism—continues to pervade peasant mentality and behavior.

The Intelligentsia

The political role of the intelligentsia in socialist societies has been a hotly debated issue. Early in this century the Polish anarchist Waclaw Machajski first suggested that socialism was an ideology invented by intellectuals for intellectuals. Much the same has been said of the Bolshevik Revolution and of the political systems of Eastern Europe.

At the outset it is important to distinguish the terms intelligentsia and intellectuals, something observers of the Polish scene have all too frequently failed to do. Let us consider the first group as that stratum of educated people that earns a living from the knowledge it has acquired and whose social function has become to serve as both managers of people and administrators of things (to adopt Leninist terms). The second group, the intellectuals, should be more narrowly construed as a substratum of the intelligentsia; they are defined by their function in society as creators of cultural and ideational (rather than material or technical) goods and also by their role as social critics, whether working from within or outside the political establishment. Although the first group is by nature amorphous and subsumes both the factory director and his secretary, the scientist and the schoolteacher, the second is more cohesive and can, for our purposes, be equated with the cultural intelligentsia and the academic community.

New class theories frequently view the intelligentsia as the dominant class under socialism. In turn, many Western observers are prone to identify intellectuals with dissidents, whatever their social origin and present class membership may be. Following this schema the intelligentsia would be treated as the polity's in-group and intellectuals as its out-group. Empirical evidence is available to help substantiate these arguments. Thus, we note that a decreasing proportion of party-state leaders is drawn directly from the ranks of the working class (though these leaders are at one in underscoring their proletarian social origins) and an increasing number from white-collar, especially administrative or apparatchik, positions. Within the PZPR as a whole the percentage of members who are of intelligentsia pedigree has risen from 10 percent in 1945 to one-third in 1985. In this respect the PZPR is gradually becoming a mass party of the intelligentsia and a cadre party of the working class.[6] Such selective facts suggest that the intelligentsia is the ascendant, if not already dominant, social stratum in contemporary Poland.

When we examine the intellectuals we do find that a substantial majority has lined up with forces challenging the authorities. Regime opposition in the 1960s was almost exclusively carried on by this group, and its casus belli at the time was government suppression of Polish cultural development. In the second half of the 1970s intellectuals formed the nucleus of the growing dissident movement, and in the 1980s they were perceived by the leadership, rightly or wrongly, as the counterrevolutionary and extremist dimension of the Solidarity social movement.

Having agreed with the substance of the traditional evaluations of intelligentsia and intellectual political roles, I need to clarify certain points. First, only a small section of the intelligentsia wields political power—those who are in the upper tiers of the party and state apparatus. A majority of white-collar workers have been siding with manual workers in the struggle for reform of the political system. Results of a survey conducted among the intelligentsia in 1985, that is, some time since the banning of Solidarity, revealed that 61 percent of respondents (engineers, teachers, economists, doctors) continued to perceive conflict between this social stratum and the political rulers. Only one-third denied the existence of such tension.[7] We can interpret this finding as evidence that the majority of the intelligentsia consider themselves outsiders in the political system. It is hardly appropriate, therefore, to speak of the intelligentsia *in toto* as possessing class power.

Conversely, to see intellectuals as a political out-group is also an oversimplification. It is true that cultural and professional associations for writers, journalists, or film directors have been extensively revamped, and leadership and membership purged, since the Solidarity period. Likewise, university government has come under closer political scrutiny: At the end of 1985 six rectors of institutions of higher education who had been elected by their institutions were dismissed by the minister of higher education, and two well-respected dissident academics were earlier removed from their posts (the historian and former Solidarity adviser Geremek, and the Poznań philosopher Leszek

Nowak). Nevertheless, a significant number of intellectuals (most notably Rakowski) and scholars (Jan Szczepański, Bogdan Suchodolski, Ryszard Manteuffel) have featured prominently in public office under Jaruzelski—a reason not by itself sufficient to dismiss them as "lumpen-intellectuals." Some have taken on the role of establishment critics, while others still remain outside the political hierarchy but have expressed varying degrees of support for the present regime. When evaluating the political role and influence of intellectuals, therefore, we need to be aware of such diverging attitudes.

A cursory examination of the economic position of the entire intelligentsia indicates, if anything, its disadvantaged status in this sphere as well. It seems inconceivable, for instance, that doctors, engineers, and economists should all earn less than welders or bus drivers (Table 5.2). On average, the earnings of white-collar workers are comparable to the earnings of blue-collar workers (Table 5.3), but the funds are put to very different uses. The ratio of car ownership within the intelligentsia is markedly higher than for other social strata, and expenditure on culture is twice that of blue-collar workers. No data are available on social background of those traveling abroad, but it stands to reason that the intelligentsia is dominant in this area as well. Polish sociologists have also reported that much of this stratum is able to pass on its socio-occupational status and educational levels to its children, another important perk of belonging to this group. Finally, the social prestige the intelligentsia enjoys in Polish society is unrivaled. Taken as a whole as well as by specific professions, it ranks at the top of this scale. What it may lack in political power, then, the intelligentsia may reclaim in economic and social spheres.

As for the social values that it cherishes, the Polish intelligentsia does not differ from its counterpart in other countries. It is in large measure materialist and consumer oriented, the more so in that a significant part of the intelligentsia's membership has only recently recorded personal success stories and wishes to savor them. When we exclude the arrivistes and nouveaux riches, the remainder of this stratum is concerned with matters of democratization, participation, and civil liberties. Intellectuals value their role as the repository, continuator, and defender of the nation's cultural heritage and as representatives of a rational enlightened force in a society led by individuals of other virtues. Intellectuals attempt to serve as the nation's social conscience, as a moral secular movement. Above affluence and economic growth intellectuals value self-fulfillment, human development, human rights, and the eradication of forms of alienation, materialism, and venality.

SOCIAL GROUPS—DISADVANTAGED AND DISAPPEARING

Next we turn our attention to groups that play (or have played) an important role in Polish society. Two of the groups examined here are sometimes considered disadvantaged or even oppressed—women and young people. A third group, Polish Jewry, has been rapidly disappearing. Let us assess the progress recorded by these groups under the communist regime.

Women

In Poland as in other communist systems women enjoy formal equality with men. It is a principle that is enshrined in Marxist doctrine and in the present Polish constitution. In fact, Polish women were among the first in Europe to be enfranchised (in 1918). Studies have shown, however, that women in socialist states—though given equal pay for equal work—are often found in inferior work. Highly feminized professional categories such as teachers and, in Poland, physicians, are those with generally low pay scales. One sociological analysis found that when all other factors were controlled, differentials in income caused by the gender factor were equivalent to six years of education; that is, for a woman to attain the earnings plateau a man is destined for, she had to complete that many extra years in school to offset her sex disadvantage.[8] It is also argued that women in Poland are rarely able to break into high managerial or political positions, that they continue to assume the burden of such traditional feminine responsibilities as shopping, housework, and childrearing, and that they are treated with ostentatious gallantry by men while actually being patronized. Dominant male attitudes, observers note, are chauvinist, and in terms of sexual freedoms there is indeed "one law for me, one law for thee." The Polish case is sometimes juxtaposed with a Western country like the United States where women must continue to struggle for formal equality (e.g., the Equal Rights Amendment) while in practice some have already freed themselves from significant cultural constraints (in particular, white middle-class women).

The extent of sexual equality in Poland depends on the weight and interpretation we assign to a number of seemingly contradictory facts. On the one hand, we discover achievements by women that have no parallel in the West. One-half of all college students and close to one-half of the work force are women. Three-quarters of graduates in the humanities, more than one-half of all doctors, and even one-third of engineers, architects, and college professors are women. Close to one-quarter of Seym deputies are now female. It is a fact, as Western detractors are quick to point out, that the feminized professions are poorly paid and that women are under-represented the further up the status and authority hierarchies one goes. For example, in the best paid medical specializations, such as surgery, less than 10 percent are women; in top-level economic management and regional administration posts the figure is between 4 and 10 percent; and in powerful or prestgious posts such as Supreme Court justices or full university professors, female participation is also less than 10 percent. In these respects the Polish pattern differs insignificantly from that in Western countries. On the other hand, women in Poland are both socialized with the values and instilled with the knowledge and skills that permit them to compete on an equal footing with men across virtually all careers. This is still not the case in the United States.

There is a staggering underrepresentation of women in positions of political leadership—more accentuated than in the West. In 1985 there was only one woman both in the fifteen-member Politburo (by communist standards a high figure) and one woman among the twenty-five or so government ministers. When we examine the opposition movements, nothing changes. Among delegates to Solidarity's 1981 national congress only 8 percent were female. Of the eighteen members (both permanent as well as "commuting" regional leaders) of the Presidium (or executive committee) of Solidarity's National Commission only one woman was appointed. Of thirty-two signatories to the KOR declaration dissolving itself, five were women. It would be encouraging to assume that such low representation stems from women's more discerning and judicious attitude to the dirty profession of politics. According to Barbara Jancar, who has written extensively about women in Eastern Europe, "Women in Communist societies may have a greater sense of practicality than men. Tied down to a job, and preferring home and family to high risk and an uncertain future, the vast majority of women have opted out of the Communist political structure both as contributors to it and as opponents."[9] The most convincing explanation remains, however, that females are barred from entering the political elite that is the exclusive preserve of a clan of men.

Governmental policies on social issues of direct concern to women appear generally to be more progressive than in the West. Divorce, abortion, and contraception are relatively easily obtained in Poland—the Catholic church notwithstanding. If the birth control pill is unpopular, it is primarily because of Polish women's concern for the pill's effects on health, not as a result of compliance with papal teachings on this subject or the pill's unavailability due to a pronatalist government policy (as in Romania). It is true, however, that as with other consumer goods, periodic shortages occur in the supply of the pill and of intrauterine devices, thereby undermining their reliability. Furthermore, contraceptive knowledge among many sections of Polish women remains elementary at best.

Under Gierek a demographic goal of 40 million Poles by the year 2000 was set, but little other than exhortation was undertaken to promote its attainment. Fully paid maternity leave of four months is official policy, and new mothers have the option of taking a three-year childrearing leave at reduced pay. State-run child care facilities are more extensive than in the West but are still outstripped by demand: In 1982, 98 percent of children in the relevant age group were enrolled in kindergartens, and approximately one-third of qualifying children were in nurseries. But the latter proportion would undoubtedly be much higher if more facilities were offered. A further constraint on larger families is the perennial housing problem, a problem felt most keenly by young couples.

The balance sheet of advantages and disadvantages Polish women enjoy is clearly mixed. Professional opportunities are greater, but traditional duties coupled with inequality of power are burdensome. As sociologist Renata Siemieńska summed up, "Relatively few women had aspired (as research has shown) to leadership positions, particularly political ones. At the same time, they did not feel discriminated against concerning access to education and the possibilities of getting a job and were convinced they received equal treatment by institutions of various kinds." In addition, women's perception of work and gender equality in Poland was, on the whole, favorable.[10]

It is not surprising, therefore, that Polish women feel insulted when told they are less emancipated than their counterparts in Anglo-Saxon countries. If no independent feminist organizations have emerged in Poland (though in the Solidarity period the government-sponsored League of Women did become more radical), it is because the party prevents the emergence of all types of autonomous movements not under its control. Furthermore, Polish women can assert themselves professionally, thereby resolving one of the chief grievances women's organizations in other countries articulate. Finally, many of the burning concerns of women—the desire for improved living standards and for a more open society—are shared by men. The absence of femininist organizations in Poland does not appear related to underdeveloped consciousness in Polish women.

Youth

Poland's communist authorities have repeatedly voiced concern about the moral and ideological upbringing of youth. This is hardly surprising: In one of the first studies of its kind, an attitudinal survey of University of Warsaw students conducted in 1958 found that only 13 percent considered themselves Marxists. The study was replicated two decades later, and the figure rose insignificantly to 18 percent. It came as a further shock to the rulers when so many young people took part in various organizations outside of party control during 1980 and 1981.

The interests, values, and goals of young people in Poland do vary. The 4 million youth who live in rural areas are primarily concerned with economic advancement and improved living conditions in the countryside. Questions of housing, social benefits, and cultural and recreational amenities are high on their agenda. The rural intelligentsia, foremost among them young teachers, has emerged as an articulate force. Yet government efforts to recruit promising young people into its Rural Youth Union have failed miserably: Its total membership of three hundred thousand represents about 8 percent of those eligible to join, underscoring again disaffection by a particular cohort group with the PZPR's political and ideological program.

In urban areas young people come from working- and middle-class backgrounds, and class affiliation significantly affects their mind set and goals in life. Working-class youth are usually found in vocational or technical schools from which they are funneled into jobs, while middle-class youth have a high probability of completing regular high school and going on to higher education. Young workers formed the core of Solidarity's rank-and-file membership and even provided some notable leaders (for example, Bujak in Warsaw), while intelligentsia youth pressed for more radical demands that at times embarrassed the union's leaders. The official organization for urban youth is the Socialist Polish Youth Union. In 1984 membership stood at less than 1.5 million, less than one-fifth of the country's young people and a 33 percent fall from the 1980 membership figure. Again, disillusionment with the union's progovernment policies has kept membership to a minimum.

Poland's three hundred fifty thousand college students are, in a sense, the vanguard of the youth movement. Their involvement in the 1968 disturbances, then in a variety of semilegal and illegal organizations in the second half of the 1970s (such as the Flying University or the critical Marxist Sigma organization), and, finally, in the radical Independent Students' Union in 1980 and 1981 has demonstrated a high degree of politicization and an organizational capacity lacking among other youth. The 1981 Łódź agreement concluded with the authorities—which followed a lengthy sit-in by the city's students and accompanying student strikes across the country—

was a stupendous, if temporary, victory. The compulsory college courses in Russian language, dialectical materialism, and military basics were to be dropped, and the rector's list, by which undeserving but politically influential young people gained admission to an institution of higher learning, was to be severely curtailed. Moreover, Polish history textbooks were to be revised and made more objective.

Within two weeks of the proclamation of martial law the Independent Students' Union had been disbanded and a series of damning articles about it published in the press. The union was, in this way, the first target of the martial law authorities (Solidarity was not dissolved until ten months later). In 1983 a new organization, the Polish Students' Association, was set up. A year later its combined membership in Poland's eighty-nine institutions of higher education was forty thousand, and at the major universities (Warsaw, Jagiellon) the proportion enrolled was close to 5 percent—this despite numerous inducements (such as foreign travel opportunities).

We should also make mention of two substrata of Polish youth. One is the children of the rich and the powerful who, predictably, enjoy incomparable privileges (foreign travel, foreign education, foreign currency, foreign clothes, foreign durable goods). The other is made up of young married couples, who suffer considerable hardship. A 1985 survey found that 80 percent of such couples relied on financial assistance from their parents, and 56 percent did not have their own apartment. Again, we are made aware of the grave inequities in various spheres of Polish society that have bred either political apathy or outright opposition to the authorities.

Finally, Polish youth are attacked by the government not only for ideological recalcitrance but for slavish aping of rival Western societies. The values, fashions, culture, and ways of thinking dominant in the United States and in Western Europe are said to have an unhealthy hold on the country's young. To a large extent this is true, but paradoxically youth's fascination with Western culture works in favor of the authorities by sublimating young people's frustrations into a harmless, superficial, and make-believe pop culture. This is a problem that is not peculiar to Poland, nor is it the most serious one the rulers face in dealing with youth.

Polish Jews

There are much larger minority groups (Ukrainians, White Russians, Germans) in Poland today than the Jewish minority. It can be argued that another religious group has suffered greater persecution in postwar Poland than the Jews: The Uniate (or Greek Catholic) church used to serve the dwindling population of Ruthenians (or

Rus) before it was banned in 1946. But the position of the Polish Jews is unique simply because there was a time when the country served as an unofficial "homeland" to world Jewry. In the Middle Ages 80 percent of all the world's Jews lived in Poland, and they constituted an integral part of Polish social and cultural life. According to Earl Vinecour, "In no other country than ancient Israel, have Jews lived continuously for as many centuries, in as large numbers, and with as much autonomy as in Poland." As late as 1939, 10 percent of the country's population (3.5 million) and 40 percent of its urban dwellers were Jewish. Not surprisingly, therefore,

> from roots sunk deep into the Polish soil for a millenium, blossomed a way of life where spiritual values and ideals blended into a folk culture, where kabbalistic mysticism and Talmudic rationality were inextricably interwoven. Bobov, Kotsk, Ger, Lublin were for them mystical utterances, rather than the names of Polish towns; paths to divinity through the gateways of Hasidic courts, rather than mere geographic locations.[11]

The Holocaust of World War II irrevocably shattered these bonds. A full 90 percent of Polish Jews were exterminated by the Nazis; only fifty thousand Jews survived the war on Polish soil. Even as the country's borders were being shifted westward, thereby causing tremendous ethnic dislocations, no people had played so central a part in Polish social life only to vanish so completely as Poland's Jewish population. New place names located so tragically on Polish soil were henceforth to become a part of the history of the Jews— Auschwitz, Treblinka, Majdanek, Chelmno, Sobibor, Belzec. Prewar Jewish districts were devastated, synagogues were systematically ravaged, and the *shtetlekh*, Jewish rural communities, vanished. Warsaw's Jewish ghetto, which covered one-third of the city's surface area and housed six hundred thousand Jews in 1939, was wiped out and razed to the ground after an abortive Jewish revolt in April– May 1943—the first instance of protracted civilian resistance to the Nazis. The poignant memoirs of Czerniaków, Korczak, and Ringelblum, inter alia, have depicted this tragic period.

As close as Hitler's final solution came to being realized, it took a series of post-Holocaust events to reduce the surviving Polish Jews by another 90 percent, to the approximately ten thousand remaining in Poland today (only two thousand of whom are officially registered as members of the Mosaic faith). In 1946, during Poland's civil war, a pogrom was instigated in Kielce by a "blood libel" that resulted in the deaths of at least fifty Jews. The period of High Stalinism forced many Polish Jews to opt for emigration, especially after the creation and survival of an independent Israel. Curiously as Jewish numbers declined so political anti-Semitism of the kind fostered by Dmowski's prewar National Democrats continued to surface sporadically within the ruling elite. At times of crises, in particular, as in 1956 (the Natolin faction), 1968 (the Moczar faction), and 1981–1982 (the Grunwald Patriotic Union), hardliners camouflaged as nationalists looked to popular support by invoking anti-Semitic sentiments. According to one writer, Tadeusz Szafar,

> Anti-Semitism, with all its odious implications, has proved to be the classic tool of diehard Communists bent on achieving or consolidating power, on tightening the screws of dictatorship. In 1980–81 this elementary fact of life was even more obvious than in 1956 or in 1968–70, if only because by no stretch of the imagination could any 'pernicious' Jewish influence be discovered in a country that was now virtually *Judenrein*.[12]

This is not the place to inquire how deep and widespread are anti-Semitic feelings in the Polish population. Some popular stereotypes of Poles depict them as incurably anti-Semitic. Extreme versions have even portrayed the Poles as aiding and abetting the Gestapo and the SS (Schutzstaffel) in the war years—a slander on a nation in the process of itself being bled to death. The case of French director Claude Lanzmann's recent film *Shoah* is representative. In it he implicates Poles with co-responsibility for the Holocaust because, he insinuates, so many Jews could not possibly have been exterminated on Polish soil without Polish-Nazi collusion. The Polish authorities have retorted that *Shoah* ignores the one hundred thousand Jews whose lives were saved by Poles. They add that Poland was the only country occupied by the Nazis in which sheltering Jews (*Judenbeherbergung*) carried the death penalty. They also insist Polish resistance leaders told the Western governments about the Holocaust and that this information was disregarded. However, the issue of an alleged latent anti-Semitism in Poles continues to preoccupy the minds of many Poles and Jews alike.

It would certainly be incorrect to say, however, that there was and is no anti-Semitism in Poland, or that there is none in other European states. It is worth pointing out that some Poles hold stereotypes of Jews that emphasize Jews' anti-Polish prejudices. Extreme versions even allege that some Jewish leaders collaborated furtively with the Gestapo in the war years and that others were responsible for the spread of Stalinist terror in the postwar years—

slurs on the nation that had been targeted for genocide by Hitler and, perhaps, by Stalin, too. All stereotypes need to be approached with extreme circumspection, if not outright rejection, and none more so than those concerning Polish-Jewish relations.

What is undoubtedly true is that the postwar communist leadership has deliberately disowned Poland's Jewish heritage. Few efforts have been made to promote Jewish culture. Although the state established a Jewish National Theatre in Warsaw in the 1950s, the twenty synagogues and the scattered Jewish cemeteries that exist at present owe much to the concern and commitment of Jewish groups abroad. Little is ever said in public about the Jewish heritage, though under Jaruzelski this has changed somewhat. In 1983, the commemoration of the fortieth anniversary of the Warsaw ghetto uprising received considerable publicity, and Jewish leaders from abroad were invited to participate. Some observers saw this largely as an attempt to bolster the flagging and isolated martial law regime. But the authorities have continued to permit the Jewish community to engage in symbolic gestures, such as a public bar mitzvah of a Kraków youth in 1985. In that same year Jaruzelski met twice with the president of the World Jewish Congress, Edgar Bronfman, to discuss the preservation of the Jewish heritage in the country. Clearly, the previously tense relations between the two communities were beginning to improve, though on a majority versus minority group basis rather than full equality between them.

Two of the most outstanding products of the Polish Jewish tradition have offered ample testimony that the spiritual heritage has not entirely vanished. Isaac Bashevis Singer—1978 laureate of the Nobel Prize for literature, born and brought up in the vicinity of Warsaw, and one of few existing novelists writing in Yiddish (among whose works is *The Magician of Lublin*)—and Artur Rubinstein—one of this century's greatest concert pianists, born and raised in Lódź, whose autobiographical *My Young Years* recalls those days—have in their life and works epitomized the best of Polish-Jewish values and the richness of its culture. In looking at the otherwise tragic twentieth century history of Poles and Jews, it is this edifying tradition that should be put at the forefront.

THE CATHOLIC CHURCH

In Chapter 1 I referred to the historical role Poland sought to play as the *antemurale christianitatis* in Eastern Europe. Late into the twentieth century Catholicism continues to exercise a strong hold over the Polish population, and, with the accession of Karol Woytyla to the throne of Peter in 1978, it seeks renewed influence in other Slavic countries such as the USSR (especially its Lithuanian, Latvian, and Ukrainian republics), Czechoslovakia, and Yugoslavia. Social and economic modernization is generally accompanied by a process of secularization, but Poland (as well as the Irish Republic) stands apart: Urbanization, proletarianization, literacy, and communist socialization have failed to shake the religious beliefs and practices of most of the population. Some observers even detect a return to Catholic fundamentalism, whose Islamic counterpart has led to the politicoreligious fervor witnessed in certain Middle East countries. Let us examine, therefore, the position of Poland's Catholic church and of its faithful.

More than 93 percent of the country's population are baptized Catholics. The remainder belong to the Russian Orthodox church or are members of Protestant churches such as the Lutherans, Baptists, or Methodists. In 1983 the Catholic church had 7,768 parishes, 14,639 churches, and 21,500 priests scattered in all parts of the country— more than twice the number in 1945 and an increase in each category of some 15 percent on the totals when Gierek took power in 1970. As the data in Table 5.5 indicate, the ratio of churches to baptized Catholics in Polish dioceses is extremely favorable when compared to corresponding ratios for selected Western European dioceses. In Przemyśl diocese, for example, there are about 2,000 Catholics per church; in the diocese of Rome there are twice that number per Catholic church (similar to the Kraków ratio), in Dublin seventeen times that number, and in Madrid thirty times that number. The position of Poland's Catholic church is clearly unique in all Europe.

In addition to churches, Poland has fifty seminaries, the only Catholic university (at Lublin) between the Elbe and Vladivostok, and more than twenty thousand catechism classes offering religious instruction to children. The ecclesiastical hierarchy consists of John Paul II, of course, and since May 1985 five cardinals—the Primate of Poland Józef Glemp, together with cardinals Macharski (Kraków), Gulbinowicz (Wroclaw), Rubin (until 1985 Vatican prefect for the Eastern church), and Deskur (head of the Vatican commission on the media). There are eighty other bishops in the country. Lay Catholic groups are represented in the Seym by way of the progovernment PAX association and the more independent Znak group. Finally, the church has consistently been viewed as the most prestigious and trustworthy institution in the country, as indicated in Chapter 2.

From 1948 to 1981 the primate was Cardinal Stefan Wyszyński— as determined and hard-nosed a figure as his nemesis for many years, party boss Gomulka. After Wyszyński's release from house arrest in 1956, church-state relations staggered from one confrontation to

Interior of one of the many churches in Warsaw's Old Town

Table 5.5 Ratio of Catholic Churches to Baptized Catholics in Selected Polish and
         European Dioceses

Diocese	Number of Churches	Catholics (in 000s)	Catholics Per Church
Krakow	494	2,144	4,340
Przemysl	767	1,550	2,020
Warsaw	387	3,120	8,062
Wroclaw	987	2,787	2,823
Barcelona	299	4,100	13,712
Berlin	32	426	13,312
Birmingham	91	329	3,615
Dublin	30	1,050	35,000
Lisbon	538	1,328	2,468
Lublijana	17	700	41,176
Madrid	69	4,102	59,449
Paris	72	1,702	23,638
Rome	609	2,731	4,484
Vienna	250	1,648	6,592

Source: J. Jarzeniec, "Poslugi Religijne," Polityka (23 November 1985)

another, and it was only with Gierek's accession that contacts were "normalized." Both Wyszyński and Woytyla threw their support behind the human rights movement springing up in the country in the late 1970s, and both took a rather cautious approach to the emergence of Solidarity in 1980. According to one Polish writer, "The ideals of Solidarity were largely those of the Catholic faith but its methods of striving to achieve social and political change were basically different from the centuries-long teachings of the Catholic Church."[13]

Under martial law the church took on various roles—a force of moderation, conciliation, and striving for national unity (for which Glemp was occasionally attacked), an administrator of aid programs to the needy and to families of political prisoners, and, at the grass-roots level, a base for clandestine Solidarity operations. The church hierarchy clearly did not seek a direct political role, and Glemp squashed attempts that might have led to the establishment of a kind of Christian democratic trade union in the place of Solidarity. Not surprisingly, criticism surfaced in the underground press that the church was "closer to eternity than to Solidarity," but the 1983 papal visit removed much of the skepticism about the church's objectives. Later that year the "battle of the crucifixes" hanging in state schools was precipitated by the secularizing zealousness of certain local leaders and was ineluctably resolved in the church's favor. Likewise, the

Girls in front of a religious shop after their first Communion

Sunday morning radio broadcast of mass—part of the August 1980 accords—continued unimpeded.

In October 1984 the brutal murder by three sadistic members of the security police of a pro-Solidarity priest, Jerzy Popieluszko, was treated by the authorities and the ecclesiastical hierarchy alike as a conspiracy by some hardliners to deliberately foment a confrontation between the two. The quick arrest, trial, and sentencing of the accused at least partially mollified public opinion and gave satisfaction to the church. Although the PRON organization, set up in 1982 to look for ways to achieve a modicum of national unity, was entrusted to a respected Catholic writer, Jan Dobraczyński, relations between the authorities and the church vacillated from proper to poor in the mid-1980s. It is obvious that the political leadership is of two minds in dealing with the church: While Jaruzelski and other moderates view it as a national, moral, and unifying force, hardliners would like to have done with it once and for all.

The church itself subsumes three different hierarchical tiers. First is the ecclesiastical hierarchy whose overriding goal is a long-term one—as in past ages, to survive long after the People's Republic has disappeared. The hierarchy's thinking is that Catholicism has existed in Poland for more than one thousand years, the socialist system a little more than forty. Because time is in the church's favor, it makes wise tactical sense for the church to engage the authorities in constructive dialogue in the hope of achieving meaningful change in the here and now. Accordingly, Glemp met personally with Jaruzelski nine times in the years 1981–1985, and there can be little question that this approach is strongly supported by John Paul II.

The pope is part of the Polish ecclesiastical hierarchy and has given it as personal an imprint as Wyszyński before him. Oftentimes, the pope's imprint is perceived unfavorably by those close to Catholicism but not to Polish traditions. In the view of Irish writer Conor Cruise O'Brien, for example, "In its spirit, the pontificate of John Paul II is a tremendous archaism, a splendid example of Polish Baroque." The pope is "a man of great astuteness, even deviousness, in tactical matters," which serve "to conceal the full depths of his traditional Tridentine Catholicity and of an authoritarianism gentle and unassuming in style, but implacable in substance."[14] It is striking how this authoritarianism, conservatism, and personality cult–though more moderate—resemble the chief features of communist rule in Poland. Perhaps, like the Soviet dissident Solzhenitsyn, it is less the form of communist rule than its philosophic premises that John Paul II finds most objectionable. The fact is that he has provided a distraught nation with moral inspiration and prudential leadership in a difficult period.

The second tier of the church is made up of the priests (particularly younger ones) in the parishes throughout the country who, in addition to performing religious duties, consider it part of their responsibility to represent and articulate the opinions of the faithful in public. Although the majority of priests place the task of ministering to souls above political goals, there are a good number who have been reprimanded by the authorities for viewing the two objectives as inseparable. Moreover, various parishes throughout the country have given assistance to Solidarity's underground network in various ways. These have been the aspects of the Polish church receiving most of the West's attention.

The third tier is composed of the more than 30 million lay Catholics in rural and urban areas, among the old and the young, within the intelligentsia and the peasantry, whose religious values and practices at times conflict with the secular materialist state policy, but most of the time don't. The composition of this group is extremely heterogenous in political terms, too: There are believers who are in the underground, those who are in the party, and those who are indifferent to politics. Lest the impression be given that a happy fusion has taken place in Poland between seemingly incompatible Catholic and communist faiths, we should underscore the fact that a practicing Catholic is never found in an important party leadership post, just as a PZPR member cannot be found in an influential position in the church hierarchy. Only at this third tier of church functioning is there some overlap.

The degree of radicalization of the three levels differs considerably. Thus, Glemp might well have been embarrassed by Popieluszko's monthly pro-Solidarity sermons while, in turn, millions of believers may have become completely disillusioned with politics of any kind. But when we fuse the three levels together, sociologist Bogdan Szajkowski's assertion makes sense that the church has a "unique role in contemporary Polish politics . . . because it intertwined moral and political authority with national, historical and cultural traditions and with the current demands and expectations of national survival."[15]

SOCIAL VALUES AND SOCIAL PATHOLOGIES

So far we have been looking at Polish society in microsociological terms, stressing the diversity within its social classes, groups, and institutions. Let us conclude by risking a more overarching approach and seeking an answer to the question—which social values and afflictions characterize Polish society sui generis and set it apart from others?

From sociological surveys we know that a number of fundamental premises and principles of socialism are shared by many Poles. These include nationalization of the means of production, agrarian reform, economic planning, and the overhaul of the prewar class structure.[16] In addition, the characteristics of a just social system identified by most respondents have included equality of life opportunities, equality before the law, and fair distribution of goods. Polish respondents have made clear that socialism offers greater equality of opportunity for upward mobility than capitalism, even if the latter system is perceived to be more effective in satisfying people's material needs.

Poles' self-image consists of both positive and negative attributes. Among the first are generosity, sincerity, valor and high spiritedness—traits that derive from the gentry model of times past and that Poland's first great sociologist, Florian Znaniecki, dubbed the model of the "man of play."[17] Negative qualities include lack of thriftiness, discipline, reliability, and industriousness. The gentry felt their economic needs would always be satisfied without any effort on their part; consequently, they disdained materialism, money, and commerce and preferred spiritual and hedonistic values. In following this model (up to the 1970s anyway), Poles have expected others to do entrepreneurial work for them (Jews, foreigners, the state). It is not surprising, therefore, that Znaniecki's "man of work" is glossed over in Polish autostereotypes.

Poles' perceptions of the world around them underscore age-old fears. In crossnational surveys conducted in the 1960s (such as "Images of the World in the Year 2000"), Polish respondents invariably ranked as most pessimistic in evaluating the extent to which they controlled their own destiny or in judging the probability of another world war. In the 1970s national pride and self-confidence increased, and the majority of Poles felt their country played a significant role in world politics, but surveys in the 1980s have indicated respondents' renewed concern with national sovereignty. What adds greater significance to these results is the fact that Poles can travel freely to socialist and capitalist countries in a way unrivaled by any other Eastern European nation. In 1985, for example, more than 90 percent of all citizens applying for passports to travel to the West received them. The major difficulty in foreign travel was obtaining a visa from a Western country. In short, Polish international perceptions are likely to be more deeply grounded in experience than in theory compared to other socialist nations.

One question asked of Poles was who their favorite and least favorite nations were. Respondents most frequently included the French and Hungarians in the first category (in a 1981 survey Americans ranked third and Russians fifth), and the Germans and sometimes Russians in the second category.[18]

It is risky to attempt identifying a distinctive Polish national character. When the attempt is made, however, it must begin with a composite of the values and vices appearing in empirical sociological studies. Several factors, often ones that pull Poles in different directions—such as historical consciousness, Catholic morality, socialist ideology, and industrial-social materialism—would have to be compared. Added to these should be such social pathologies as the alcoholism, increasing drug use, graft, and atomization of society found across all social classes and groups in contemporary Poland. Another serious malaise—sometimes perceived to be the result of Polish attitudes as much as of communist policies—is the destruction to the environment wrought in recent decades.[19] Although all rapidly industrializing countries pay little heed to environmental protection, the stereotype of the Pole as a *balaganiarz*, or creator of disorder, presupposes a link between spreading pollution and widespread Polish attitudes.

After we have sketched such a judgmental and irreverent composite of Polish national character, we may still find, in the final reckoning, that Poles share many of such characteristics with Slavs in the rest of socialist Europe. The most we can hold out for is, therefore, that "being Polish" is a factor that should be included in any analysis of uneven economic, political, and social development in the region.

In recognizing the nation's social heterogeneity and the differing, possibly conflicting, interests of its classes and groups, we can appreciate more fully the remarkable unity and coalition of interests that Solidarity was able to sustain, even if for a brief time. It may have been optimistic to expect that such unity would persist once an initial victory had been achieved. But the authorities should not assume that existing social differences cannot again be overcome in a spirit of solidarity.

NOTES

1. A. Pravda, "Political Attitudes and Activity," in J. Triska and C. Gati (eds.), *Blue-Collar Workers in Eastern Europe* (Boston: Allen and Unwin, 1981), p. 47.

2. See G. Kolankiewicz and R. Taras, "Poland: Socialism for Everyman?" in A. Brown and J. Gray (eds.), *Political Culture and Political Change in Communist States* (New York: Holmes and Meier, 1979), pp. 101–130; G. Kolankiewicz, "Poland, 1980: The Working Class under 'Anomic Socialism,'" in Triska, *Blue-Collar Workers*, pp. 136–156; T.A. Jones, D. Bealmear, and M. Kennedy, "Public Opinion and Political Disruption," in J. Bielasiak and M. Simon (eds.), *Polish Politics: Edge of the Abyss* (New York: Praeger, 1984), pp.138–168.

3. A. Pravda, "The Workers," in A. Brumberg (ed.), *Poland: Genesis of a Revolution* (New York: Vintage, 1983), p. 90.

4. A. Korbonski, "Agriculture and the Polish Renewal," in Bielasiak, *Polish Politics*, p. 92.

5. C.M. Hann, *A Village Without Solidarity* (New Haven, Conn.: Yale University Press, 1985), p. 56.

6. G. Konrad and I. Szelenyi, *The Intellectuals on the Road to Class Power* (New York: Harcourt Brace Jovanovich, 1979), p. 179.

7. S. Kwiatkowski, "Inteligent—kto to taki?" [Who is the Intelligentsia Member?] *Polityka* (30 March 1985).

8. This and other data were collected by a team of sociologists at the University of Warsaw in the course of a national study of social stratification

during the early 1970s. Many of the findings have not been published; the one cited in the text was obtained privately by the author.

9. B. Jancar, *Women under Communism* (Baltimore, Md.: Johns Hopkins University Press, 1978), p. 121.

10. R. Siemieńska, "Women's Political Participation and the 1980 Crisis in Poland," *International Political Science Review* 6, no. 3 (1985):343; also see her "Women, Work, and Gender Equality in Poland: Reality and its Social Perception," in S. Wolchik and A. Meyer (eds.), *Women, State, and Party in Eastern Europe* (Durham, N.C.: Duke University Press, 1985), pp. 503–528.

11. E. Vinecour, *Polish Jews: the Final Chapter* (New York: New York University Press, 1977), p. 1.

12. T. Szafar, "Anti-Semitism: a Trusty Weapon," in Brumberg, *Poland*, p. 121.

13. T. Kaminski, "Poland's Catholic Church and Solidarity: A Parting of the Ways?" *Poland Watch* no. 6 (1984): 76.

14. C. Cruise O'Brien, "The Liberal Pope," *New York Review of Books* 32, no. 15 (10 October 1985): 13–14.

15. B. Szajkowski, *Next to God . . . Poland* (London: Frances Pinter, 1983), p. 226.

16. S. Nowak, "Values and Attitudes of the Polish People," *Scientific American* 245, no. 1 (July 1981): 49.

17. F. Znaniecki, *Ludzie teraźniejsi a cywilizacja przyszłości* [The People of Today and the Civilization of the Future] (Warsaw: Książnica Atlas, 1935).

18. These results are taken from A. Jasińska-Kania, "National Identity and Image of World Society: The Polish Case," *International Social Science Journal* 34, no. 1 (1982):93–112.

19. An article published in a Warsaw daily claimed Poland had the most polluted environment in Europe. See *Życie Warszawy* (30 August 1985; 11 September 1985).

FURTHER READINGS

E. Allardt and W. Wesolowski (eds.). *Social Structure and Change: Finland and Poland Comparative Perspective.* Warsaw: PWN, 1978.

J.R. Fiszman. *Revolution and Tradition in People's Poland: Education and Socialization.* Princeton, N.J.: Princeton University Press, 1972.

W.W. Hagen. *Germans, Poles, and Jews.* Chicago: University of Chicago Press, 1980.

C.S. Heller. *On the Edge of Destruction: Jews of Poland Between the Two World Wars.* New York: Columbia University Press, 1977.

D. Lane and G. Kolankiewicz (eds.). *Social Groups in Polish Society.* London: Macmillan, 1973.

W. Majkowski. *People's Poland: Patterns of Social Inequality and Conflict.* London: Greenwood Press, 1985.

J. Malanowski. "Polish Workers." *International Journal of Sociology* 14, no. 3 (Fall 1984).

J. Marcus. *Social and Political History of the Jews in Poland 1919–39*. New York: Mouton, 1983.

D. Mason. *Public Opinion and Political Change in Poland 1980–82*. Cambridge: Cambridge University Press, 1985.

A. Matejko. *Social Change and Stratification in Eastern Europe*. New York: Praeger, 1974.

E. Mendelsohn. *Zionism in Poland*. New Haven, Conn.: Yale University Press, 1981.

A. Micewski. *Cardinal Wyszynski*. San Diego, Calif.: Harcourt Brace Jovanovich, 1984.

P. Potichnyj (ed.). *Poland and Ukraine Past and Present*. Edmonton, Alberta: Canadian Institute of Ukrainian Studies, 1980.

K. Slomczyński and T. Krauze (eds.). *Class Structure and Social Mobility in Poland*. White Plains, N.Y.: M.E. Sharpe, 1978.

S. Starski. *Class Struggle in Classless Poland*. Boston: South End Press, 1982.

A. Szymanski. *Class Struggle in Socialist Poland*. New York: Praeger, 1984.

N. Tec. *When Light Pierced the Darkness: Righteous Christians and the Polish Jews*. New York: Oxford University Press, 1986.

B.D. Weinryb. *The Jews of Poland*. Philadelphia: Jewish Publications Society of America, 1972.

6

Polish Culture and National Survival

A nation lacking statehood is unlikely to disappear if its culture is maintained and flourishes, for culture is the measure of a nation's will to survive. Nowhere is this thesis confirmed more convincingly than in nineteenth-century Poland and, critics of communism would add, in the Soviet-dominated People's Republic. Although the nation was politically subjugated by others, its poets, artists, and composers kept alive the spirit and values of the population, preserved and beautified its language, devised other means of national expression, and aroused hope and confidence where otherwise there was only despair and defeat. For these reasons, inter alia, the prestige of the writer or the artist in Polish society attains a level seldom approximated in Western countries. By the same token, the series of national disasters induced by unwise statesmanship during the centuries has reduced the prestige of politicians in Poland to an unparalleled low point; it is not surprising that power has been taken over by a still highly regarded military leadership.

In short, many countries have their own national poets or composers, but Poland during its history has had a more desperate need of them. If Polish culture has remained in the shadow of the anguished and introspective literary tradition of Russia and of the grandiose and assertive artistic movements of the Germanic peoples, it may perhaps be the result of its need to bow to two exigencies, functional as well as creative.

In this chapter I examine the development of Polish culture from its foundations through the years of partition into the twentieth century. I then look at Polish culture since World War II and contrast in particular its evolution in the Solidarity and martial-law periods, concluding with a brief assessment of contemporary popular culture.

Les jeunes filles en fleurs

DEVELOPMENT OF A POLISH CULTURE

The first writings about Poland that we know of come from the early chroniclers, such as Gallus Anonymous (ca. 1100) and Jan Dlugosz (1415–1480), who wrote in medieval Latin. The astronomer Copernicus (1473–1543), born in Toruń, also authored his *De Revolutionibus Orbium Coelestium* in Latin, but in his lifetime works already were being written in the vernacular and published by Kraków-based printers. At this time another great achievement was recorded in Kraków: The magnificent wooden altar triptych in the Church of the Virgin Mary was carved during a twelve-year period by Wit Stwosz (1440–1533).

The inadvertent "father" of Polish literature was Mikolaj Rey (1505–1569): Born into a gentry family where little Latin was used, he began to compose poetry in Polish. It was less than an auspicious beginning for Polish literature or for its Golden Age of culture, however: According to contemporary Polish poet and 1980 Nobel Prize laureate Czeslaw Milosz, Rey indeed symbolized "merry old Poland" of medieval times, but "whether he can be called little more than a glutton, a drunkard, a lecher, a gossiper, a man of obscene language, or a blasphemer is doubtful."[1]

A more upright representative of Polish Renaissance humanism was Jan Kochanowski (1530–1584), a poet and dramatist whose *The Dismissal of the Grecian Envoys* (describing the unsuccessful mission to Troy to obtain the release of Helen) served as an idiom to explore the nature of statesmanship, patriotism, and political nemesis—themes that were to recur in Polish history. Kochanowski's *Laments*, highly charged verses constituting a "monument to a father's sorrow" on the death of a beloved daughter, stands as one of the masterpieces of all Polish literature.

The Golden Age was perhaps most distinguished by its architecture—Wawel Castle (containing splendid Arras tapestries), Sukiennice market square, and Jagiellon chapel, all in Kraków—that fused Gothic and Renaissance, Polish and Italian forms. By the seventeenth century Renaissance town buildings and country mansions were springing up throughout the country: in Zamość, Sandomierz, and Lublin in the southeast; Kalisz and Poznań in the west; Toruń in the north; and Warsaw in central Poland, which became the country's new capital after 1596. The entire length of Warsaw's Royal Way, extending from the castle in the Old Town past Ujazdów Castle and the Lazienki estate to Wilanów—former country home of Jan Sobieski situated on the outskirts of the city—offers splendid examples of the architecture of this and subsequent periods.

The wars with Sweden in the middle of the seventeenth century caused widespread destruction of Polish social and cultural life, and the Polish baroque that followed did not produce any outstanding men of letters. However, the short-lived enlightenment period of the second half of the eighteenth century, which coincided with the reign of Poland's last king, Stanislaw August Poniatowski, engendered such authors as the poet-bishop Ignacy Krasicki (1735–1801) and the radical-minded publicists Hugo Kollataj (1750–1812) and Stanislaw Staszic (1755–1826). In their writings all three were concerned with methods of strengthening the political system and the moral education of Poland's citizens.

The decades following the partitions of the late eighteenth century may have represented a political catastrophe for the nation, but they were a high-water mark for its literature. Elsewhere in Europe Byron was writing *Don Juan*, Pushkin *Eugene Onegin*, Hugo *Lucretia Borgia*, and Heine *The Book of Songs*. In Poland three romantic poets stand out in this cultural neo-Renaissance—Adam Mickiewicz (1798–1855), Juliusz Slowacki (1809–1849) and Zygmunt Krasiński (1812–1859). The first—most often regarded as the country's national poet—is best known for his complex four-part *Forefathers' Eve*, a drama of proto-Wagnerian sweep and pathos. Part 3, written last (after the 1830

Warsaw's Square viewed through a window

Artisan ware in a fancy shop window along Warsaw's Royal Way

insurrection), is the most evocative: It is a morality play based on
the apocalyptic vision of the principal character, Conrad—poet, freedom fighter, prisoner of supernatural forces, and savior of the Polish
nation. *Pan Tadeusz*, an epic poem describing the gentry of old Poland
and Lithuania, is another magnum opus written by Mickiewicz:

> Lithuania, my country, you are like health:
> how much you should be prized only he can learn
> who has lost you. Today your beauty in all its splendor
> I see and describe, for I yearn for you.

Of Slowacki's dramas, *Kordian* is unique in its status as "history
in the making" and in its presentation of the political manifesto of
the romantics:

> Unseal the national urn and place the ashes in my hand!
> I will resurrect the people and buskin on tomb will stand.

His other historical works concerned with Poland included *Anhelli*,
a poem in prose, as well as *Horsztyński* and *Balladyna*, both tragic
dramas.

Krasiński's *The Un-divine Comedy* is a further high point of
Polish romantic, revolutionary-centered literature. Its eerie pre-Marxian
motifs of conflict and upheaval may make it the work most accessible
to a Western audience. A reader with an acquired taste for romantic
literature might go on to read the poetry of Cyprian Norwid (1821–
1883) and attend performances of the comedies of Alexander Fredro
(1793–1876). Perhaps the most significant fact about these writers is
that all were forced into exile in the 1830s. Thus, Mickiewicz was to
die in Istanbul and Slowacki in Paris. From this fact descends to us
the widespread belief that all great Polish literati are to be found
outside the country, in emigration. I will return to this subject later.

No survey of Polish romanticism would be complete without
mention of the country's greatest composer, Frederic Chopin (1810–
1849). Contrary to conventional wisdom, there were indeed significant
composers in Poland before Chopin. The Renaissance was distinguished by the song collections of Mikolaj Gomólka (1535–1609), the
early baroque by the compositions of Mikolaj Zieleński (1550–1615),
and the later baroque by the instrumental works of composer (as
well as architect and poet) Adam Jarzębski (1590–1649). It was the
genius of Chopin, however, that gave tonal expression to the pathos
of the poets and the revolutionary designs of the radical democrats.
The most Polish of his works are probably his mazurkas, polonaises,

fantasies, and scherzos. The piano competition carrying his name, held every five years in Warsaw, is one of the great cultural events of contemporary Poland and one of the world's blue-ribbon musical competitions. In Chopin's lifetime Polish opera was born; its progenitor was Stanislaw Moniuszko (1819–1872), who underscored national motifs in works such as *Halka* and *The Haunted Manor* at a time when all symbols of "Polishness" were being suppressed.

When the next insurrection failed, in 1863, the political reaction was to turn away from the redemptive martyrdom of the romantics towards organic work, and cultural positivism became the vogue. A new triad of writers dominated the age—Boleslaw Prus (1845–1912), Eliza Orzeszkowa (1841–1910), and Henryk Sienkiewicz (1846–1916). Prus's two most significant works had very different settings. *The Doll* was the touching story of an industrious Warsaw shop assistant and his petite bourgeois world. The principal character, Wokulski, nevertheless had the heart of a romantic—illustrating that the break with the previous period was torturous. *The Pharaoh*, by contrast, was a colorful allegorical account of an ancient Egyptian ruler, Ramses XIII, whose reform-mindedness was to prove more enduring than his reign. The novel presented the characteristic positivist view that society was an organism greater than the sum of its parts. It clearly offered hope to a country that at the time of publication had been partitioned for one full century.

Orzeszkowa was remarkable for the far-ranging social sensitivity she displayed in her many novels. In *Marta* she described a well-bred woman who, in spite of courage and willpower, met a tragic end as a result of *force majeure*—the man's world she could never conquer. In *Meir Ezofowicz* Orzeszkowa wrote of life in the Jewish ghetto of a provincial town, while in *The Boor* and *On a Winter's Evening* she offered a Polish rural counterpart to Zola's French urban realism. Her most highly regarded novel was *On the Banks of the Niemen*, which depicted a kaleidescope of characters and the ambiance and social stratification in rural eastern Poland. Here love could not surmount the rigid barriers of class. Orzeszkowa was a novelist who never achieved the international renown she merited.

By contrast, Sienkiewicz became the most popular and famous of Polish writers, the country's first Nobel laureate, who even outshone his contemporary of Polish origin, the English writer Joseph Conrad. The best-selling *Quo Vadis*, about ancient Rome, and the corresponding Slavic epic *The Teutonic Knights* demonstrated extraordinary creative and organizational talents. Three lengthy novels about seventeenth-century Poland—*With Fire and Sword*, *The Deluge*, and *Pan Wolodyjowski*—have become Polish classics and have been turned into movies. Several generations of children have been brought up on his *In Desert and Wilderness*, set in Arabia, while *Portrait of America* recounted his visit to this country. Sienkiewicz's versatility, if not his prose style or moral conscience, makes him one of the country's foremost novelists.

Significantly, Jan Matejko (1838–1893), an artist who dealt with similar historical themes and whose inspiration Sienkiewicz readily acknowledged, became one of Poland's most respected nineteenth-century painters. Together with the romantic artist Piotr Michalowski (1801–1855), they represented Poland's otherwise insignificant contribution to painting up to then. Even with Matejko, however, the desire for historical accuracy and for an art that would serve the nation overrode concern with artistic values. Finally, the most notable example of Polish positivism in practice was the research into radium and polonium carried out by Maria Curie-Sklodowska in Paris at this time.

At the turn of this century, Poland was swept by a cultural movement that elsewhere in Europe became known as modernism or neoromanticism. The Young Poland school possessed no program or manifesto, though as Milosz observed, "Art that creates values in a world deprived of values became for 'Young Poland' an object of worship."[2] In literature neoromanticism found its most eloquent expression in the social novels of Stefan Zeromski (1864–1925). For instance, his *Homeless People* depicted the reaction of the intelligentsia to the immiserization of the masses, and *Before the Spring* described the injustices and backwardness that persisted after Poland had regained statehood in 1918. Wladyslaw Reymont (1867–1925) wrote a four-volume novel, *The Peasants*, that reflected a belated Polish phenomenon equivalent to the 1870s Russian *narodnik* ("going to the people") movement. His unfavorable characterization of Lódź urban society in *The Promised Land* also exhibited the fashionable radicalism of the time. In 1924 Reymont was awarded the Nobel Prize for literature.

Perhaps the most creative cultural figure of the period was Stanislaw Wyspiański (1869–1907), whose plays and painting exude an energy that transcends political and ethical concerns. Polish nationalism is clear in his historical play *November Night* and his symbolic play *Liberation* and also in the bizarre and pulsating *The Wedding*, which recalled the betrothal of a peasant girl to, predictably, an intellectual, attended by painters, poets, priests, peasants, and haystacks! The joyous atmosphere at the outset is transformed into a haunting introspective finish, and *The Wedding* deserves the status of a twentieth-century masterpiece.

Interest in the countryside produced a pair of great landscape artists in Jacek Malczewski (1854–1929) and Józef Chelmoński (1850–1914). In music a worthy successor to Chopin was found in Karol Szymanowski (1882–1937), whose experimentation with folk music themes conveyed wistful airs. Only a small part of his varied repertoire (which includes the opera *King Roger*, the oratorio "Stabat Mater," the ballet *Harnasie*, choral works, symphonies, and chamber music) has found its way into Western concert halls. Even more obscure to Western music lovers are the symphonic poems and other lyrical works of Mieczyslaw Karlowicz (1876–1909). The obscurity of Szymanowski and especially Karlowicz is perplexing given that their output, like that of the whole Young Poland movement, displayed greater vitality and subtlety than the more highly regarded, stirring, but often insipid output of Polish romanticism.

Cultural developments in the interwar period were marked everywhere by surrealism. The most enigmatic, if not most outstanding, figure of this period was Stanislaw Witkiewicz, or Witkacy (1885–1939), dramatist, philosopher, and painter extraordinaire. An early exponent of the theatre of the absurd (or at least nonsensical) and of the grotesque, a surrealist and existentialist before his time, the self-proclaimed founder of the school of "erotology" who was frequently inspired by drug-induced hallucinations, Witkacy was not fully appreciated in his lifetime—which was cut short by his suicide the day Russian forces attacked Poland in September 1939. One of his plays bore the apposite title *The Madman and the Nun, or Nothing Is So Bad It Can't Become Worse*—"Dedicated to All the Madmen of the World (*y compris* other planets of our system as well as planets of the Milky Way and other galaxies) and to Jan Mieczyslawski. The title of his analytical study is no less beguiling: *Nicotine, Alcohol, Cocaine, Peyote, Morphine, Ether + Appendix*. His paintings are no less bizarre. One of Poland's most eminent literary critics, Ludwig Krzyżanowski, had scant praise for Witkacy:

> The iconoclast, having destroyed every vestige of previous systems of public life, political and social ideologies, not excluding philosophical systems, sails forth on the ocean of nihilism, the only thing he believes in being human urges, instincts connected with the satisfaction of the digestive and sexual organs. Thus ends the vision of the struggles of the 20th century man."[3]

Witkacy was not considered for a Nobel Prize in literature.

A more sophisticated writer was Witold Gombrowicz (1904–1969), who gained international literary renown in the postwar period after settling in the West. His prewar "antinovel" (not dissimilar to the postwar French *roman nouvel*) *Ferdydurke* anticipated his laterworks such as *Pornografia* and *Cosmos*. Gombrowicz, too, was concerned with literary form and with the illogicality of life.

Finally, more catholic and aesthetic tastes were reflected in a movement of young poets that became known as the Skamander group. In the works of Julian Tuwim (1894–1953), Antoni Slonimski (1895–1976), and Jaroslaw Iwaszkiewicz (1894–1980)—all of whom developed their creative powers further in People's Poland—we observe a return to classical, often lighthearted, lyric rhymes. In its time Skamander overshadowed the dadaist poets represented by Alexander Wat (1900–1967), and the Zagary group—or school of catastrophists—in which Milosz began his apprenticeship. It was this latter group, in fact, that displayed the clearest vision of the world on the edge of a cataclysm, as Milosz's verse pointedly makes clear:

> The world trembles, the trees fall silent, when a just man walks,
> but this too sinful age will bring forth no saint
> —thus you taught us; a stream of boiling lava
> will extinguish the cities and Noah will not escape in his ark.
>
> "To Father Ch."

CULTURAL POLICY AND CULTURAL OUTPUT IN PEOPLE'S POLAND

Despite the general skepticism of Polish intellectuals about the socialist system, some of Poland's cultural intelligentsia were indeed influenced by socialist ideology and subsequently produced literary works of great artistic merit. The leading figure in the "proletarian" school of poetry, for example, was Wladyslaw Broniewski, perhaps best known for his patriotic call to arms on the eve of World War II:

> Rouse yourself from sleep—fight.
> Stem the flood.
> Bayonets ready!
> There is need for blood.

Much of the early literature of People's Poland was concerned with the war. Two of the most promising poets, Krzysztof Baczyński and Tadeusz Gajcy, died fighting in the 1944 Warsaw uprising. Others who survived, such as Tadeusz Rożewicz (in the volumes *Anxiety* and *The Red Glove*) and Wislawa Szymborska (poems published between 1945 and 1948 in *Dziennik Polski*), spoke of the impossibility of returning to normal life in the aftermath of the war's inhumanity and carnage. Prose writers like Jerzy Andrzejewski (*Ashes and Diamonds*), Miron Bialoszewski (*Memoir of the Warsaw Uprising*), Tadeusz Borowski (*This Way for the Gas, Ladies and Gentlemen*), and Roman Bratny (*Kolumbowie. Birthdate 20*) touched in various ways on the German occupation, the extermination camps, and the postwar struggle for power between Communists and non-Communists. In painting and sculpture, too, the horrors of war were starkly portrayed, as the 1968 Royal Academy exhibition in London on "A Thousand Years of Polish Culture" bore witness. Among the cultural intelligentsia there was little criticism of, and in fact there was oftentimes sympathy for, the socialist experiment in those years.

The Stalinization of Polish life of the late 1940s compelled artists to follow the precepts of socialist realism that subordinated artistic values to the need to glorify present and future socialist accomplishments. Artists' responses to the political and cultural climate of the time varied: Some writers, better forgotten, embraced the principle and extolled the socialist reality in the idealistic way prescribed.[4] A few committed themselves to the doctrine but quickly became disillusioned (Andrzejewski, Kazimierz Brandys, Tadeusz Konwicki). These novelists were to form the core of the "contestators"—those challenging the authorities—in later decades. Their view is perhaps best summed up in the remark of one writer, Stanislaw Dygat: "There are two things I don't regret . . . joining the party and leaving the party."[5]

Some writers sought to evade socialist realism by choosing nonpolitical genres. Stanislaw Lem (of *Solaris* fame) chose science fiction; interestingly, when he moved to Switzerland in the 1980s it was not for political reasons but to have ready access to scientific journals hard to come by in Poland. The poets Konstanty Galczyński (associated with the prewar *Quadriga* review) and Adam Ważyk (who became famous for his 1955 anti-Stalin "Poem for Adults") turned to literary translation. Some opted for silence or "internal emigration," as it is sometimes called; these included Tadeusz Breza, author of *The Office* and *The Bronze Gate*, which are revealing essay-novels about the Vatican's corridors of power (Breza was a seminarian before joining the Communist party). Others preferred authentic emigration like Milosz or, later, Marek Hlasko—the self-styled Hemingway clone who authored rough-and-tumble books like *The Eighth Day of the Week* and *The Graveyard*. One writer, Borowski, a dogmatic Marxist, chose suicide.

As with collective farms, the Polish October signaled a relaxation of the leadership's commitment to socialist realism, though lip service continued to be paid to it. Gomulka soon identified the cultural intelligentsia as the source of the revisionist cancer he sought to destroy and three prominent liberal periodicals, *Nowa Kultura, Po Prostu,* and *Przegląd Kulturalny,* were closed down. Kazimierz Brandys caught the duplicity of the time in a short piece he wrote about two turds by the side of the road: One says to the other "Do you feel it? It's thawing. Now we can really start stinking."[6]

In general, the party's policy on culture during the past three decades has been neither exclusively repressive nor liberal. There have been none of the arrests, show trials, imprisonments, and expulsions that occurred in neighboring Czechoslovakia, East Germany, or the Soviet Union, even though the intelligentsia has (as we noted in the preceding chapter) regularly challenged the authorities. However, disaffected and disapproved-of authors such as Brandys (whose earlier socialist realism novel *Citizens* gave way to the recent critical *Warsaw Diary*) or Konwicki (*The Polish Complex* and *A Minor Apocalypse*) were forced to turn to opposition publishing houses (such as Nowa and Krąg) in order to have their work see the light of day. Others, through frustration, were eventually driven out of the country.

Several writers managed to produce works of significant artistic merit while taking care not to run afoul of the censors. Chief among these were the "new wave" poets Stanislaw Grochowiak, Adam Zagajewski, and Zbigniew Herbert. The first dwelt on the themes of the inseparability of love and death and of the beauty of ugliness. The second, in Milosz's words, "left behind that poetry of political commitment—noble-minded but often one dimensional—and embarked upon a new adventure, a search in a labyrinth where meditation on the flow of time brings together the historical and the metaphysical."[7] The latter, much of whose poetry has appeared in English translation, adopted a cerebral approach, classical logical structure, free verse style, and intrinsic faith in human nature that allowed him to transcend all politics and address universal topics:

> Now you have peace Hamlet you accomplished what you had to
> and you have peace The rest is not silence but belongs to me
> you chose the easier part an elegant thrust but what is heroic death
> compared with eternal watching with a cold apple in one's hand
> on a narrow chair with a view on the anthill and the clock's dial
>
> Adieu Prince I have tasks a sewer project
> and a decree on prostitutes and beggars
> I must also elaborate a better system of prisons
> since as you justly said Denmark is a prison
> I go to my affairs This night is born
> a star named Hamlet We shall never meet

What I shall leave will not be worth a tragedy

It is not for us to greet each other or bid farewell we live on
archipelagoes
and that water these words what can they do what can they do
Prince

"Elegy of Fortinbras"

The substantive merit of Herbert's poetry reinforces Milosz's ad-
monition to modern Polish writers that, however disenchanted they
may be with the political system, they should never permit politics
to interfere with the creative process.[8]

Because of the nature of the idiom, the Polish theater has served
as the avant-garde of contemporary cultural life and has shown
greatest resilience in the face of the government's attempts to impose
on it political and stylistic conformity. The most experimental was
Jerzy Grotowski's now defunct pantomime theater in Wroclaw, which
stressed an acting technique centered on total expressiveness of the
body. The most political has been the Theater of the Eighth Day
based in Poznań: In the works it performs (Stanislaw Barańczak,
presently at Harvard, was once its in-house playwright) the theater
explores the nihilism of life under socialism. According to one critic,
"When other theaters have pointed to symptoms of social disorders,
Eighth Day pointed to the existential root."[9]

Several other theater directors have distinguished themselves
through highly avant-garde productions. Kraków-based Tadeusz Kantor has created what theater critic Jan Kott has termed "the theater
of essence": "Essence is the human drama freed of accident and of
the illusion that there are choices." In fact, "in Kantor's theater the
living are already corpses" and the "doubles of the dead."[10] In Warsaw,
Józef Szajna's internationally respected Studio Theater emphasizes
light, shadow, and the extension of the proscenium in its method,
while the more established Janusz Hanuszkiewicz, director of the
National Theater, has put on controversial productions of classic Polish
drama. The Old Theater in Kraków may be the country's premier
stage, and Wajda's adaptation of Dostoevsky's *The Possessed* (seen in
London in the 1970s) and his 1980s' production of *With the Passing
of Years, With the Passing of Days* were memorable achievements.

The most creative contemporary Polish dramatist is in all likelihood Slawomir Mrożek, who now lives in Paris. He is also concerned
with existential themes and has developed a theater of political satire
that is unrivaled. Mrożek's targets are not just the socialist system
(*The Police*) but the "progressive" ideas popular in the West (*Tango*).
Individuals locked in uncharacteristic situations (*Out at Sea, Striptease,*

and possibly his greatest play, *The Emigrants*), is another recurring theme in Mrożek's plays as well as in his satirical short stories (*The Elephant*). The inspiration of Gombrowicz's chaotic world (such as his *The Marriage Ceremony*) is clearly evident in much of Mrożek's output.

The artistic avant-garde has had the greatest impact in contemporary Polish music. Beginning with the early compositions of Grażyna Bacewicz (such as her quartets) and culminating in the sweeping operas and oratorium of Krzysztof Penderecki (*Saint Luke Passion*, the Auschwitz oratorio *Dies Irae*, *The Devils of Loudon*, and more recently an operatic version of Milton's *Paradise Lost*), in its inventiveness and scope Polish music has become the equal of other countries in the region that earlier produced such innovative composers as Stravinsky, Prokofiev, Bartok, Kodály, and Janáček. Other internationally acclaimed Polish composers are Witold Lutoslawski and the late Tadeusz Baird. Every year since 1956, the Warsaw Autumn, a festival of contemporary music, is held in the Polish capital.

The Polish school of film is closely identified with Andrzej Wajda, and rightly so. This director has sustained a high level of cinematographic activity for thirty years, beginning with the classic *Canal* and *Ashes and Diamonds* in the 1950s, continuing with *Landscape after the Battle*, *The Birch Grove*, and *Hunting for Flies*, and subsuming more recent films highly critical of Poland's socialist development such as *Man of Marble* (about the Stalin era), *Without Anaesthesia*, *The Conductor*, *Man of Iron* (about the birth of Solidarity), and the allegorical *Danton*. For his pains Wajda, under martial law, was removed from his posts as chief of the Polish Film Makers' Association and head of the "X" film production group in Lódz. Wajda's politics, as he would readily acknowledge, have been equivocal and resemble the attitudes of the journalist in *Man of Iron* who only gradually is won over by the free trade union movement.

A second international vedette of Polish cinema is the erudite Krzysztof Zanussi. A recurring theme in his works is intellectuals confronted with the dilemma of moral integrity (*The Structure of Crystal*, *Camouflage*, *The Spiral*, and *The Constant Factor*.) Finally, Jerzy Kawalerowicz was making good films as early as the Stalin period (*The Village Mill*) and has continued to produce interesting work since (for example, the remarkable *Mother Joan of the Angels*, *Night Train*, and, more recently, *Chance Encounter on the Ocean*.) But he is not as widely acclaimed in the West, perhaps because of his membership in the PZPR and the Seym. Generally, "establishment" artists of People's Poland have a difficult time obtaining critical recognition in the West.

Our survey of postwar Polish culture must make mention of the leading graphic artists who have transformed the poster into a vibrant artistic medium. The doyens are Franciszek Starowieyski and Waldemar Swierzy. The world's first poster museum was opened in 1968 in Wilanów, near Warsaw, and the International Poster Biennale has been held in Warsaw since 1966.

Contemporary Polish painting reflects the multiplicity of styles and idioms that are apparent in art galleries throughout the world. There is the abstract expressionist Tadeusz Brzozowski, the neoimpressionist Eugeniusz Markowski, the op art exponent Ryszard Winiarski, the pop art and lyric abstractionism (more specifically tachism) of theater director Kantor, the figurative surrealism of Jerzy Nowosielski, the neodadaism of Wlodzimierz Borowski, and the primitive art of Nikifor. The school of colorism—the dominant artistic current before the war, which subordinated form to color—has successors to its founder Jan Cybis such as Adam Marciński. In turn, the prewar abstractionist (and inventor of unism) Wladyslaw Strzemiński has strongly influenced Zbigniew Makowski among others. Also noteworthy are the works of Henryk Stazewski and Magdalena Abakanowicz. Finally, in sculpture Wladyslaw Hasior has achieved fame for his assemblages that make frequent use of fire and water.

The question arises whether this flowering of Polish culture has been the result of the shrewd and financially supportive policy of the communist leadership, or whether it symbolizes an energetic, creative, defiant response of Polish artists to the constricting or indifferent attitude of the communist rulers. Successive leaders have reiterated the principle that the party will not interfere in the artistic realm (that is, in experimentation with form, style, and idiom) provided that the cultural intelligentsia refrains from overt or veiled political attacks on the authorities (that is, works that express hostility toward socialism). As then vice premier Rakowski asserted in May 1982, when a National Council on Culture and a Cultural Development Fund were set up, ostensibly to provide further autonomy and aid to artists: "The limits of freedom are the good of the human community, the good of the national community, the good of the socialist Polish state which in our conditions is the only guarantee of this community."[11]

Within this framework works of high artistic merit can be and are produced in Poland. The truly great artist can function in the People's Republic; emigration is not a sine qua non to achieving artistic fulfillment. Some who emigrate for political reasons show only mediocre talents in the end. At the same time, the writer, painter, or composer who stays behind confronts many hardships apart from the artistic caprices of the established authorities. Artists' materials, film, paper, rehearsal sites, and grants are in very short supply and are likely to be allocated according to political criteria. If in capitalist societies the demands of the market have limiting effects on artistic creation, under Polish socialism the political sensibilities of the leaders and their appendages, the cultural establishment (such as the boards of the Writers' Union, the Film Makers' Association, the exclusive Composers' Union), together with the conformity that political institutions often require impose serious restraints on the artist.

So as better to illustrate the vagaries of cultural policy, let me sketch cultural life in Poland, first, in its present two highly polarized forms (official versus underground culture), then, in two very different periods (under Solidarity and under martial law).

CULTURE BEFORE AND AFTER MARTIAL LAW

In no other sphere, perhaps, has the struggle between the political authorities and the opposition movement remained so bitter and enduring in the Poland of the 1980s as in the cultural sphere. Several reasons can be advanced to explain this phenomenon: 1) the state possesses a monopoly in the exercise of coercion (notwithstanding the spectre cultivated by the rulers in early 1982 of an armed movement prepared to engage in a civil war with the authorities), thereby enabling it to destroy all the organized (but not the spiritual) forms of opposition; 2) the means of expression employed by the liberal cultural intelligentsia (above all, the extensive underground press) are not easily susceptible to total state eradication; and 3) the writers and artists are themselves highly polarized, with one group ardently asserting its allegiance to the regime and the other just as fervently wishing to change it. Let me briefly develop this theme of co-existing official and alternative cultures.

In the face of the state's ability to stage imposing displays of force (riot police, the army, networks of informers), all that was left for those sharing Solidarity's vision of a self-governing Poland was to engage in symbolic politics. The most apposite and effective form of such politics was to confront the rulers with an elaborate and alternative culture. Autonomous organizations (of professionals, farmers, and workers) were swept away under martial law, but the technical base for publishing remained in large part intact, and publishing served as the spearhead of the cultural confrontation with the Jaruzelski administration. If, as is estimated by Solidarity's Interim Coordinating Commission (TKK), some five thousand individuals in Warsaw were left in the "real" underground by 1985, there was a much broader

A peasant selling flowers in front of a bookshop

infrastructure, consisting of "normal" people, who serviced the clandestine press—the chief disseminator of this alternative culture. These
individuals, drawn from all social classes, helped carry out editorial,
printing, and distribution functions, providing "average" Poles living
in the cities with regular alternative reading material.

Initially, the underground press concentrated on the publication
of political information: Examples are such newssheets as *Tygodnik
Mazowsze*, which claimed a press run of 15,000 copies per week, and
such periodicals as *Zapis* and *Krytyka*. In recent years, however, the
underground press also has published novels, short stories, and poems
by writers whose works were banned by the authorities. Although
by no means a new development in People's Poland—this practice
had already begun under Gierek—it now took place on a much
broader scale. Among the more popular authors of the underground
some may be familiar to Western readers because their writings have
appeared in English. These include Tadeusz Konwicki, Marek No-
wakowski, and playwright Janusz Glowacki (now living in the West).
It is ironic, therefore, that in probably no other socialist state has
cultural output become so diverse and critical as in "normalized"
Poland.

However, we should take care to judge works, whether from
the underground or the establishment, on the basis of literary and
artistic merits. A considerable amount of the cultural output of banned

writers has little to recommend it other than that it is proscribed by the regime. In turn, a number of novelists closely associated with the authorities, whose books are vigorously disseminated by the official publishing houses, have on occasion produced works of significant literary quality: for example, Roman Bratny, the late Jaroslaw Iwaszkiewicz, and even Jerzy Putrament and Wojciech Zukrowski (who was elected head of the overhauled writers' union in 1986). In examining the ongoing struggle between official and alternative cultures, therefore, it is crucial that the reader keep an open mind about both forms of output. The key point to emphasize is that the authorities have largely failed in eliminating the rival culture and penetrating society with the official version of social and political reality. The political ramification of this failure is that Poland remains not quite as "normal" as the other socialist states—a source of concern to both Jaruzelski and the socialist bloc states.

Let us briefly return to the Solidarity and martial law periods— both highly exceptional in postwar Polish history—in order to underscore the stark contrast between the two different types of culture. The following account is based on the author's personal exposure to both during those years and may help illustrate the nature of and rift between the two.

For the vast majority of the population who did not actively struggle against the military rulers after martial law had been imposed in December 1981, the most disturbing changes introduced were the curfew, the travel restrictions, the disconnected telephones, the broadcasting of just one radio and one television program, the publication of only two (the two least popular) newspapers, and the ban on public gatherings, which closed down theaters, cinemas, and concert halls. For the political opposition it was paramount that these deprivations be countered. Some of the first protests consisted of generalized throwing of newspapers into gutters and turning television sets around to face windows. When theaters and the opera house reopened more than a month later those performers who had in some way "collaborated" with the military authorities were ridiculed, either by public laughter at their first appearance or by endless ironic applause after the performance.

In this way culture became a major battleground. For the Jaruzelski administration the sterilization of culture constituted an important means of inculcating a martial law ethos in the population. To suggest the scope of the changes, it is worth contrasting cultural diffusion before and after 13 December 1981.

In the week preceding martial law, a superb film, *Wahadelko* ("Pendulum"), which had been gathering dust on censors' shelves for years, was shown on state television. It portrayed a neurotic middle-aged man who depended unscrupulously upon his younger sister. His calculating mother, whom he despised, had been mythologized by the party for her contributions in the past. Through these connections she had access to a variety of material privileges until one day she began to have doubts about the way she had become trapped in the system. After December 13 such introspective films gave way to World War II epics like *Do Krwi Ostatniej* ("To the Last Drop of Blood"), which glorified the joint Polish-Russian assault on German positions near Lenino.

Another example: On the opening day (11 December) of the Congress on Polish Culture televised proceedings included the prophetic statement of the president of the Writers' Union, Jan Józef Szczepański, that there were those who considered the congress had as much significance as the orchestra playing while the *Titanic* sank. With martial law the proceedings were suspended, and instead a graying, hunched-over, little-known professor from the Agricultural Academy was shown presenting cheesecake and flowers to five wide-eyed teenage conscripts on patrol on a snow-covered Warsaw street. The commentator pedantically added that this was the professor's way of expressing gratitude to the army for having prevented civil war.

Or: Before martial law radio talk shows, patterned on the U.S. model, had begun to thrive. One show solicited listeners' questions on the economic reform program, and these were answered by the minister of finance. In January 1982, however, an army commissar who now supervised radio broadcasts objected to the airing of an all-night taped music program on the grounds that it contained an offensive song. This was a Polish hit *Za Ostatni Grosz* ("With My Last Penny"). The disc jockey insisted there was nothing political in the song, but the commissar replied: "Aren't you aware there has just been a price increase?" The tape was edited accordingly.

Or: On the evening of 12 December *Dreszcze* ("Chills"), a film depicting the political indoctrination of scouts in the 1950s, was playing in a Warsaw cinema. The audience reacted with hilarious laughter when the scout leader, an upstart party member confused by the 1956 Poznań events, spoke of the "subversive forces" and "American imperialism" that were behind the bread riots. For the rest of that month these same catchwords were used daily by the media, without any qualms, to castigate Solidarity and its supporters.

The existence of Solidarity helped underscore the absurdity of certain contradictions that had arisen in the cultural sphere. Three sets of contradictions were particularly striking: 1) an official ideology propagating socialist norms juxtaposed with an inverse bias latent in society against all things socialist; 2) official encouragement of experimentation and innovation in the arts set against the adherence by cultural institutions to established modes and patterns; and 3) promulgation of the goal of equal access to the arts set against the persistence of closed or selective admission to much cultural activity. Let us look at some examples.

An illustration of the first was audience reaction in Warsaw's Great Theater to a 1979 performance by the Cuban National Ballet, directed by the legendary prima ballerina Alicia Alonso, of an original work on the life of Victor Jara. *La Tierra Combatiente* ("The Combat Ground") portrayed the torture and death of the Chilean folk singer, and the choreography called for the production to end with the raising aloft of the hero's red cape. This was taken as a cue by many theatergoers to begin whistling, despite a flawless interpretation by the ballet company. Many ordinary Poles, like their leaders, had come to judge art in terms of political criteria.

In an inverse way Mrożek's *The Ambassador*, which premiered in Warsaw in October 1981 and was directed by Kazimierz Deymek (whose production of *Forefathers' Eve* in 1968 precipitated the March events), evoked a crude anti-Russian reaction even though the web of allusions in the play had far more universal connotations. The propensity to see anti-Sovietism in all satire, together with the general boycott of all things Russian, are unhealthy if understandable cultural reactions. Thus, several screenings of the Oscar-winning film *Moscow Does Not Believe in Tears* had to be canceled because no tickets had been sold, while the artistically vacuous Hollywood creation *Nickelodeon* played to packed, receptive audiences.

An example of the second contradiction—the latent conservatism of the cultural establishment in a supposedly progressive socialist system—was perhaps best dramatized at the 1980 Chopin Piano Competition. The remarkable Yugoslav pianist Ivo Pogorelič overwhelmed Warsaw music lovers and critics with his technically brilliant and highly original interpretations of the composer's works. But the eight Poles (and the socialist bloc majority) on the twenty-six-member jury were unimpressed with the brash and irreverent Pogorelič, and he was not even permitted to reach the competition finals. No less an authority than the Argentine concert pianist Martha Argerich resigned from the jury in protest. Subsequently, Pogorelič's career has flourished while the competition winner, a Vietnamese pianist who had to practice in a cellar while U.S. bombs dropped on Hanoi, remains unknown in the West. In art as in other fields, originality and innovation are increasingly discouraged by the real socialism found in Poland.

Yet an equally dogmatic and similar attitude was taken, paradoxically, by the organizers and patrons of a musical review, *Strike Songs of 1980*, held in Warsaw's Palace of Culture exactly a year later, in November 1981. We might have expected that Solidarity-sponsored cultural events would depart from the socialist model; instead some appeared to be patterned on it. The atmosphere was so somber, self-congratulatory, and programmed (not to mention it was closed to the general public) that it recalled a party *akademia*—a bizarre concoction of light entertainment and serious speechmaking held in conjunction with socialist red-letter days.

This brings us to the third contradiction—the proclaimed goal of bringing art to the masses and the actual practice of limiting public access to culture. The problem of closed performances (no tickets available to the public, no prior announcement made of a performance) has been acute in People's Poland. Perhaps understandably the documentary film *Workers '80* about the birth of Solidarity was not publicized by state media, and screenings were confined to select clubs. But a rare performance of the Yiddish masterpiece *Dybbuk*, about traditional Jewish customs and supernatural spirits, held in November 1981 at the Jewish State Theater, was reserved for an invited audience that only filled the first four rows of seats. The reason for the limited audience was that it included several members of the Central Committee and two members of Britain's House of Lords. It would be wrong to draw general conclusions based on a few examples. Nevertheless, whenever an attractive cultural event takes place in Poland and demand for tickets is great, those with personal connections or imposing party credentials who can flash an identity card (*legitymacja*) attesting to membership in the *nomenklatura*, or socialist ruling class, have priority. So much for the socialist system that makes art accessible to the people.

The imposition of martial law not only eliminated these contradictions of cultural life: For more than a month martial law eliminated culture altogether. It was not until 22 January 1982, that the arts were revived in Warsaw with the inaugural concert of the Szymanowski centennial. This time members of the National Philharmonic did not appear wearing Solidarity badges as they had when Soviet violinist Vadim Brodsky performed on 4 December. The mournful opening bars of Szeligowski's *Epitaphium on the Death of Karol Szymanowski*, followed by Baird's *Voices from Afar* (specially commissioned for this occasion though the composer did not live to see the premiere), seemed eerily appropriate to the conditions of martial law.

Many writers, artists, and intellectuals were interned in those
months. Bitter verses were written from the camps:

> Is this what you wanted, General Jaruzelski,
> that we humbly genuflect towards the east again?
> that barbed camps spring forth on our soil again?
> that precious Polish blood pour from our veins again?
> Is this what you wanted, General Jaruzelski?
>
> Anonymous, 1982

Those who were not detained protested in various ways: Two
actors high in the party-state structure resigned their posts, while
others in the theater left for the West, either temporarily or for good.
For a time actors and other performers boycotted state television.
The flagship literary periodical *Kultura* was closed down and its
editorial staff dispersed after the staff stubbornly refused to sign
declarations of loyalty to the socialist system as the authorities required.
Only in mid–1985 did a newspaper bearing the same title (and nothing
else) begin to publish. The television, cinema, and theater programs
that were put on were designed, as then minister of culture Tejchma
put it, "to provide relaxation for the public weary after each day's
burdens."

In the past Polish artists captured the essence of the country's
socialist reality, as was evident at the exhibition "Thirty-five Years
of Polish Art," staged in the Zachęta Gallery in 1979. There will
doubtlessly be sequels to the ironic hyperrealist painting "Awaiting
Socialist Dawn," depicting two fashionably clothed dandies sipping
brandy on their villa veranda as the sun rises on the horizon. The
revealing original photographs of the 1956, 1968, 1970, and 1976
events, on display in Castle Square in 1981, now have a supplement
when the next such exhibition can be staged. Generally, the art of
the underground (posters, postage stamps, drawings in the clandestine
press) has flourished since 1982.

This may appear paradoxical but the cultural event that, in the
author's personal view, most powerfully dramatized the spirit of
freedom and integrity that Polish society sought to reconstruct during
the Solidarity period took place before August 1980 and involved a
Russian actor and songwriter. It was a performance of *Hamlet* by
Moscow's Taganka Theater, and the actor was the squat, forty-two-
year-old, lantern-jawed Vladimir Vysotsky, stretched out against a
desolate gray stage prop, strumming a guitar, and in gravel voice
reciting Pasternak's "Night's Darkness Is Directed upon Me." The
actor and his Hamlet embodied the fury, simplicity, courage, and

honor that were shown by so many Poles later that year. At the end of the performance, moved by the reception he was given, Vysotsky stripped off his neck the gold-plated chain of the prince of Denmark and hurled it into the audience. One month later the first workers' strikes broke out in Lublin; two months later Vysotsky was dead of a heart attack.

In January 1982 another closed spectacle was held in Warsaw—the trial of workers from the Ursus tractor factory accused of having organized a strike under martial law. One Pole who had been able to gain admission declared: "It is tragic that people like this are being tried." Then, after describing the simplicity and honor of those defending themselves he added: "But it makes me proud that such noble people are being tried." His words somehow recalled the image of Vysotsky as Hamlet.

POPULAR CULTURE

It would be a misrepresentation of Polish culture to depict it exclusively in terms of its highbrow components—poetry, novels, classical music, the fine arts. For the majority of people, exposure to culture is largely limited to the film offerings of the two state television programs, to the pop and light music broadcast by the country's four state radio stations, and to war novels available at every kiosk. In this respect modern Polish society is scarcely distinguishable from its counterparts in other industrialized societies. This is in spite of the fact that most people accept the slogans promulgated in the Solidarity period that "the press lies" and "television lies."

In fact, the media are scrupulously controlled for both information and cultural content by party-state authorities. From 1946 to 1981 a Main Administration for Control of Press, Publications, and Public Performances exercised censorship of all the communications media. The method of controlling what was disseminated was far more complex than generally assumed in the West. In the case of English-language literature, for example, works might be banned on the basis of an author's very name (George Orwell), loose morals (Henry Miller), origins (Vladimir Nabokov and Jerzy Kosinski), false values (Jack Kerouac), or metaphors (Ken Kesey). Individual passages, even sentences, might cause cancellation or postponement of the publication of a book. It is said that the translated version of Günter Grass's *The Tin Drum* was held up for years because it contained one offensive phrase—"the lice on the collar of a Russian soldier." In works published in Poland and, presumably the rest of the socialist bloc, no Russian soldier is supposed to have lice on his collar. If these are criteria

Children outside a provincial church in the month of May

used to censor foreign literature, the Polish writer is under even greater pressure to conform to the authorities' standards if he or she hopes to have a work published.

One of Solidarity's demands in 1980 was to replace the existing censorship system. In 1981 a new law was indeed passed by the Seym that eased censorship regulations, and a Censor's Office was established that was to answer to the Council of State, an allegedly representative body. The law was effectively nullified by martial law, however, and the old criteria have been resurrected.

At present, dissemination of both news and culture is manipulated, the first crudely, the latter more subtly, to reflect the values the rulers wish to inculcate. The pervasiveness of U.S. pop music, rock videos, Miss Poland pageants, football games, shallow musicals, and romance-filled television miniseries is a way the leaders tell the masses, "You aren't missing anything the West has." Mass culture for mass society is now crossnational, proving the validity of McLuhan's "global village" thesis. Recreation, leisure, and light entertainment are viewed by the authorities as desirable substitutes for activism, critical-mindedness, and enlightenment.

In rural Poland peasants do occasionally practice age-old rituals and seasonal customs. Traditions differ greatly from one region to the other. In Little Poland, for example, on St. Stephen's Day (the second day of Christmas), "the cows are given straw, pieces of bread, and the wafer from under the Christmas Eve tablecloth, the horses—hay from under the table, the poultry—crumbs of all kinds." Elsewhere, "the farmers make the rounds of beehives to announce to the bees 'the news of the birth of the Holy Infant.' It is a widespread belief (for instance, in the Lublin region) that the bees then awake for a moment and answer with joyous buzzing."[12]

The state has lent support to efforts to preserve local folklore. Regional cultures seek to survive by maintaining dance troupes (such as Mazowsze or Śląsk), musical festivities, the colorful local costumes, craftwork (such as woodcarving or pottery), and dialects (such as those of the mountaineers or the Kashubs). Time is on the side of modernization and uniformity, of course. Less and less often can we find traditional folk culture practiced in the Polish village, and more and more the ether waves carry mass culture to the most rural of regions. This is a loss—and not just for the cows, horses, poultry, and bees.

NOTES

1. C. Milosz, *The History of Polish Literature* (Berkeley: University of California Press, 1983), p. 56.

2. Ibid., p. 327.

3. J. Krzyżanowski, *A History of Polish Literature* (Warsaw: PWN, 1978), p. 612.

4. For a portrait of four such writers see C. Milosz, *The Captive Mind* (New York: Random House, 1981).

5. Quoted in K. Brandys, *A Warsaw Diary 1978–81* (New York: Random House, 1983), p. 98.

6. Ibid., p. 149.

7. C. Milosz, "Three Poems by Adam Zagajewski," *New York Review of Books* (24 October 1985):34.

8. Yale University Conference, "Contemporary Poland in Historical Perspective," May 1984. Quoted in *New York Times* 27 May 1984, p. 8.

9. J.C. Goldfarb, *On Cultural Freedom* (Chicago: University of Chicago Press, 1982), p. 100.

10. J. Kott, *The Theater of Essence* (Evanston, Ill.: Northwestern University Press, 1984), pp. 160–161.

11. "Culture and the State," *Polish Perspectives*, no. 3 (Summer 1982):8.

12. C. Baudoin de Courtenay Jędrzejewicz, "Polish Peasant Rituals and Seasonal Customs," in M. Giergielewicz (ed.), *Polish Civilization* (New York: New York University Press, 1979), pp. 5–6.

FURTHER READINGS

For an extensive bibliography of Polish literature in translation see C. Milosz, *The History of Polish Literature*. For current studies see the journal

Polish Review and the Yearbook of Central European Culture, *Cross Currents,* published by the University of Michigan.

M.K. Albright. *Poland: The Role of the Press in Political Change.* Praeger: New York, 1983.
J.L. Curry (ed.). *The Black Book of Polish Censorship.* New York: Vintage, 1984.
L. Erhardt. *Music in Poland.* Warsaw: Interpress, 1975.
J. Fuksiewicz. *Film and Television in Poland.*Warsaw: Interpress, 1981.
A. Gillon and L. Krzyżanowski (eds.). *Introduction to Modern Polish Literature.* New York: Hippocrene Books, 1982.
S. Hornik. "The Art and Fire of the Polish Poster." *The Smithsonian* 13, no. 10 (January 1983):88–97.
M.G. Levine (ed.). *Contemporary Polish Poetry 1925–75.* Boston: Twayne Publishers, 1981.
B.M. Maciejewski. *Twelve Polish Composers.* London: Allegro Press, 1976.
B. Michalek. *The Cinema of Andrzej Wajda.* New York: Barnes, 1973.
C. Milosz (ed.). *Postwar Polish Poetry.* Berkeley: University of California Press, 1983.
J. Waśniewski. *The Polish Poster.* Warsaw: WAG, 1972.
A. Wojciechowski. *Contemporary Polish Art.* Warsaw: Interpress, 1974.

7
Conclusion

We have encountered a number of contradictions in this study of modern Poland. It is a socialist state that prizes the virtues of law and order, of pragmatism and conservatism. It has achieved much in the past forty years and takes utmost care not to jeopardize its successes. But Poland is also a rebellious nation that espouses an odd mix of values, originating in the traditions of romanticism, radicalism, and religiosity. The Polish people are intolerant of the repeated errors of the party-state authorities, the complacency of the ruling elite, and the geopolitical constraints facing the nation. To the state's Realpolitik Polish society advances an idealistic self-governing republic; to the leadership's *asekuracja* (or cautious pursuit of self-interest) it often offers bravado; and to the long-term socialist vision of justice and plenty it demands the addition of material rewards and moral rectitude in the here and now. State and society appear locked, therefore, in constant tension with each other.

Of the many dilemmas that face modern Poland and will determine its future, I have singled out three for evaluation in this conclusion. They are: 1) the need to synchronize the conflicting exigencies of the socialist utopian vision and the seemingly incorrigible everyday actuality of socialist life; 2) the perennial problem of reaching an optimal equilibrium in Poland's relations with Russia and with the West; and 3) the necessity for bringing into congruence socialist structures and societal attitudes.

UTOPIA AND REALITY

Some Polish specialists hold that the country's current serious problems are the result of the propensity to sacrifice the present for the future—in other words, of the thrust to achieve the socialist vision. Thus, journalist Ryszard Kapuścinski has written: "Here everything is based on a certain principle of asymmetrical verification: the system

179

promises to prove itself *later* (announcing a general happiness that exists only in the future), but it demands that you prove yourself now, *today*, by demonstrating your loyalty, consent, and diligence. You commit yourself to everything; the system to nothing."

According to this scenario Marxist-Leninist ideology plays a crucial role in Polish politics, if only by subordinating current requirements to the future utopia. The sense of time is distorted by it: "The present too is deprived of certainty and of a spirit of encouragement: we feel we are its guests or even its victims, not its creators or rulers. And the future appears more like an ambush and a mystery than a crystal palace in which servants are about to switch on the lights and prepare for us a feast."[1]

A diametrically opposite evaluation of ideology's role in Polish politics is offered by philosopher Leszek Kolakowski. It is his contention that all that is left of Marxism and its vision in contemporary Poland are "mummified remains."[2] The leaders, he claims, have ceased to believe in or pursue with any great commitment the communistic ideals of human emancipation, social justice, and egalitarianism. Marxism-Leninism performs the function, at most, of an operative code used by the rulers to reconcile rhetorically their acclaimed fundamental goals with their diurnal policies and practices.

Whatever the influence of ideological goals in affecting present development, it is clear that Poland suffers from ideological retardedness compared to other states (and perhaps societies) of the Soviet bloc. We need only note terminological distinctions that set it off from a number of other socialist countries. Poland continues to be called a People's Republic, whose leading force is a workers' party, at the same time that Romania, Czechoslovakia, Yugoslavia, and the USSR have proclaimed themselves socialist republics that (except for Romania) are led by communist parties.

That Marxism-Leninism has not prospered in Poland may be due to a reason other than the saddle not fitting the cow (to cite Stalin's 1945 metaphor). The official state ideology, Marxism-Leninism, is a hybrid of the thought and traditions of Poland's two chief historical adversaries—Russia and Germany. It is hard to imagine a doctrine emanating from a source more alien to Poland than this composite of Germanic idealism and Russian opportunism. Accordingly, the adversarial basis of Polish Marxism-Leninism may partly explain why this ideology has had difficulty taking root in Polish society.

This is not to claim that socialist ideals are foreign to the country. This is a simplistic view that holds that socialism is fundamentally incompatible with the country's national traditions and values. I would like to argue, however, that Poland's indigenous socialist tradition—its greater liberalism and internationalism—needs to be represented more fully when rulers seek to square practice with utopia.

RUSSIA AND THE WEST

It is no exaggeration to assert that, historically, Russia was not amicably disposed toward Poland. But one of the principal barriers standing in the way of Polish society's rational understanding of the country's present objective position in the international alliance system is, it seems, the transposition of past animosities to current affairs. In Chapter 3 I noted how pivotal relations with the Soviet Union are to Poland's foreign as well as domestic policies. The postwar achievement of a very imperfect *modus vivendi* with the USSR continues, nonetheless, to be regarded as totally illegitimate by large sections of the population. In fact, the likelihood of closer social and cultural ties between the two societies has diminished over time. As novelist Kazimierz Brandys observed:

> Poles do not know how to think about Russians and Russians do not
> know how to think about Poles. Instead of thinking, both sides engage
> in knee-jerk responses, the result of a mutual psychological conditioning.
> . . . The last forty years have set things back a century and a half.
> Polish consciousness is still at the level expressed in *Forefathers' Eve*.
> And Russian consciousness is still on the level of Dostoevsky's 'treach-
> erous little Poles.'[3]

Poland's political prospects would be greatly improved if both nations shed such stereotypes of each other. This is a problem that transcends objective factors and extends to the subjective sphere. It will not easily be resolved so long as the mistakes and illiberalism of Polish rulers are blamed on their role as Kremlin surrogates.

Attitudes to other neighbors (East Germany and Czechoslovakia) are scarcely better. It may be fundamentally sound not to place great faith in the Central Europe concept or an alliance system based on it, for the interwar period underlined its inefficacy and transience. Nonetheless, the key to a more autonomous and democratic Poland lies precisely in the "spread of the Polish bacteria" to adjacent state organisms. Poland's failure to do so in the Solidarity period was due primarily to the fact that Poland evoked little sympathy among the nations with which it has been squabbling for centuries. National images die hard, but Poles should make efforts—commensurate with their struggle for liberalization at home—to project themselves as well disposed toward other peoples of the region.

Finally, Polish society must become aware that in purely geographic terms it lies, at best, on the periphery of the Western world. It is illusory to hope this will somehow change. Even if the system of rival military and political blocs in Europe disappears one day, Poles will need to remain attentive to regional interests while becoming more open to Western influences. Put succinctly, interdependence, not dependence on either East or West, is the optimal direction for Poland's foreign policy.

SOCIALIST STRUCTURES AND SOCIETAL ATTITUDES

In the foregoing discussion I have imputed a certain intransigence to the attitudes of Polish society. I must also note that the political system, in reflecting the values of this society, has exhibited a great degree of inflexibility of its own during the past forty years. A country attaining a relatively advanced stage of industrial development, such as Poland has, becomes too complex to be governed by a single politicobureaucratic force claiming to possess a monopoly on political wisdom and administrative expertise. Institutional arrangements that prevent societal interests from achieving meaningful participation in policy formulation are both archaic and counterproductive. The leading role of the party in society should not be interpreted as exclusive. Perhaps the party's role would be better redefined as the leading role in the state, that is, in the making and implementing of policy. The process of interest articulation, aggregation, and feedback would, in this view, be left to institutions independent of the party.

In addition, as loathe as communist leaders are to recognize the need for second-stage reforms that would go beyond the economic dimension, this is precisely what can enhance the prospects for social harmony and order in Poland in the long term. The urgency of such a second (or, perhaps more accurately, third) stage becomes clear when we examine the course of political development in postwar Poland. The most substantive political transformations took place in the years 1954–1958, when the country discarded the Stalinist political ethos (if not necessarily the institutions and processes) and replaced it with the values of a modern civic society. The most notable changes were the reversion from the use of state repression to that of repressive tolerance in dealing with dissenters and the nurturing of a more even balance between coercion and consent as the bases of system legitimacy. When, therefore, we compare present-day Poland to the Poland of 1958, rather than to the immediate postwar or Stalinist periods—

a comparison that is bound to exaggerate the degree of political development—we find that the intervening decades consisted almost exclusively of economic transformation that gave rise to certain social changes as well. In short, the Polish polity today seems to have evolved very little from its 1958 formation. Whether under Gomulka's Polish October or Jaruzelski's 1980s reformism, relations between the state and society are characterised by a similar degree of paternalism, manipulation, and selective intolerance by the former and inefficacy, frustration, and apathy by the latter. It is time that political and economic progress be effected hand in hand. Such a symbiosis should constitute the essence of the third stage of postwar development; this symbiosis alone can bring into alignment the interests of both state and society and affect economic growth and political liberalism.

Poland is an overwhelmingly Catholic nation, and this offers certain opportunities as well as dangers to the leaders overseeing the construction of socialism. Let us refer to the overarching thesis about Catholic societies expounded by Glen Dealy: "Catholic man is public man. He defines himself in terms of a code of excellence that derives (originally) from the public or political sphere. He thinks, acts, and has his being within a framework of public values." Dealy contends that a Catholic country is essentially a *"caudillaje* society"—it is characterized by "a style of life according to which everyman attempts to be a leader or caudillo" in a public setting. The author then adds that "Catholic man pursues public power the way Protestant man strives for public wealth."[4]

If Dealy is right, then the values of Catholic man are intrinsically participant- and public-oriented. They are ideal for a society engaged on a megaproject such as Poland's building of socialism. If the authorities are serious about completing this project, they could mobilize this Catholic nation by finding outlets for its value aspirations. Without appropriate structures into which such aspirations could be channeled, however, the rulers run the risk that the values will cut against them, that these values will be operationalized in extraconstitutional structures. It is this potentially advantageous challenge that Poland's communist leaders have studiously ignored for forty years and that make the country's future political prospects as murky as ever.

Finally, in this study I have tried to show that Poland is both a homogeneous and a diversified society. In ethnic, religious, and spiritual terms Poland is remarkably unified. The Polish people value the same heroes and the same glorious episodes in their history, are deeply patriotic, and can unite on occasions to move mountains— the insurrectionary tradition best exemplies this latter point. But

Poland is also more diverse than appears on the surface. There are different agendas, different interests, and different objectives for various sections of this society. In these respects Polish society is largely fragmented, and cleavages cut across class and strata lines. We are left with a contradiction that can best be resolved if we adopt the concept of "fragmentation in homogeneity." This concept most satisfactorily does justice to the complexity of Polish society; moreover, it can explain why socialist Poland has been shaken by a series of profound crises, which demonstrate the rebellious Polish tradition, and still has managed to withstand these crises and survive, which suggests the resilience of the Polish nation-state. We have found no evidence in our analysis that, at some future juncture in Poland, both tragic and heroic elements will not reappear.

NOTES

1. R. Kapuścinski, "A Warsaw Diary," *Harper's* 271, no. 1622 (July 1985):14.

2. L. Kolakowski, *Main Currents of Marxism*, 3 vols (New York: Oxford University Press, 1978), vol. 3, p. 465.

3. K. Brandys, *A Warsaw Diary 1978–81* (New York: Random House, 1983), pp. 173–174.

4. G.C. Dealy, *The Public Man* (Amherst: University of Massachusetts Press, 1977), pp. 3–7.

Abbreviations and Acronyms

AK	Home Army
CMEA	Council for Mutual Economic Assistance
Comecon	Council for Mutual Economic Assistance
CPSU	Communist Party of the Soviet Union
DiP	Experience and the Future Group
EEC	European Economic Community
GDP	Gross Domestic Product
GL	People's Guard
IMF	International Monetary Fund
KiK	Club of Catholic Intelligentsia
KOR	Committee for Workers' Self-Defense
KPP	Polish Communist Party
KRN	National Council of the Homeland
MFN	most favored nation
NATO	North Atlantic Treaty Organization
ND	National Democracy Party
OECD	Organization for Economic Cooperation and Development
OPEC	Organization of Petroleum Exporting Countries
PKWN	Polish Committee of National Liberation
PPR	Polish Workers' Party
PPS	Polish Socialist Party
PRON	Patriotic Movement for National Rebirth
PSL	Polish Peasant Party
PZPR	Polish United Workers' Party
SD	Democratic Party
SDKPiL	Social Democratic Party of the Kingdom of Poland and Lithuania
TKK	Interim Coordinating Commission (Solidarity)
UB	State Security

UNRRA	United Nations Relief and Rehabilitation Administration
UPA	Ukrainian Insurrectionary Army
WOG	Large Industrial Association
WTO	Warsaw Treaty Organization
ZOMO	Motorized Units of the Citizens' Militia
ZSL	United Peasants' Party

Index